We Sang
and
Whistled
Then!

We Sang and Whistled Then!

The Glory Years of the American Popular Song

John H Evans

Library of Congress Control Number:		2021901529
ISBN:	Hardcover	978-1-6641-1431-9
	Softcover	978-1-6641-1430-2
	eBook	978-1-6641-1429-6

Print information available on the last page.

Rev. date: 02/15/2021

To order additional copies of this book, contact:
Xlibris
UK TFN: 0800 0148620 (Toll Free inside the UK)
UK Local: 02036 956328 (+44 20 3695 6328 from outside the UK)
www.Xlibrispublishing.co.uk
Orders@Xlibrispublishing.co.uk
803838

C O N T E N T S

An introduction to the piano

The author with his Granddaughter Katy at the age of 15 months.

To the pals of my youth, Kenneth Arthur, Colin Cooper,
David Cox, Dilwyn Davies, Arbant James, John May,
Michael McCarthy, Colin Middleton, Arthur Molyneux,
Bryn Scourfield, Haydn Scourfield, and Glyn Stokes.

Acknowledgements

My sincere thanks to:

- Professor Michael Bagshaw of King's College London, who took time out from a busy schedule to read the manuscript and write the foreword.
- Winston G Ramsey, editor and owner of the magazine *After the Battle*, for his many suggestions concerning the Second World War
- Arthur G Molyneux, who despite his ninety-one years, read the manuscript and still shows a sharp and keen eye for the written word
- And finally, my two wonderful children, Sian Marianne Evans and Gavin William John Evans, who helped me to survive the toughest period of my life and without whom this book would not have seen the light of day

Foreword

Many books and articles have been written about popular music and film music, particularly that of the 1930s and 1940s.

Many scholarly books and articles have been written about the Second World War (1939–1945), describing and discussing the politics and the battles and the eventual outcomes.

But this is the first book to be published that seamlessly intertwines both themes, each enhancing the understanding of the other.

John Evans grew up in the Rhondda, South Wales, and vividly describes the feelings and emotions he experienced during his formative years prior to and during the Second World War. He skilfully incorporates his voyage of discovery of popular and film music of the time, relating it to the events going on around him and further afield.

I first knew John many years later when he had abandoned school teaching to become a commercial pilot and aviation entrepreneur. He inspired me then with his intelligence and personality and he went on to significant achievements in aviation, making a difference to the industry, which persists to this day.

However, it was only on reading this semi-autobiographical book that I came to understand his musical skills and his deep and wide-ranging knowledge of areas well beyond aviation. His observation and analysis of the events leading up to the Second World War certainly taught me things I didn't know, in many cases changing my preconceived perspective of events and their outcome.

Anybody can search the literature for the life stories and output of the music composers. What John has done is to skilfully interweave this with the contemporary events to produce a highly readable and entertaining book, which will educate you and enthral you in equal measure. Enjoy it.

Professor Michael Bagshaw
King's College London
July 2020

Poem on The Book

Playing classics leaves me with sweaty palms
But it takes a greater toll on Beethoven and Brahms.

I prefer the music of Gershwin, Berlin, Porter, Rogers, and Kern,
Which gives me greater pleasure than a high-value tax return.

'They Can't take That Away from Me' and 'Night and Day'
Remain superb music that still holds sway.

And Berlin's 'White Christmas' takes me back in time
To my family and friends and the drinking of wine,

While the lyrics of Lorenz Hart still gives a thrill
When I hear the music of 'My Heart Stood Still'.

But my admiration never ceases and time flies
When I listen to Kern's 'Smoke Gets in Your Eyes'

Then there was Gershwin, arguably the best, which can be played for hours without rest,
And his music with its jazz-infected brilliance can be improvised in many ways because of its resilience.

It was he who won plaudits galore
When he played his *Rhapsody* in 1924.

Along came Porter with his 'Begin the Beguine'
That can best be enjoyed with a glass of gin.

'Come Fly with Me; was a Jimmy Van Heusen song;
He flew his own plane, and girls tagged along.

And Harold Arlen with 'Over the Rainbow' and 'Blues in the Night'
Won many Oscars and set the world alight.

Many followed, like Ellington the Duke, Dubin, Youmans, and Styne
Not forgetting Mercer, Warren, Carmichael, and Hammerstein

Also, Fields, Caesar, Donaldson, Brown, and Fain
Vernon Duke, Ranger, Monaco, Burke, and Lane

Then Harburg, Noble, Robin, and Steiner.
There were few as good, and none were finer.

Theirs were the best accompaniment of the '30s Depression
And the sadness of World War II that followed in succession.

They provided the music that made living worthwhile,
That was whistled and sang and had such great style.

Indeed, the music of Gershwin, Porter, Warren, Rodgers, Kern, and Berlin
Were the best ever from theatre, cinema, and the alley of pan and tin.

There were many others I could not include,
So I hope they will forgive me and not feel screwed.

Preface

Research into what eventually became this book began in the last decade of the nineteenth century. I have long played the songs from the Great American Songbook beginning in my early teens. However, my knowledge of the composers and lyricists who provided this wonderful music remained a mystery. I first looked up the dates of their births and deaths.

I was astonished to find that the majority of them were born in the last decade of the nineteenth century and the first decade of the twentieth. Somehow that struck me as being somewhat incredulous.

Having played this music for over seventy-five years, I had arrived at the conclusion that I had no favourites among these music marvels. At that point, I looked at my collection of books and found seven or more books about George Gershwin and, on average, a mere one or two each on all the others. At that point, I realised that it was Gershwin who had provided whole new chords, key changes, and rhythm and mood changes that fascinated me and that few, if any, of the others had touched.

In no time, a whole new generation of talent emerged and opened up a seam of golden melodies. Even established composers like Jerome Kern and Vincent Youmans began to swing a little with 'Can't Help Loving Dat Man' and 'Time on My Hands', both of which I enjoy playing. Then of course there was the strange case of Harry Warren whose standard joke was, 'Even my friends don't know who I am.' Indeed, it was Harry's songs that were more famous than he was himself. Who can ever forget 'I Only Have Eyes for You' and 'Chattanooga Choo Choo'?

There have been many times when I've played a tune and somebody has asked me, 'Is that song by Gershwin?'

Yes of course there were, other standout composers, like Kern, Berlin, Porter, Carmichael Warren, Arlen, and Rodgers, all of whom produced great melodies. But somehow Gershwin led the way, and with his legendary ego, style, and class, still found time to help other composers along the way up and congratulate them when they arrived.

It was in the 1920s that he did the unthinkable when he broke into classical music with his *Rhapsody in Blue* and then *An American in Paris* and his piano Concerto in F. In the 1950s, I learned to play 'Porgy and Bess', another amazing piece of music by Gershwin, which still tests me today. I can't think of any other composer who could have written such an astonishing piece of music. Perhaps his greatest gift was to introduce jazz into almost everything he wrote.

He and his fellow musicians created a body of music that today is still played and admired around the world in what is termed *standards*. As time moves inexorably on, more of these songs seem to reappear in television commercials. These melodies will never be forgotten, and I hope that, in some small way, *We Sang and Whistled Then* will help to reawaken the musical soul that exists in the human brain and see it re-emerge again into the bright light of day. Many of the songs when written were about love, and Gershwin, Ira this time, wrote these lyrics to his brother's music, 'Our Love Is Here to Stay'. I would like to think that the songs in this book are also here to stay.

Introduction

There is a magic to music—a feeling created that removes one from the humdrum constraints of everyday life to a wonderful make-believe world where, as famous lyricist E. Y. (Yip) Harburg put it in 'Over the Rainbow', troubles melt like lemon drops and dreams really do come true.

In this book, you'll meet the men of the early twentieth century who wrote the most wonderful creative music the world has ever known. Their music was matched by the brilliance of the lyricists, who were indeed the poets of the modern age. These men created a superb anthology of popular music, a canon that today is justifiably known as the Great American Songbook.

What I find extraordinary is that so much wonderful music came from composers who were born between 1895 and 1915? How did that happen? Perhaps there is a God after all!

The magic of playing the piano music, certainly for me, rests with the melody of the piece. It is the heart of the matter, which, when combined with the lyrics, results in a harmony of sound. Such harmony creates a glamour and illusion that pleases the ear and raises one's thoughts to a higher level, remaining in the memory for many a year. Such music sustained the nation during the Second World War and helped maintain the people's morale through those dreadful years. Such music made us all the dreamers of dreams.

This book is largely concerned with the music that filled our ears between the years 1925 and 1955, a time known as the golden years of the American popular song. On the plus side, this period included the invention of the talking pictures; radio; the microphone;

and, following the Second World War, the magnetic tape (a German invention). The negative side, of course, includes the Wall Street Crash of 1929 and the Second World War.

It is well known today that music positively affects the thinking process and has a major effect on general intellect and emotion. When people say they are not musical, that is, in my view, akin to saying, 'I'm not alive.' Music has also been linked to the language of love—in the early days of our civilisation, the sexes charmed each other with musical noises and rhythms. Various forms of dancing, which George Bernard Shaw described as 'a perpendicular expression of a horizontal desire', also took centre stage. Without doubt and on many fronts, music talks to us, and many people decode their feelings through music and dancing quite easily, while others find it far more difficult. What is certain, however, is that music is interpreted in a variety of different ways. I have been reliably informed that musical activity stimulates not just the left or right sides of our brains but most of our brain cells at the same time. It is no wonder, therefore, that when I sit at the piano and play a Gershwin tune, I feel that I have been transported back to the New York of the 1920s—a time before my birth.

Most people today are aware that America is a melting pot of races. The black population arrived in the United States against their wishes, and between 1880 and 1925, more than two million Jews arrived and were very pleased to do so. They had left Europe, with its hotbed of social unrest, pogroms, and economic hardship, and immigrated to a free country—the United Stated of America. In Germany, following the rise of the Nazi Party into government, Dr Goebbels, the propaganda minister, spoke as follows: 'The age of extreme Jewish intellectualism has now ended, and the success of the German revolution has given the right of way to the German spirit.' According to Louis P. Lochner, the head of the Associated Press Bureau in Berlin at the time, Goebbels made this statement after Nazi raiding parties had gone into public and private libraries and thrown into the streets books that Goebbels, in his supreme wisdom, had decided were unfit to be read by Nazi Germany.

For some two thousand years, the Jews had been a people without a home. The very first time in my life that I heard the term 'Jew', it was in the context of 'the wandering Jew'. What it meant I had no idea. And several interpretations today can be found in a number of books, such as Evelyn Waugh's *Helena* (1950) and Robert Nichols's *Golgotha and Co* (1923). However, my own belief today is that the term 'wandering' really meant what it said literally. The Jews had sought a permanent home for many years, and it wasn't until the Balfour Declaration of 1919 that they succeeded in creating the State of Israel. Sadly, this act also created a continuing animosity between the Arabs and the Jews that continues to this day.

In the United States the Jews were free to fit in, and they created and defined a new American culture through music and film to which we in the Western world became captive. Today that period of music is known as the golden age of popular music. It was the explosive mixture of Jewish and Afro-American musical themes that created a totally new era of popular music, which set the world alight and brought hope and pleasure to the masses. It popularised composers like Jerome Kern, Irving Berlin, George Gershwin, Cole Porter, Richard Rodgers, and Harold Arlen. Here I must also add the name of Harry Warren, who wrote countless standards for mostly second-rate films and buried himself in Hollywood. He himself admitted that even his friends didn't know who he was.

It was the lyrics of a song that people sang and remembered, and it was the lyrics quite often written by university-trained and well-read people who became household names and who had the knowledge and skill of the vernacular to write the words that were truly American. Some of these greats were Lorenz Hart, Ira Gershwin (brother of George), E. Y. Harburg, Johnny Mercer, and Oscar Hammerstein. These men wrote lyrics that distinguished them from the other lyricists and musicians of the Great American Songbook.

Most of the Jews who arrived in the United States started their journeys from somewhere in Europe, and while most of them felt it expedient to keep their Jewish identities, they did little to advertise it. Artie Shaw described how he was bullied in school because of his name, Arthur Jacob Arshawsky. He soon realised that America was essentially a Gentile country, and success only became his when he Americanised his name. George Gershwin was born Jacob Bruskin Gershowitz but became the most American of all Jews when he changed his name. Bob Dylan had been born Robert Allen Zimmerman, and there were many others who changed their names, like Al Jolson, Barbra Streisand, Harry James, Frank Loesser, Richard Rodgers, Stephen Sondheim, Billy Joel, the Marx Brothers, Max Steiner, and Harold Arlen.

Jews had certainly created an over-representation in the popular music industry and the film industry, yet there was no great wave of anti-Semitism as a consequence. By the 1920s, Jewish production companies in Hollywood would list the following: Selznick, Goldwyn, Fox Films, United Artists Corporation, Paramount, and the Universal Film Company. For the Jews who did much to build this new culture and helped create Hollywood, it really must have seemed that the United States of America was indeed a truly free and great country.

This new music was brought to life by now-famous vocalists. There were many, of course, like Dick Haymes, Vaughn Monroe, Helen Forrest, Frank Sinatra, Kitty Kallen, and Ella Fitzgerald, but the most famous of all was Bing Crosby, who has been said to have the world's friendliest voice. Tony Bennett had stated that, at his peak, Crosby was bigger than Elvis Presley and The Beatles combined, and Decca Records added that Crosby's voice had been heard by more human beings than anyone who had ever lived on planet Earth. When I listen to Crosby, I am always struck by his laid-back affability. He came to typify Middle America, but his appeal was global and reached out to all ages, sexes, and races. Certainly, he was my family's favourite singer, and even my grandfather, who was no lover of the radio, always turned it on if Crosby was singing. He was one of the first singers in the world to exploit the possibilities and intimacy of the microphone. He also had the ability of making the lyrics ring true. Tommy Dorsey used to tell Sinatra, who was then a vocalist with his band, 'There's only one singer you ought to listen to, and his name is Crosby.'

Crosby had many business interests, and by 1940, he was the biggest name in show business in America. He had arrived on the music scene at the same time as a new wave of technology that had begun to transform the industry. With the microphone, electrical recording combined with the explosion of radio on both sides of the Atlantic, paving the way for a new style of singing. Up to that point, singers had needed the lung power for their sing in to reach the back of the hall. Now things changed dramatically.

By 1935, there were more than thirty million radio sets in Britain. Unlike the freedom of ownership of radio stations in the United States, in Britain, listeners had little alternative but to listen to the British Broadcasting Corporation, known throughout the world as the BBC. Demand, however, existed for popular music, especially jazz and dance band music. As a result, the International Broadcasting Company was set up, and the broadcaster hired airtime from overseas stations, which then broadcast popular music programmes. The most popular of these stations was Radio Luxembourg. These programmes only ceased when the European War began and the Luxembourg's transmitters fell into German hands.

After the war, the pre-war status quo resumed. By the time the Second World War started, 96 per cent or more of homes in the north-eastern part of the United States had radios. In the south of the country, the percentage was rather lower. Even there, one radio existed for every two homes. Consequently, World War II music could be distributed to a vast audience, and coast-to-coast broadcasting in America became possible.

The first piece of sheet music I ever played on my piano was 'Beautiful Dreamer'. The composer was an American, a famous American with the name Stephen Foster and widely referred to as the 'Father of American Music'. He wrote that piece of music the year he died in 1864 and, as I have already pointed out, well outside the musical parameters of this book. I believe I first heard the music when it was sung by Bing Crosby, accompanied by the John Scott Trotter Orchestra early in the Second World War. 'Beautiful Dreamer' was a favourite piece of music in our house when I was a child, and my father loved to sing it. Stephen Foster lived from 1826 to 1864, a short life, but during that time he created a legacy of superb melodies. In 1847 his first hit was 'Oh Susana', and he followed this with 'Old Folks at Home' written in 1854. The latter piece became the official state song of Florida in 1935. 'My Old Kentucky Home' had been composed a year earlier, and that became the state song of Kentucky in 1878.

Continuing in a nostalgic mood, I have always been surprised at what we as human beings take for granted. I have played a variety of pianos over a period of seventy years but never asked myself who invented and created the first one. Well that honour fell to Bartolomeo Christophori (1655–1731) of Italy. His invention was first called 'clavicembalo cel' e forte piano and shortened today to the now common name 'piano'. The world owes him a great deal.

Music found a notable role for itself during the Second World War. The music spoke of love, absence, nostalgia, glory, and an eventual return to peace and happy days when the war ended. In Britain, the most popular stars were George Formby and Gracie Fields. Both of them were regarded as wartime heroes, as they performed at various theatres of war but also because they came from the working class. The wartime leader, Prime Minister Winston Churchill, was far less popular with his fellow countrymen and women—he having come from a small social elite circle. The most popular songs early in the war were 'Kiss me Goodnight, Sergeant Major', 'We're Going to Hang out the Washing on the Siegfried Line', and 'Run Rabbit Run', among others. Perhaps the best remembered was a song sung by Vera Lynn (the forces' sweetheart), 'We'll Meet Again'. Even today, all these years later, the song still evokes past memories and, for many, still brings tears to the eyes.

The songs that America broadcast at that time were far too numerous to list here, but I have made an effort to include the ones I remember for each year of the war beginning in 1939 and ending in 1945. That was a difficult task, as a number of dates could have been used—for example, when the song was written; when it was first played and sung; or, lastly, when it was recorded. I would like to think that I have placed most of them in their correct time frame.

The Second World War saw the death of more than 60 million people, yet today the young seem to have little knowledge of it and of the significant events that occurred during it. Consequently, for each year of the war following the music that was played and sung, I have selected an event of note that happened then. Sometimes this will be a famous battle, for example Stalingrad in 1943; other times, it will be a change in government, such as the 1944 Education Act in Britain, which had far-reaching consequences for millions of children. This act safeguarded the future of the English public school (for the well off), while at the same time ignoring the talents of almost three quarters of its secondary state school children. Indeed, it was so selective and bad that I found it necessary to include it in this book. I saw the results at close hand, having spent almost ten years teaching in the secondary school system in England and Wales, before embarking for the rest of my working life as an airline pilot in the Civil Aviation Industry both in the United Kingdom and abroad.

I have played the piano from the young age of eight years and gradually through the years grew to love the instrument. However, like all love affairs, it was not always constant. And it was my mother's inventiveness and my father's strength of personality that placed me firmly back on track when I strayed. Like most children learning the piano at that time, I learned musical pieces that were classical or semi-classical in nature. It was early in my teenage years that I encountered American popular music for the first time. However, it was sometime later that the composers like Jerome Kern, George Gershwin, Irving Berlin, Richard Rodgers, Cole Porter, and others became known to me.

You will have become aware that nearly all the composers and lyricists mentioned in this book are men. That was not a choice of mine but, rather, a reflection of how society was structured before the Second Word War. It was the social changes brought about by the war that fundamentally changed the role of women in Britain and the United States at that time. However, in the field of music before the war, one woman stood out, and she was regarded as one of the boys. Her name was Dorothy Fields, and she was a fine pianist and a superb lyrics writer. She wrote over four hundred songs during her career, and it is said that she taught Jerome Kern to swing, and that must have taken some doing. With Kern, she wrote some remarkable lyrics for 'The Way You Look Tonight', which won them both Oscars. She and Kern also wrote 'I Won't Dance' and 'A Fine Romance' among many others. Fields wrote many lyrics for Broadway shows and Hollywood films. Her lyrics are lovely to sing and had touching simplicity of expression with the gift of being able to match the rhythms of colloquial speech to music. She teamed up with Jimmy McHugh and wrote beautiful lyrics for songs like 'I'm in the Mood for Love' and 'I Can't Give You Anything but Love.'

In the mid-forties, she had an idea to write a stage musical with a cowboy theme as a fictionalised account of Annie Oakley, a female sharpshooter of the Wild West. Rodgers and Hammerstein were persuaded to produce the show with Irving Berlin writing the music. As he always wrote the words to accompany his music, he did so for this show, and Dorothy Fields and her brother Herbert Fields wrote the book of the show. *Annie Get Your Gun* opened at the Imperial Theatre New York on 16 May 1946 and was a great success. Dorothy Fields's good friend Ethyl Merman (for whom the part was written) played Annie Oakley, and it was the biggest Broadway hit in Merman's career. It ran for 1,147 performances.

The choice of music in this book is mine, and if I have omitted some favourites blessed by others then I apologise. However, my choices are eclectic, and most of them result from musical programmes I heard in my early years. Today, I play most of them on the piano and regard them as old friends.

When my pals of my youth would walk home from the cinema (we called it 'the pictures' then), we would inevitably break into song. 'Home on the Range' and 'Don't Fence Me In' were favourites. More often than not, some of us would forget the words and then resort to whistling the tune. Hence, this book is dedicated to my former friends, many of whom are no longer with us. So, the title just had to be *We Sang and Whistled Then*.

Note: The wartime president of the United States was Franklyn Delano Roosevelt, and he acknowledged that his favourite song was 'Home on the Range'. The most popular version was sung by Bing Crosby, and he recorded it in 1933, 1938, and again in 1939. The composer was Daniel E Kelly, and the lyrics were provided by Dr Brewster M. Higley, both Americans. It became the state song of Kansas in 1947 and the unofficial anthem of the American West and also of our group of young boys.

CHAPTER 1

The Dire 1930s

The Rhondda, South Wales, in the 1930s was a place and time when human civilisation in Britain entered its darkest chapter. That decade was a byword for mass poverty, unemployment, and violence with a world war hovering just over the horizon. Fortunately, I was too young to realise all this, so I missed the soup kitchens, dole queues, and hunger marches to London from South Wales and Jarrow in the North of England. Mass unemployment seemed endemic, and in the United States, joblessness reached 25 per cent. Social unrest seemed universal, and fascist and nationalistic movements began in Italy, Spain, and Germany. In our own Rhondda Valleys, communism was rife, with its centre in Maerdy at the apex of the Rhondda Fach (the small Rhondda). In the 1930s, almost each village was created around a coal mine, both the villages and the coal mines had grown to a huge extent since the year 1850. So, what had been two beautiful valleys was soon turned into a large urban conurbation.

For the benefit of people living outside Wales, the Rhondda Valleys are comprised of two separate valleys, with both valleys connected at the town of Porth at the southern end.

In 1807, a poet considered the Rhondda as 'a wonderful place of such beauty as the imagination would find difficult to surpass'. The valley had a few sparse farms and a beautiful clear river running its length. The name Rhondda translated meant 'The river's speaking aloud'. Similar to the Irish expression 'a babbling brook', while Llwynpia translated meant the 'magpie's bush'. The continued search for the black gold (anthracite coal) had, by the early 1900s, tuned a once beautiful landscape into a scarred industrial one.

The Rhondda became a part of the southern Welsh coalfield and, at around the size of 1,000 square miles, was the largest in Britain. It was this coal that drove the ships of the Royal Navy and the Merchant Marine in two World Wars. Indeed, it was the coal that made the name 'Rhondda' famous throughout the world. However, the human cost was high; pit explosions between 1844 and 1965 killed well over 1,000 men, including my great grandfather in the Maerdy explosion on 23 December 1885. Thousands more were killed by black lung disease (CWP) or pneumoconiosis. This disease resulted from a long exposure to coal dust. There were no CT scans in those days. In George Orwell's *The Road to Wigan Pier*, he stated that, 'if there is one man to whom I do feel inferior, it is the coal miner.' I echo those sentiments, as one who came largely from families who had arrived in the Rhondda to work in the coal mines.

The people of the Rhondda were largely made up of immigrants; the lure of coal and the wages that the industry paid was far better than that paid to labourers on the land. Five thousand or more people from the county of Somerset arrived in the Rhondda and many more from other parts of England. The Irish arrived in large numbers, and the local Llwynypia Colliery shaft was sunk by a Scotsman, Archibald Hood, and opened in 1863. His statue still stands proudly today with his outstretched arm pointing to the site where his colliery was built.

The Italians also arrived, not to work in the mines but to open ice cream parlours throughout the Welsh valleys. I believe that one had the surname Bracchi; consequently, all such cafés thereafter were called Bracchi shops. These became a very important part of the social life of the area, and some still remain, although the coal mines have all now disappeared. Because of the vast numbers of immigrants arriving in the Valleys of South Wales, the original Welsh language was 'drowned out' by the main commercial language of English. However, the resilience of the Welsh people rose to the occasion, and today in late 2017, almost a million people either speak Welsh or are busy learning the language. I have a friend living in the village who was born in

Yorkshire, married a Welsh girl when only seventeen years of age, and worked in a number of Welsh mines for over fifty years. Derick lost his wife some years ago and suffers from a disabling lung disease. Nevertheless, at the time of this writing, he is learning to speak Welsh at the youthful age of almost ninety years. What a man!

My grandfather on my father's side of the family had reached the Rhondda in 1891 and, by the turn of the century, had married a beautiful local teacher. He established Royal Stores, a grocery business and a confectionery shop next door. Within a year or so, he had been persuaded to join the local Labour Party, which at that time was sweeping across the valleys of South Wales. Soon he was chosen to be their candidate to fight the communists in the local elections of 1938. Having won that contest, he rose to become the council leader and chairman and the de facto Lord Mayor of Rhondda with its population of 160,000 plus people. Maerdy had, by this time, become known as 'Little Moscow', a title it retains to this day.

I remember as a young boy standing in the windowsill in the upstairs lounge of Royal Stores one Sunday afternoon watching the men assembling in front of the Workman's Hall. Behind a banner and a variety of flags, the men began their march on their way to the next village of Ferndale a few miles lower in the valley. My grandmother then entered the room, and I asked her why the men were marching. Her reply was short and curt. 'Come down from the window, boy. They are not nice people.'

In the same lounge stood a beautiful upright piano, which my grandfather had bought for his daughter, my Aunt Peggy, during the First World War. It was always kept tuned, and it possessed a wonderful rich tone. I played it every time I arrived in Maerdy. It had my name engraved on the piano lid, well not exactly my name, but that of a relation of mine based in Fishguard in West Wales, who was a piano distributor. His name coincided with mine—at least the first and last names did. Today, over a hundred years later, the same piano now resides with another aunt of mine living in North London, and I am given to understand that it plays as well as ever.

The main music of our young lives rested undoubtedly with the valley chapels. Apart from the usual array of hymns all sung in Welsh, there were musical concerts held in the vestry, which inevitably we were persuaded to attend. Salem Chapel was our focus of attention on a Sunday. Here we stood and joined the chorus of hymns with some vigour. We boys shared a couple of benches on the right-hand side of the chapel, while the regular elders filled the central aisles. The star singing performance was Ellyn, who attracted our interest largely because of her enormous bosom (my mother's description). Ellyn was a middle-aged spinster of substantial proportions, roughly eleven stone or more of major attachments and gossip. However, when she struck the high notes, the chapel windows rattled, and the lights flickered. She made the choir redundant, and the chapel deacon (all men) looked on at her in unstinting admiration. She certainly was a large mass of female pulchritude. Had Marilyn Monroe or Jane Russell visited our chapel, they would have certainly fled back to Hollywood to get a refit. She sat next to Cassie, a lady of roughly the same age and size. Cassie was the local 'do-gooder' and the leading air raid warden in our neighbourhood during the war. She, like Ellyn, was a leading soprano with very large shoulders. Indeed, she looked like the local blacksmith in a skirt but, nevertheless, was universally admired for her good works in the neighbourhood. She and Ellyn made a formidable pair, regarded by our gang as a rather frightening combination. But oh boy, could they sing!

The half dozen or so chapel deacons sat in front in a semicircle around the altar facing the audience. The head deacon was Diaphragm Davies, so called by us boys. He was a large man with a booming voice, which often changed key when he sang and, thereby, confused the organist. At Christmastime, we often sang carols outside the front of his house, but never once did he answer the door. He was a mean man and a poor example of Christian charity. So we changed tack and knocked his door—keeping very quiet. When he opened the door and saw only the vague images of little boys, he roared with anger. We fled in all directions, safe in the knowledge that, in the blackout he had no way of recognising any of us. We then tied thread to his door knocker and, from a safe distance—hidden behind a bush, tree, or fence—would pull the string and listen to his door knocker clanging away. His roar when he appeared must have disturbed the roof tiles, and we still ran for our lives.

Another deacon was known as 'Danny One Arm'. He was a kindly man and sold toffee apples to us at the school gates during the week. He had lost his arm in a colliery accident. But unlike Mr Davies, Danny was a nice man and was always friendly and cordial to us boys. Consequently, no tricks were ever played on Danny. And when we sang at his front door one Christmas, we were surprised when he asked us all to enter his house and poured each one of us a drink—telling us not to tell our parents. We all loved Danny, and I have often wondered what became of him.

Sometime later when I was in the grammar school, we often played our Saturday rugby matches on the Cambrian ground at Clydach Vale. This pitch was situated almost on top of a nearby mountain. I played rugby there on numerous occasions but never really enjoyed the experience. A severe hailstorm occurred on one occasion, and hail stones the size of large marbles roared across the playing field. The players formed a large scrum on their knees, protecting their heads and faces as well as they could. I stood behind one of the upright posts and made myself as small as possible. The surface of the field was usually very muddy, and one day in torrential rain, the referee called a halt to the proceedings and explained that he had lost one of his eyes (a false one). Both teams scrambled around in the mud and luckily found it. The referee cleaned off the mud on his jersey and then reinserted it into his eye socket, and the game continued. Sometime later, I was told that the referee had lost his eye in the retreat to Dunkirk earlier in the war. *What a great chap!* I thought.

We boys called Tonypandy the capital of the Rhondda—largely, I suspect, because of its innumerable public houses and, far more important from our point of view, the three cinemas, or picture places as we called them. The Picture Drome stood behind Tonypandy square and was the most run-down. The Empire Theatre stood in the middle of the town and was certainly the largest, having two balconies. The uppermost was known to us as the 'Gods'; it had the cheapest seats in the house. The third cinema and the most posh was the Plaza at the far end of the town. All three were within a distance of three-quarters of a mile and were readily accessible, with seats ranging from nine pence (old money) to one shilling and six pence (1.6 d). All my pals lived in, and thus, we were the boys of the 'Magpie's Bush'. In the late 1930s and onwards for the next decade, these three cinemas became our window on the world. My favourite programme, which stirred my imagination and a love of history, was *The March of Time*. The programme was an American Innovation, which began in 1935 and was shown continually in British cinemas until 1951, a date that coincided with the advent of television in our homes.

The Pathé News was another source of information at the cinemas. Société Pathé Frères was founded in Paris in 1896, and its newsreels were shown in Britain cinemas from 1910 until 1970. Charles Pathe adopted the national emblem of France, the cockerel, as the trademark for his company. Indeed, each newsreel was preceded by the vision and sound of a crowing cockerel.

My father worked as the chief engineer at the local hospital and one day brought home a blue rugby jersey with the cockerel emblazoned on its front. This had been given to him by the hospital's chief superintendent, a Dr Watkins who had played rugby for Wales against France sometime before the war. It was customary then, at the end of each international game for the players to exchange jerseys—which was why I possessed a French rugby jersey with its cockerel emblem. However, I never associated the cockerel of *Pathe News* with the cockerel on my French rugby jersey. But then, of course, my age had not reached double figures.

Even before the declaration of war on that September Sunday morning, the valley had begun its preparation for war. Light industrial factories were opened to provide alternative employment to the coal industry. The first of these was the factory of Alfred Polikoff an Austrian Jew who had fled the racism of the Third Reich. He had been encouraged by the British government with its financial support to open a manufacturing unit in a valley of South Wales, a 'special area' and one of the four 'depressed areas' in the country as designated by the Government as early as 1934. The factory eventually employed 1,500 people and was soon producing large quantities of military uniforms. The valley was now being brought onto a war footing, like other parts of the country. By January 1940, ration books had been distributed, and food rationing began. People now had to register with a grocer for butter, margarine, lard, sugar, tea, cheese, bacon, and eggs and with a butcher for any sort of meat. Petrol rationing put an end to most private motoring, although there were few car owners in the valley. In my street, Sherwood, only one person owned a car, and he kept it in a garage and made friends with it on wet Sunday afternoons. By early 1941, clothing was also rationed, as were sweets and chocolate, while ice cream simply disappeared from shops, cafés, and restaurants.

Street lights, mainly gas in the valley, were now permanently turned off and a strict blackout enforced. Sticky tape criss-crossed windows to stop glass shattering and sandbags were piled high to protect important buildings, like the council offices and police stations.

The introduction of conscription saw thousands of young men called up for the forces, while many others volunteered. Those too young or too old were not conscripted or were excused on medical grounds or because they were already working in a 'reserved occupation'. They had the option if their occupation permitted to join the Home Guard, originally called the Local Defence Volunteers (the LDVs), created in March 1940. The age limit for the Home Guard was between seventeen and sixty-five years and recruited male volunteers only. They practised drilling, largely to boost public moral, and guarded public facilities at night. The firearms practise was carried out with the newly arrived American-produced rifles.

Many civilians were required to perform fire-watching duties at their places of work at night. My father worked all day at the local hospital and returned there night after night for his fire-watching duties.

Designated public air raid shelters, as well as Anderson shelters, were now erected, the latter in some of the gardens of private houses. These were corrugated steel structures erected over a three- to four-feet hole in the earth. Two million were issued free all over the country, but supplies soon ran out, as steel was needed for more urgent requirements. Gas masks were issued, and people were expected to have an apprehensive understanding that, in this war, civilians were liable to find themselves in the front line. Air raid wardens, first recruited in 1937, enforced the blackout, and salvage drives saw young people making their contribution to the war effort by enthusiastically collecting scrap metal, railings, and old pots and pans. In fact, the practical use of these materials was negligible, but it all had a valuable psychological effect in making people believe that they were contributing to the war effort.

The major problem of unemployment, which had stricken the valleys' communities in the 1920s and the 1930s, was banished. Now unemployed males entered the military, and older men too found work in the new ordnance factories close to the Rhondda, at Hirwaun in the north and Bridgend in the south. Also, for the first time, women now found work in them too. These two new factories employed a total of 45,000 people. Even closer to the valley was the greatly expanded Treforest Industrial Estate, where a further 17,000 jobs were created.

Women were now drawn increasingly and compulsorily into war work. In fact, the mobilisation of women was taken further in Britain than in any other belligerent country, allied or enemy, with the sole exception of Russia and, later, America. In March 1941, women aged twenty to thirty years (later lowered to nineteen years) became liable to conscription for war services into such organisations as the Women's Land Army and the Royal Observer Corps. Indeed, many women in the eighteen-to-forty-year-old age group were now subject to direction of labour; in other words, they were told where they were to work. Later that directive was extended to the forty-to-fifty-year-old age group. However, mothers with young children were excused this rule.

Many women, of course, joined the army. They served in the ATS (Auxiliary Territorial Service), the Air Force, the WAAFS (Women's Auxiliary Air Force), and the Navy WRNS (Women's Royal Naval Service). By the end of the war, some 10 per cent of the British Armed Forces were women. Also, for the first time, women were admitted to some trade unions. And incredibly, for the first time, some women began wearing trousers. Many of the older generation were positively scandalised by this and even more so to see women drinking and smoking in public houses. A social revolution was under way, giving women a new self-confidence in what was essentially a male-dominated community. Such events brought about profound change in the valleys of South Wales and elsewhere across the country.

It was shortly before 6 a.m. on Friday 1 September that German forces invaded Poland. They proved conclusively that fast-moving armoured columns operating with close air support would make the trench warfare of the First World War obsolete. Soon, the Russians also joined this invasion from the east, and poor Poland was doomed. A new word was entered the lexicon of the English language—a terrifying new word called 'Blitzkrieg', meaning 'Lightning War'. All our hopes of peace were now shattered, and while we hoped for the best, we feared the worst. The nation was in turmoil, and we were now told that the prime minister would soon be addressing the nation on Sunday 3 September. The nation now waited and prayed, but we boys continued to play, sing, and whistle.

CHAPTER 2
You're Swinging It

My dear mother believed that I had some talent for music. How she arrived at that decision remains a mystery to this day. She had lost my baby brother at birth, so she made me the centre of attention during my formative years, largely because I had inherited a defective gene, which gave rise to bouts of asthma from time to time—a condition that, even today, has no known cure. As a result, I was labelled a 'delicate' child, a term that irritated me beyond belief. Consequently, I grew up attempting to prove I was anything but delicate and received much opprobrium for my efforts. Being good at various sports did much to alleviate my condition and allowed me to compete on an almost level playing field with my compatriots.

By the time I'd reached the age of eight years or so, my mother decided that I should begin my musical education. And soon a new piano arrived at the house, courtesy of a great uncle who, among his many holdings, had acquired a music shop in Cardiff. My first piano teacher was a Mr Hammond, a very quiet man who gently persuaded me to learn the lines and spaces of the treble and base clef. He knew full well that I was something of a rabble-rouser even at my young age and I rather resented learning the piano, whilst my pals enjoyed their freedom outside. This constant intrusion into my private life thoroughly annoyed me and caused a certain amount of family friction.

This reached an unfortunate conclusion one evening during a lesson when I revolted against what I considered the simple; banal; and, in my view, sissy tunes I was being forced to play, like 'Buttercups and Daisies'. I pretended to faint and fell to the floor. Poor Mr Hammond was at a complete loss, and he left the room to inform my parents. My father quickly arrived on the scene, put a firm boot into my behind, dragged me back onto the piano stool, and clipped me hard across the ear. With tears running down my face, I suddenly began playing 'Buttercups and Daisies' with some zeal, as if my life depended upon it. I believe now that had my father not acted in that fashion, my piano playing days would have ended there and then, and my life would have become so much poorer for it.

Mr Hammond, a lovely man, had been sorely tried by my antics, and so a new teacher, in the form of Mr James, soon arrived on the scene. Now it appeared necessary for me to attend at his home for lessons, and my messing about ceased abruptly. Now for the first time, it appeared that I had a certain flair for piano playing. But how my mother could have known that remains a mystery.

Within a year with my new teacher, I was entered for my first examinations. This was the elementary examination of the London College of Music. It took place on a very cold February day, and the one-hour train journey was followed by the long trek across Cardiff to the examination centre on Cathedral Road. My examiner that day turned out to be a genial gentleman by the name of Professor Harold Watts. He allowed me to sit down near the room's solitary gas fire to warm my hands. As a matter of fact and in a friendly tone, he began asking me questions on the theory of music, which I was able to answer quite easily. When my fingers were sufficiently warmed up, I began to undertake the playing part, which consisted of a series of scales and a study. The final part consisted of a minor and a major piece of music, which I completed successfully.

Some weeks later, my mother and I were standing in the front garden of the house when Mr James walked up the street towards us, grinning broadly. John passed with honours, he said, and, in addition, had the best result in the country for that examination. To say that my mother was elated and proud would be an understatement, and I was so pleased for her sake. I was happy with the result particularly when I was presented with a book of opera by the London College. I was far less pleased, however, when I heard my mother and Mr James describing me as a potential classical pianist. I knew enough about that idea to realise that such an ambition meant many hours a day practising the piano musical pieces for which I had little affection. The one fact of the examination results has remained with me to this day. The results paper showed the marks entered for each part played. The marks were out of ten, but dear Professor Watts had entered eleven out of ten for scales, which merely proved what a fine gentleman he really was.

Early one Christmas and bored with my toys, I ran down the back garden and knocked the door of my friend's house. David was playing with his fort and lead soldiers in the middle room, where I joined him. He had a little field gun where you pulled back a lever and loaded a matchstick into the barrel. Then when you released the lever, the matchstick would be propelled a few feet, knocking over a few lead soldiers. *What great fun*, I thought. And I became totally engrossed in this exciting activity for an hour or so.

Then David's sister, Eirwen entered the room and began playing the piano. She played a piece I had heard on the radio called 'The Teddy Bear's Picnic'. Eirwen was a few years older than me and played the piece well. When she finished, she stood up and gave the sheet music to me as a Christmas gift. I thanked her for the present and then went home and did my best to play the piece on my piano.

The music of 'The Teddy Bear's Picnic' had been composed by an American, John Walter Bratton, in 1907. The lyrics were added in 1932 by the Irish songwriter Jimmy Kennedy. As a child, I remember hearing it played and sung by Henry Hall and his orchestra. The music was also used in a Dad's army episode, 'The Big Parade', in 1970. My favourite rendition of the song was recorded by the Canadian singer Anne Murray in 2015.

'Beautiful Dreamer' was another song I liked, which I first heard sung by Bing Crosby. The music had been written by the American Stephen C. Foster in 1862, and Crosby had recorded it on 22 March 22 1940 with the John Trotter Orchestra. It was one of my father's favourites and I still play it today.

In such a small way and beginning with the two musical pieces mentioned, I began my torturous move away from classical music to the more popular genre. Another piece of popular music that remained in my memory was 'There's a Small Hotel'. Up to that time, I had played a number of pieces of music but took little notice of the names of the composer and lyricist printed on the top right of the lead sheet. The cover of 'There's a Small Hotel', however, attracted me. It showed a lovely looking blonde with long legs on a background of red, which for me in those days was an extremely lurid attraction but mild by today's standards. As a result, the names Richard Rodgers and Lorenz Hart stuck firmly in my memory. From that moment on, I began to remember and look out for the names of all the composers and lyricists who had made the songs what they were.

When they evacuated London children to our village in 1939, our family grew by one. But the whole group of them seemed to have arrived en masse from St Pancras, London. Audrey was about fourteen years of age when she first appeared in our street. At that time, I had not reached my teens, but when she passed me one day in the street, she reached out and brushed my forehead with her fingers and gently caressed my hair. An electric shock ran through me, and I ran indoors quickly and sat down in our middle room alone and in a daze. I recognised instantly that this was 'sex', far too important a word to bandy about, so I swore to myself to keep this discovery a secret.

During the following summer, cricket took pride of place, and so I packed all the cricket gear into a long bag and carried it alone down the street to the Tennis. The Tennis ground had been created when a cutting for the Taff Vale Railway had been made and thousands of tons of soil had been deposited to the east of the railway line. All this had been completed towards the end of the nineteenth century. The net result had been the creation of a fine group of playing areas suitably level and grassed, which provided successive generations of village children with a play area second to none for the next fifty years or so. The area initially housed at least six or more tennis courts of grass, clay, and concrete surfaces and, in addition, sported a bowling green and a large pavilion for the older generation. The whole area, around four to five acres or so, stood some thirty to forty feet above the level of the houses and adjacent railway line. The backdrop on the

Western side was the mountain with its mass of trees. In all, it was a beautiful area for sport, and when the tennis club ceased to exist in the early 1930s, the whole area became a playground for the youth of the area. We called it the Tennis. In the summer months, the Tennis became Our Lord's or Oval cricket ground, and in winter it became Wembley or Ninian Park (home of Cardiff City Football Club) or Hampden Park Glasgow or anywhere where our imaginations took us.

It was towards these Elysium fields that I dragged the heavy cricket bag that day. Where were my many pals? I asked myself. They had all seemed to have gone missing. The answer was soon to become evident when, on the far side of the field, six or more of my chums seemed to be wrestling together in a large heap. As I watched their antics, the reason soon became evident; from the bottom of the melee emerged Audrey, her clothes in complete disarray. The thought occurred that perhaps all my friends had also suddenly become aware of sex. I suddenly realised that girls as they got older seemed to develop strange lumps and curves, and I guessed that must have something to do with it. My aunt Mali had a very large bosom, almost two feet wide and very thick. She was a big name in her local Baptist chapel, and I couldn't figure out how sex fitted in with that. I really thought that, at night, she must have taken off her bosom and placed it on her bedside table.

This sexual spasm came to a head some weeks later when I bumped into Audrey on my way to the Tennis. Now Audrey had a variety of lumps and curves in various places, and having seen her in action, I guessed she knew all about sex. I was startled when she suggested that we should meet in the woods for a date. Intrigued and excited, I agreed and was not unduly troubled when I found that she had a younger local girl in tow. We sat on the grass verge elevated above the road and exchanged pleasantries. Suddenly she turned towards me and suggested coyly that we should exchange gifts. I failed to grasp her meaning, so she put it colloquially and in explicit terms. 'Well, if you show me yours, then I'll show you mine.' Well I was slow but not that slow, so I exclaimed sharply that my mother was expecting me home for tea.

I fled as fast as my legs could carry me and only felt safe when I entered the house. My mother, having discovered that I had been out with Audrey, warned me not to do so in the future, as Audrey was not a nice girl. Sex became, at least for the immediate future, a much less important facet in my life.

I never saw Audrey again, and she was dispatched to a new location, probably to the Outer Hebrides in Scotland. As a result, life returned to normal and, for the immediate future, football and cricket filled all my available free time.

* * *

Having had my lunch, I crossed the street to call on my pall Dill. As he was having his dinner, his father, an ardent communist, asked me into his study to listen to one of his favourite pieces of music. As I had just entered my teens, I knew little of classical music. My musical education to date had been limited to the pieces I had learned for my examinations and the popular songs I had heard on the radio. Mr Davies put on a record, and we both sat back and listened in rapt attention.

I had never heard anything quite like it before, and to state that I was awestruck would be an understatement. The piece of music was Tchaikovsky's Piano Concerto in B flat minor, and it was played majestically by one Benno Moiseiwitsch. His playing has been described as brilliant yet poetic. And without doubt, it disturbed my young senses that day. The music so impressed me that immediately I ran back home and persuaded my mother to buy a copy of the score on her next visit to town. I have to admit that the piece of music I learned to play was a watered-down version and clearly much easier to play than the original score. Nevertheless, it was sufficiently difficult for a young boy of ten years to master. That visit to Mr Davies' study I still remember quite clearly. But I was well into my adult years when I was able to see and hear Moiseiwitsch playing the piano for the first time on YouTube.

Benno Moiseiwitsch was born in Odessa, Russia, in 1890 and died in London in 1963. He moved his family to the United Kingdom and played his first concert in Reading in 1908. His playing was quite brilliant and poetic, features that must have enchanted me earlier as a young boy. He favoured the romantic composers, most particularly Rachmaninoff. Indeed, Rachmaninoff considered Moiseiwitsch his 'spiritual heir', and both these pianists have given me much pleasure with their playing over the years. Rachmaninoff was, of course, a composer of wonderful melodic music and the last in the tradition of the great romantic composers of the twentieth century. However, a paradox existed, in that critics sniffed at his compositions, but the working people loved them. During the first decade of the twentieth century Rachmaninoff's fame in Russia grew rapidly, bordering on idolatry. His romantic music is emotional, and Tchaikovsky's influence on him was quite obvious. Eventually, he became one of the most significant figures in the musical world and a worthy successor to Tchaikovsky. Following the Russian Revolution, he accepted an invitation to play concerts in Scandinavia. He stopped in Petrograd on 23 December 1917. As no trains were running, he travelled north through Finland on a sledge until he reached the Swedish frontier. He longed to leave Russia, but he could not have known then that he would never return again to the country of his birth in his lifetime. Sergei Rachmaninoff, born 20 March 1873, died 28 March 1943.

My second introduction to the classical genre occurred in much the same way. I was sitting on my front gate in idle fashion when I heard Frank call out to me. Frank was a local bus driver and a classical music collector and aficionado. 'John, if you're free, come in and listen to this.'

I ambled along and sat with Frank and his wife and found myself listening to the wondrous tenor tones of Jusse Björling singing 'Nessun Dorma' ('None shall sleep'), from Pucinis's opera *Turandot*. To say I was overwhelmed by his voice, again would be an understatement. His voice reminded me of a glacier, pure and ice-like, and he sang the high notes in an almost effortless manner. He was of course called the Swedish Caruso, a term well merited. He was born in Borlänge, Dalarna, Sweden, on 20 February 1911. Dalarna was an area that became familiar to me in later years, as my wife's family came from that area of Sweden.

While on the subject of tenors, I seemed to have completely missed out the name of the German Joseph Schmidt, who at that time was also known as the German Caruso. He was born in 1904 and grew to only four feet eleven inches in height. I was a mere child at the time, and the cloak of war that surrounded us acts as my excuse for having missed him. Being a Jew, Schmidt was thrown into a refugee camp, starved, and ill-treated. By a stroke of good fortune, however, he managed to be transferred to Switzerland, where he was a mere two weeks from freedom in 1942 when he had a heart attack and died. I would have missed hearing his magnificent voice but for a duet he recorded with that melodious American soprano Grace Moore, which fortunately can be found on YouTube. The piece they sang was from *La bohème* re-recorded in 1974.

Germany, in fact, appeared to have a production line in tenors, and another favourite of mine was Fritz Wunderlich (1930–1966), another who died young in a house accident, only a few weeks before he was to make his debut at the Metropolitan Opera in New York City singing Mozart's Don Giovanni by Puccini. The production line continues to the present day with the most wonderful voice of Jonas Kaufman.

By the time I had reached thirteen years and three months, I had passed both the intermediate and senior examinations with the London College of Music and would, without too much difficulty, play most of the music placed in front of me. As a consequence, my parents probably considered that I had arrived in the promised land, and I was now free from any pressure to continue on the same path. Similarly, I was also seduced into believing I had arrived and ceased to consider any move upward into the associate examination with the London College. It proved to be a huge mistake. Although I had no desire to teach music, the added knowledge would have created a new dimension in my understanding and playing of the piano. I guess we all make mistakes in our choices when we are young, and that was certainly my first.

Like my father, I, it appeared, also had a keen musical ear and listened to the latest musical offerings from the BBC. Leaving the grammar school on a Friday afternoon, it became my habit to visit Gregory's Music Shop in Tonypandy to peruse the popular song sheet music on display. Each sheet of music cost six pence (old money) but then climbed to one shilling. My limited pocket money was spent this way. My parents never objected to my playing this music, and my father would often stand behind me when I played and sing away. Despite the shortages of almost everything during the war years, singing was not one of them.

After the pictures, the gang of us boys would walk home on a Saturday night and, suddenly as if on cue, break into the song of the day. If the words were not known, we would hum or whistle and then return to our old favourite, 'Home on the Range'. We knew the words and harmonised in our fashion, which gave us a certain amount of pleasure. 'Don't Fence Me In' was another song that took our fancy. I was surprised many years later to discover that the words and music of that song had been written by Cole Porter. Very un-Cole Porter-like I thought! Porter did claim, however, that it was one of his least favourite pieces of music. However, when Bing Crosby recorded the song with the Andrew Sisters in 1944, it sold over a million copies and topped the American chart for eight weeks. This merely showed what a good judge of a song our gang proved to be. What we were never aware of, however, was that most of the songs we sang and whistled then were largely American in origin.

Before World War I, or the Great War as it was then called, American music was in many ways a reprise of European music, mostly in the Viennese style. The greatest exponents of this music were Victor Herbert, born 1859; Rudolf Friml, born 1879; and Sigmund Romberg, born 1887. All three wrote popular music in the fashion of Viennese operettas, and all three composers emigrated to American from Europe.

Herbert's most popular pieces were 'Naughty Marietta' (1910) and 'Sweethearts' (1913). His 'A Kiss in the Dark' became a world-famous waltz. He was present at New York's Aeolian Hall on 12 February 12 1924 when George Gershwin premiered his *Rhapsody in Blue* for the first time. Also present that night were Sergei Rachmaninoff, John Philip Sousa, Igor Stravinsky, and Fritz Kreisler, among others. In 1935, the very successful film *Naughty Marietta* was released, featuring Jeannette MacDonald and Nelson Eddy, who sang what has become an enduring and favourite song of mine, 'Ah Sweet Mystery of Life'. In 1939, Victor Herbert and his music were celebrated in a Hollywood film simply called 'The Great Victor Herbert'.

Rudolf Friml was both a composer and pianist. His best-known works were 'Rose Marie' and 'The Vagabond King', both great favourites of my father, who loved singing them. Indeed, to this day, I still preserve and play a rather battered score of 'Rose Marie'. Friml wrote this in 1924, and he collaborated on it with lyricist Oscar Hammerstein II and Otto Harbach. This operetta, together with the 'Vagabond King' and the 'Firefly', were all made into films.

Sigmund Romberg wrote his best-known operettas in the 1920s, with the 'Student Prince', the 'Desert Song', and 'The New Moon'. And once again, the wonderful voices of Jeanette MacDonald and Nelson Eddy were heard on screen. (Jeanette MacDonald died on 14 January 1965 aged sixty-one, and Nelson Eddy died on 6 March 1967, aged sixty-five.)

In the late 1930s, all three composers began to fall out of fashion. However, the music of Ivor Novello on this side of the Atlantic remained popular well into the 1940s.

Nearer home, my family was delighted to hear a piece of music composed by Franz Lehar, with lyrics by Heryer and F. Lohner Beda. The song was from the operetta *Das Land des Lasheins* (written in 1929). Translated, it was known as 'You Are My Hearts Delight' from the operetta *The Land of Smiles*. What pleased my father most was the mesmerising voice of the Austrian tenor Richard Tauber. He was born in the Austrian town of Linz of a Jewish family on 16 May 1891. He had a lyrical flexible tenor voice and sang with an exquisite Germanic inflexion. His singing at the same time revived Lehar's flagging career.

When Tauber was assaulted by Nazi thugs in Germany, he returned to his native Austria but, following the Anschluss, left for Britain, where he remained throughout the Second World War. He had a slight squint in his right eye and consequently always wore a monocle, even when singing. As a family, we adored his voice, and one of his songs I remember from my youth was 'Girls Were Made to Love and Kiss', a piece I still play on the piano. Yet again, it was written by that genius Franz Lehar from the operetta *Pagani*. When Tauber was resident in London, he produced the operetta *Old Chelsea* in 1942, which proved to be a bestseller. And the song 'My heart and I' became one of his most popular recordings. Tauber died on 8 January 1948 and was buried in Brompton Cemetery London. In many people's view, including my own, Tauber's voice was unique and his passion evident; the changing tones of his voice when singing were truly amazing.

A new form of music was now being heard in America, formed by the rise in jazz and ragtime, combined with the popular songs of the great innovators, who were largely Jewish. Perhaps Hoagy Carmichael said it better than anyone else when he wrote both the music and the lyrics to the song 'The Old Music Master':

> Along about 1917
> Jazz'll came upon the scene
> Then about 1935
> You'll begin to hear swing
> Boogie Woogie and Jive

Perhaps Hoagy knew more than most, as he was a composer, lyricist, pianist, actor, and bandleader. Among his world-famous songs were 'Stardust' (one of the most recorded songs of all time), 'Georgia on my Mind', 'Skylark', and 'Ole Buttermilk Sky'. He remained active from the 1920s through the 1970s.

The new American music was a monument to swing, sophistication, and syncopation. It was melodic; rhythmic; and, with certain limitations, could be played with various and multiple improvisations and was synonymous with the arrival of the radio set. Between the two world wars, jazz had begun to take hold in the United States of America. It had moved north from New Orleans to the cities of Detroit, Chicago, and New York. And by 1927, Americans had bought over 100 million of the so-called phonograph records. Paul Whitman, the self-termed 'King of Jazz', considered this music to be a genuine force, and in this, he was subsequently proved correct. However, a large part of so-called Middle America debunked this music, and some, mostly whites, considered it to be the music of the devil.

As early as 1911, Irving Berlin's song 'Alexander's Ragtime Band', had swept across the world. Strangely, however, there was no ragtime in it. Nevertheless, it did much to confirm that the jazz idiom was a musical force of the future. By the time of my arrival on this planet, the world of popular music had evolved from the jazz style of the 1920s to the swing and syncopated music of the '30s. Most sheet music told of love and 'I love you' lyrics invariably fitted into the thirty-two-bar popular song format of the time. The overall effect was a more sophisticated sound, and most of the big hands adopted this style. Is it any wonder then that my mother would shout from the kitchen, 'You're swinging it,' when I played the piano?

Such music now dominated the airwaves, and the larger mainstream bands embraced this style, largely by dropping their string section and using an anchoring rhythm section supported by the brass and wind section. Later it became quite common for a band or, if it grew, an orchestra to have a soloist centre stage with the musicians improvising on the music's central theme. By the late 1930s and early 1940s, swing had become the most popular musical style, and the music was clearly enhanced by the singers (crooners) who grew largely out of big band tradition. The best known were Bing Crosby; Frank Sinatra; and, later, Nat King Cole. It was said by some, that Crosby crooned, Nat King Cole sang, and Sinatra spoke in tune.

Gypsy swing music also emerged in Europe, with Django Reinhardt and Stéphane Grappelli, while later some rock and roll artists like Jerry Lee Lewis, Fats Domino, and Elvis Presley included many swing standards in their repertoires. Even Robbie Williams with his 'Swing When You're Winning' was reminiscent of the Sinatra style and sold over seven million copies in 2001.

Swing music, I believe, is almost endemic to our musical psyche and is likely to be reprised as a natural force for as long as the human race has the ability to play musical instruments and to sing and whistle. Alongside the music, an amazing culture of popular songwriters and lyricists emerged, such as the world had never seen and is unlikely to see again. These tunesmiths produced the most amazing pieces of music, and the lyricists, in anybody's language, would be recognised as the world's modern poets. It is difficult—indeed nigh impossible—for me to consider a world without the music of Jerome Kern, George Gershwin, Irving Berlin, Richard Rodgers, and Cole Porter. Alongside them were the lyric writers Ira Gershwin, Lorenz (Larry) Hart, Johnny Mercer, Oscar Hammerstein II, and the like. The world would have been a much poorer place without them.

Perhaps the golden age of American popular music all began on 27 December 1927 with the arrival of the musical play *Showboat* when it opened on Broadway. This show made a star of Paul Robson, that magnificent baritone/bass singer. *Showboat*'s music was composed by

Jerome Kern, and the lyrics were written by Oscar Hammerstein II. It was a new departure for Broadway musicals, as it told a story that depicted social and racial themes in an America seriously divided on racial grounds. Previous musicals had been derived from Viennese-style operettas, many of them written by composers like Sigmund Romberg (*The Desert Song*) and Rudolf Friml (*Rose Marie*) and, in Britain, Ivor Novello (*Glamorous Nights*). Friml, like Romberg, had been born in the old Austrian-Hungarian Empire and had emigrated to the United States. Others like Franz Lehar also wrote wonderful melodies like 'The Merry Widow', as did Victor Herbert with his 'Oh Sweet Mystery of Life'. I heard all these songs as a young man and later played the music on the piano. Without any doubt, my enduring love of musical melody was born at that time.

It was in the 1920s that the new revolution in American music took place. This new music reflected the rhythm, vernacular, and everyday life of Americans and American life in general. It became the most famous art form in the world and spread like wildfire across the planet.

On Friday afternoon, I would arrive at my grandparents' home in Maerdy. Having made the customary greetings, I sat myself down at the piano in the upstairs lounge as per usual and began playing my latest purchased sheet music. I remember a piece called 'All Through the Day' from the film *Centennial Summer*. The information was printed in black on the front cover, together with the actors who played in the film, namely Jeanne Crain, Cornel Wilde, Linda Darnell, and William Eythe. I now understand that the film was anything but exceptional but brightened up considerably by the music, the score of which was nominated for an Oscar in 1944.

By that time, I had begun to take note of the composer and the lyricist name on the lead page. Consequently, I became aware, for the first time, of the name Jerome Kern (as the composer) and Oscar Hammerstein II (as the lyricist). Sadly, the Oscar nomination that year was awarded posthumously, as Kern died on 11 November 1945 while preparing to write a score for a new musical to be called *Annie Get Your Gun*. As a result, Irving Berlin was asked to compose the words and the music for the show, which became a worldwide hit.

Kern, born on 21 January 1885, became one of the most important composers of the twentieth century. He wrote more than seven hundred published popular songs, including some of the best remembered, 'A Fine Romance', 'All the Things You Are', 'The Way You Look Tonight', 'Smoke Gets in Your Eyes', and 'Long Ago and Far Away'. In my humble opinion, he was the supreme melodist of the American theatre, cinema, and Tin Pan Alley.

There is little doubt that Kern strode the stage at the beginning of what is called American Popular music. Indeed, he, with Irving Berlin and George Gershwin, were at the initial cutting edge of the movement. Kern, like his two compatriots, was of Jewish decent, and as a baby, Kern was wheeled around Jerome Park in New York. This clearly suggested the name of the park to his parents as a suitable name for their child. It may also be of some interest to British readers that the park was owned by the Jerome family whose daughter, Jennie, married Lord Randolph Churchill, whose son was Winston Churchill, the future prime minister of Great Britain.

American music of the twentieth century coupled the best of American jazz with the almost religious undertones of Jewish genius. These characteristics distinguished it from the music of other countries and left its undying legacy on the world. Today the music is known as the Great American Songbook—long may it prosper!

CHAPTER 3

The War Begins and Disaster in France, 1939–1940

My mother and I were in the kitchen that morning, waiting on an announcement by Prime Minister Neville Chamberlain. He had served the country in that capacity since May 1937. The wireless set, as we called it then, stood on the shelf above a cupboard and required a chair to stand on in order to switch on or change a station. At precisely 11.15, the BBC announcer introduced the prime minister. The day was Sunday, 3 September 1939.

In his sombre voice, the prime minister began. 'I am speaking to you from the Cabinet Room in 10 Downing Street. This morning, the British ambassador in Berlin handed the German government a final note, stating that unless we heard from them by eleven o'clock that they were prepared at once to withdraw their troops from Poland, a state of war would exist between us. I have to tell you now that no such undertaking has been received and that consequently this country is at war with Germany.'

Even as a young boy, I could discern the sadness and even fear in his voice as he spoke the words 'this country is at war with Germany'. My dear mother was sobbing as I rushed out to the passage to answer the knocking on the front door.

David Brown a neighbour, was a burly man dressed in his army uniform, entered. He wore his three stripes with pride as he quickly strode into the kitchen to talk with my mother. It appeared he had already received his calling-up papers and was on his way to the railway station. My mother and David embraced in tears as David spoke of his impending departure.

The following week, he departed for Singapore, and no more was ever heard from him. He was part of the British Army, who succumbed to a much smaller Japanese force. That defeat was probably the worst defeat this country suffered in the war. Two months later, David's son died of a malignant disease, and his mother left the area for good a few weeks later, unable to face the all-too-familiar surroundings. This was a small part of the detritus of war, which had barely begun.

The country now entered a phase of waiting. The British Expeditionary Force shipped off to France, and the French sat comfortable and complacent within their impregnable fortress, the Maginot Line.

The next eight months would go down in history as 'The Phoney War' (a British spelling of the American 'phony') and known thereafter by the French as the 'Drôle de Guerre'. The French Maginot Line had been named after French Minister of War André Maginot and had been built in the 1930s to deter any invasion by the Germans. It stretched from the Swiss frontier to the borders of Luxembourg, and there it stopped. To continue building to the English Channel would have cost an excessive amount of money, and the French government did not wish to offend neutral Belgium.

In turn, the Germans constructed the Siegfried Line, a similar line of defensive forts and strongpoints extending 390 miles, and in part, facing the Maginot Line. The Germans commonly referred to it as the 'West Wall'. The popular song 'We're Going to Hang out the Washing on the Siegfried Line' was first broadcast in Britain on 11 October 1939, and it became a favourite among the troops and civilian population alike. Essentially, the lyrics made fun of the Germans in general and the Siegfried Line in particular. However, both the British and the French failed to take account of the brilliance of German

General Erich von Manstein, who would become the greatest strategic mind on any side during the Second World War.

The German general staff, under the direction of Franz Halder, could not be more innovative than to plan a virtual rerun of the First World War's Schlieffen Plan. This would operate like a door hinged on Switzerland and closing down to the west of Paris along the Channel Coast. This plan was a compromise and satisfied no one. But Manstein had already discussed his plan with General Guderian, the leading tank expert in the German Army who would lead the attack. Guderian was to attack north of the Maginot Line through the Ardennes, with the maximum number of Panzer units in its Army Group A, reinforced from Army Group B in the north. The latter would act as a diversion, drawing the British and French troops farther into Belgium. At the same time, Army Group A would attack through the Ardennes, the weakest part of the French line manned by second-level French divisions.

Manstein met Hitler on 17 February 1940 and persuaded him that such an attack would be decisive. Hitler agreed, and the attack succeeded brilliantly. Having crossed the River Meuse near Sedan on wooden pontoons and under fire, the German troops ascended the heights opposite, supported by continuous and terrifying Stuka bombing attacks. Soon the Guderian panzers were able to cross the river and fan out across the plains of Picardy. It was not the French who tried to hold back the Panzers but Hitler and the German general staff. Their own speed of success alarmed them, as their thinking processes were attuned like that of the French to the war of 1914 to 1918.

Within a week, Guderian and his Panzers had reached the Channel Coast, and the war for them was almost over. The British evacuated most of their troops from the port of Dunkirk, and within a few weeks, the French would seek an armistice. Although the British Expeditionary Force escaped with most of its forces from Dunkirk, they left behind over 90,000 of their fellows and most of their heavy weapons, transport, and tanks.

No more would we hear, 'We're going to Hang out the Washing on the Siegfried Line'. It appeared that the Germans had had the last laugh after all. But had they?

When General Alanbrooke was recalled from Dunkirk on 29 May 1940, he was informed by Anthony Eden, the foreign secretary that he was to lead a new army back to France through the port of Cherbourg. To say that Alanbrooke was appalled by this order would be an understatement. He realised that such instructions had come from Churchill, who was treating him and his troops as cannon fodder, in a lame attempt to support an already defeated French Army. Alanbrooke warned Eden that such an operation had no chance of success and would probably end in disaster. Alanbrooke had attended school in France and spoke fluent French and he was fully aware that the French Army was in the throes of complete collapse.

Some days later, when in France, he was telephoned by Dill, the then CIGS (Chief of the Imperial General Staff) who then put him through to Churchill, who questioned Alanbrooke's disposition of his forces. This was both insulting and a gross interference with a general in the field without any knowledge of the prevailing conditions. Churchill then told Alanbrooke that he had been sent to France to make the French feel that the British were supporting them. Alanbrooke's riposte was quite marvellous when he replied that it was impossible to make a corpse feel.

When Alanbrooke was close to losing his temper, Churchill agreed and re-embarkation soon began from the Normandy and Brittany ports. The French Army stopped fighting on the 17 June. By 19 July, Alanbrook was promoted the commander in chief of all Home Forces with full responsibility for defending Britain against the threat of the now likely German invasion.

CHAPTER 4
The Phoney War

'We're Going to Hang out the Washing on the Siegfried Line' was described by mass observation as the first great hit of the war. The song was composed by Michael Carr, born in Leeds but brought up in Dublin. He also composed the freedom concerts in 1942. The famous words were written by Jimmy Kennedy, who hailed from Northern Ireland. By using the first-person plural in the song, the appeal to the general public was great; and it suggested that the war would be short, and Britain would eventually prevail.

In France at the same time, the most popular song among the French was the beautiful melodious love song 'J'attendrai' meaning, 'I will wait for you'. It was first broadcast in 1938. It has been a favourite of mine ever since. I first heard it played in the television series *Das Boot* in 1981. The music was composed by Dino Olvieri, and the French lyrics, written by Louis Poterat.

It was the War in North Africa, however, that created the most popular song of World War II. Radio Belgrade, then in German hands, first broadcast the beautiful song 'Lili Marleen'. It was sung in German by Lale Anderson, and soon it became a favourite, among not only the German troops but the Allied troops as well. Three verses and the lyrics (poem) were written by Hans Leib, and he combined the nickname of his friend's girlfriend, Lilly, with the name of another friend Marleen. In 1938, it was set to music by Norbert Schultze and recorded by Lale Andersen, whose correct name was Elisabeth Carlotta Helena Berta Bunnenberg. (I think I will stick with Lale Andersen). Her voice was sensuous, husky, and extremely nostalgic and was listened by us all, becoming a favourite among British listeners, as well as the troops.

The song 'Roll Out the Barrel' became famous in the late 1930s. The composer was Jaromír Vejvoda, a Czech musician who wrote the piece in 1927. The English lyrics were written by Lew Brown and Vlademir Tirnan. The Glenn Miller orchestra recorded it in 1939, as did Benny Goodman. Another such song was 'Bless em All' (the long and the short and the tall). This song had been composed in 1917 by Robert Kewley with lyrics provided by Fred Godfrey. It was first recorded by George Formby in 1940. It proved very popular among us boys and was probably the first time in my life that I heard 'the F word'—as in, 'F em all'.

The RAF had its own version of the song, a parody of 'Bless em all':

> They say there's a Lancaster leaving the Ruhr,
> Bound for old Blighty's shore.
> Heavily laden with terrified men,
> All lying prone on the floor.

They also sang the following, to the tune of the German National Anthem:

> Home presents a dismal picture, dark and dreary as the tomb.
> Father has an anal stricture; mother has a prolapse womb.
> Sister Mary has aborted for the forty-second time.
> Brother Tom has been deported for a homosexual crime.

I have no information as to who wrote those words, but they must have created more than a few laughs in the aircrew mess.

Another wartime favourite was 'Kiss Me Goodnight, Sergeant Major'. The music is credited to Art Noel, and the words were provided by Don Pelosi. The boys loved singing the lines of this song—some of which I can still remember:

> Don't forget to wake me in the morning

And bring me a nice hot cup of tea
Kiss me goodnight, Sergeant Major
Sergeant Major, be a mother to me

Vera Lynn probably became well known to the public with her rendering of the song 'We'll Meet Again'. It was composed and written in 1939 by Ross Parker and Hughie Charles. It was recorded by Lynn in 1942, by Benny Goodman and his orchestra, and by the Ink Spots in 1943. It was popular because it emphasised optimism for the future:

We'll meet again
Don't know where
Don't know when
But I know we'll meet again some sunny day.

Sadly, many of our men in the forces who sang these words early in the war never did return home.

It was an English composer, Eric Coates, who composed three pieces of music that are well remembered from the war years. The first was 'Calling All Workers' which was broadcast on both the Light and Home Service programmes starting June 1940 and lasted until September 1967. The music programme was called *Music While You Work*. The piece was played at the beginning and the end of each programme. It was also played in factories throughout the land and is said to have improved productivity.

The second piece was 'The Sleepy Lagoon', with lyrics provided by an American lyricist, Jack Lawrence, who wrote the words early in 1942. I remember hearing this music for the first time when I was in the sick bay at my boarding school in Cowbridge Wales. The matron, a kindly soul, had put her wireless set (radio) in the sick bay so that I could listen to the BBC.

The third piece was the music he wrote for the radio show called *In Town Tonight*. The programme started in 1933 and lasted until 1960. Its theme music was the Knightsbridge March, written by Coates in 1933. The show started with the voice saying, 'Once more we stop the mighty roar of London traffic.' The programme then consisted of a series of interviews with famous people who happened to be 'in town tonight'. At the end of each show, the same voice would then say, 'Carry on, London,' and the traffic would resume on its way.

Coates also wrote a musical march in the 1950s, which became a very famous piece of music when it was used as the background music for the film *The Dam Busters*. Most people think this piece of music had been written for the film and because of the film it became Coates's most famous compilation. However, the music had been written some time earlier, and when Coates was asked to provide the music for the film, he lifted the piece from his archive and it fitted into the film admirably. I last heard it at Millfield School in Somerset, when the school entertained the Central Band of the RAF. That night, the band played 'The Dam Busters March' in honour of their guest, Johnny Johnson, the last living British member of the Dam Busters raid of 1943.

George Formby, like Gracie Fields, was born in Lancashire. He followed his father into show business and was a comedian and ukulele player. He took his father's name and learned his trade in the music halls singing comical songs. By the 1930s, he had become a major star and made a number of films through producer Basil Dean, the head of Associated Talking Pictures (ATP). George was offered a seven-year contract by Dean, which resulted in the making of eleven films.

An early film contained the song 'When I'm Cleaning Windows', with its suggestive lyrics. Although Lord Reith, director of the BBC, banned the song from the airwaves, it was reinstated after the royal family heard the song at the *Royal Variety Performance* and rather enjoyed it.

In 1937, George made a film called 'Feather Your Nest', and out of it came the song 'Leaning on a Lamp-Post'. The music for this song was written by Noel Gay, and the lyrics, by Andrew Eyton. It became one of George's most popular renditions and one of the most remembered songs of the war years.

In all the films he made, he was depicted as a working-class lad with an affable sense of humour and a cheeky resilience. Many of his songs annoyed some of the public but amused others largely through George's mastery of the double entendre. Examples of such songs were, 'When I'm Cleaning Windows', 'Chinese Laundry Blues', and 'My Little Stick of Blackpool Rock'. Indeed, the Lord's Day Observance

Society filed lawsuits against the BBC, as the BBC played this music on a Sunday. As a consequence, George issued a statement stating, 'I'll hang up my ukulele on Sunday, only when our lads stop fighting and getting killed on Sunday.' No more was heard on that subject.

By 1940, George Formby had become the highest-paid entertainer in Britain. He had applied to join the army but had failed the medical, so he joined the Home Guard as a motorbike despatch rider. Soon, however, he was called up to join ENSA (Entertainments National Service Association), formed in 1938 essentially to entertain the troops throughout the various theatres of war. As a result, George travelled to France, the Middle East, and Canada doing what he did best—singing and playing his ukulele.

Shortly after his death in 1961, the George Formby Society was formed at the Imperial Hotel Blackpool. Four conventions are held there each year. A television documentary has been made by the comedian, Frank Skinner, of such a convention that, I must say, I found hilarious. Watching a theatre full of people all playing their ukuleles whilst watching their hero George Formby playing the same music on a screen in front of them—this had me rolling around in laughter. Anyone can join the society, whether you can play a musical instrument or not. What is important, however, is that the music of George Formby is kept alive and the huge part he played in entertaining our troops during the Second World War is never forgotten.

The year 1940 carries a very special memory for me. It was the first film I ever saw with my parents. The film was Walt Disney's *Pinocchio*, with its music 'When You Wish Upon a Star'. That year, it won the Oscar for the composer Leigh Harline, with lyrics by Ned Washington. In 1934, Washington was signed by MGM (Metro Goldwyn Mayer), and he relocated to Hollywood. He wrote full scores for feature films for Paramount, Warner Brothers, and Disney. He worked with many of the greatest composers of the time, including Victor Young, Max Steiner, and Dimitri Tiomkin. Between 1940 and 1962, he won the best original music award twice—the first time for *Pinocchio* and, in 1952, for the song 'Do Not Forsake Me Oh My Darling' for the film *High Noon*. During that period, he was nominated for eleven Academy Awards.

Many of the songs that were played in Britain during the Second World War were composed by Noel Gay. That of course was not his real name but one assumed as a nom de plume. He was born with the name Reginald Moxon Armitage in 1898 in Wakefield, Yorkshire. He learned to play the piano at a young age. And by 1926, as an unknown composer, he began writing music for London Review a music magazine. He was on his way to the offices of the BBC to sign a contract when, as he was passing a West End theatre, he saw that Noel Coward was appearing in a show with one Maisie Gay. Consequently, from then on, he used the name Noel Gay—a name that was to take the West End by storm for the next twenty-five years.

Gay eventually wrote the music for forty-five songs, six London shows, and twenty-eight feature films. He wrote music for many of the biggest stars of the day, including George Formby, Gracie Fields, Flanagan and Allen, and Arthur Askey, among many others. His best remembered songs were 'Run Rabbit Run', 'The Sun Has Got His Hat On', 'Hey Little Hen', and 'Let the People Sing' (made into a film). However, the two most famous of his songs were 'The Lambeth Walk' and 'Leaning on a Lamp-Post'. The latter piece was made famous by George Formby.

George Formby's wife and manager, a lady called Beryl, was by all accounts a real 'tough nut' and generally not a nice woman. She had already stated publicly that George had written the song 'When I'm Cleaning Windows'. The sheet music I possess clearly confirms this.

This, of course, was far from the truth; indeed, it was a pure invention. The song had been composed by Henry Cliffard, with lyrics by Fred E. Cliffe as early as 1936. As a consequence, George received one-third of the royalties of a song that he was not legally entitled to. Beryl had browbeaten the real authors of the piece, threatening that, unless they allowed George's name to be on the sheet copy, then he would not be performing any more of their music.

She attempted to try the same trick on Noel Gay but failed. He was not a regular Formby composer and had been smart enough to ensure that, having written 'Leaning on a Lamp-Post', he obtained the copyright to it. Beryl then threatened to sue him if George's name was not included in the credits. She only conceded defeat when Gay threatened to inform the media that such were George's musical talents that he was incapable of tuning his own ukulele. Beryl consequently withdrew her threats, and Gay was added to an already long list of enemies. In many ways, this was a shame, as Gay confessed later that he would have liked to compose more songs for the ukulele maestro.

Sadly, he died in 1954 at the young age of fifty-six years. His music was melodious and often funny, and it helped to shake away the gloomy forebodings of war. For that alone, he is still remembered today, and I very much enjoy playing and singing his songs with my children and grandchildren.

Gracie Field was both a comedienne and a soprano. She had a lovely voice, and I first heard her singing the song 'Sing as We Go' early in the war. The music had been written in 1934 as a morale-boosting anti-depression song from a film of the same name. It was a good marching and singing number, and everybody seemed to know the words and sang it with gusto.

A second song of note was 'Wish Me Luck as You Wave Me Goodbye'—a very apt piece for its time. Both songs were written by the Welsh composer Harry Parr Davies, and the lyrics of the second piece were written by the famous novelists J.B. Priestley and Gordon Wellesley. The latter was later nominated for an Oscar for his writing adapted for the film *Night Train to Munich*.

Gracie's favourite song and also her theme music was 'Sally', and her first film was *Sally in our Alley*, a 1931 film and box office hit. However, she found film-making boring and much preferred live audiences, with whom she had a wonderful rapport.

In 1933, she set up Gracie Fields Children's Home and Orphanage at Peacehaven in Sussex, for children of those working in the theatrical profession who were unable to look after their own children. She lived in Peacehaven in Sussex and often made a point of visiting the orphanage, where the children called her Aunty Grace.

In 1936, she signed up with ENSA and later travelled to France to entertain the troops after war was declared. She carried on this work throughout the war visiting troops in the Middle and the Far East. After the war in 1951, she opened the Festival of Britain in London, and in 1956, she became the first actress to play Miss Marple in the US television production of Agatha Christie's *A Murder Is Announced*.

Gracie had been born in Rochdale in Lancashire in 1898, and in 1978 she was granted the Freedom of the Town. Seven months before her death in 1979, she was honoured by the queen and became a dame of the British Empire. She died in her home in Capri, Italy, and will always be remembered for the huge contribution she made to the morale of the people during the Second World War.

Note: Harry Parr Davies became Gracie's piano accompanist for much of her early career. He was born in Briton Ferry, South Wales, in 1914 and died in his early years when he was just forty-one in 1955. Harry wrote over two hundred published songs.

A favourite piece of music of mine originated in a 1928 London show called *That's a Good Girl*, produced by the then famous, Jack Buchanan. The song was called 'Fancy Our Meeting', with music by Joseph Meyer and Philip Charig. The lyrics were written by Douglas Furber, a lyricist and playwright (1885–1961). Furber began song lyric writing with an Australian composer, Emmett Adams. It was Adams who later wrote 'The Bells of St Mary', which had been published in 1917. In 1945, it became a major hit when sang by Bing Crosby in the film of the same name. The film was enormously popular and became the highest-grossing film of 1945 and the most profitable in the history of RKO Pictures.

In *Funny Face*, an American lyricist appeared—the first time I had registered his name. That name was Ira Gershwin. Ira, of course, was the brother of the famous American composer George Gershwin (more on both can be found in chapters 11 and 12 'Composers of the Glory Years' and 'Lyricists of the Glory Years' respectively).

Vera Lynn was another famous entertainer of the time. Her songs are still widely remembered, particularly 'We'll Meet Again', 'A Nightingale Sang in Berkeley Square', and 'Yours'. She became a very popular artist and was known as 'The Forces Sweetheart'. Vera was born in Essex in 1917 and on writing this in 2020 she recently celebrated her hundredth birthday. Her rendition of 'We'll Meet Again' still stirs a huge nostalgic effect in people. It is a British song composed by Ross Parker, with lyrics by Hughie Charles. For the troops going abroad, it was an optimistic send-off, but sadly, many never returned. The music was recorded by Benny Goodman and his band in 1942 and by the Ink Spots in 1943 and is still being sung and recorded to the present day.

Another favourite song of mine at the time was '(There'll Be Bluebirds Over) The White Cliffs of Dover'. 'Just you wait and see.' My mother and I used to sing this song together, and my thoughts always drifted to the line, 'And Jimmy will go to sleep in his own little room again.' Whoever Jimmy was, I felt myself feeling sorry for him.

Walter Kent, an American, composed the music, and it was published in America in 1941 prior to America entering the war. The lyrics were written by another American, Nat Burton, who had never visited this country. So contrary to the meaning of the words of the song, there are no blue bird's resident in Britain. Indeed, they are not indigenous to Europe, and furthermore, they are not migratory.

Not to worry; the words and the music were great. The song reached the top spot in the United States in 1941 and 1942 and was recorded by Jimmy Dorsey and Glenn Miller, among others—to name a few, Bing Crosby, Connie Francis, and Jim Reeves. In 1995, it was recorded by Robson and Jerome and reached the top spot in this country, selling more than two million copies.

Another song previously mentioned was 'A Nightingale Sang in Berkeley Square'. When I was a youngster, I spotted the sheet music in my aunt's piano stool. I was on cloud nine when she sang and played it for me. The words were written in 1939 by Eric Maschwitz, and the music by Manning Sherwin. Perhaps the most famous rendition was in October 1940 by Glenn Miller and his orchestra, with vocals by Ray Eberly. Many others recorded the song, including Sinatra, Nat King Cole, Bobby Darin, and of course Vera Lynn.

Arthur Askey was another notable entertainer during the Second World War. His favourite catchphrase was, 'Hello, playmates.' As a comedian, he came to prominence in 1938 as a part of the BBC comedy radio show *Band Wagon*, with his partner Richard Murdoch.

Note: Arthur Askey, with his featured song 'The Busy Bee', became a television, radio, and film personality and entertained the troops when he was in ENSA during the war.

I best remembered him in the film *The Ghost Train* in 1941. This was a really compelling mystery for a young boy, and the story was written by Arnold Ridley, better known as private Godfrey, who plays the old dodderer in the television series *Dad's Army* and acts as the platoon's medical orderly. The music for *Dad's Army*, contrary to many people's belief, was not a Second World War song. The theme tune, 'Who Do You Think You Are Kidding, Mr Hitler', was Jimmy Perry's idea and was intended as a pastiche of wartime songs. Perry himself wrote the lyrics and composed the music with Derek Tavemar. A retired Bud Flanaggan was persuaded to come out of retirement to sing the song for a large fee, thus giving *Dad's Army* an authentic world war touch. The series, however, did contain many genuine wartime songs between the different scenes.

Following the German invasion of France in 1940, Jerome Kern wrote the music, which was entitled 'The Last Time I Saw Paris'. The lyrics were written by Oscar Hammerstein, and the music was written by Kern, in memory of the Paris he had known before the war. The song won the Academy Award for the best original song of 1941. In the music, Kern had inserted the sound of the Parisian car horns. This he had copied from Gershwin's *An American in Paris*, with, of course, Gershwin's permission. It was sung by Anne Southern in the 1954 film of the same name, a romantic drama produced by Metro Goldwyn Mayer. For film buffs, it is interesting, as Roger Moore made his debut in this film.

The music 'My Sister and I' was written as a tribute to the refugee children of Europe, inspired by the book of the same name by Dirk Van Der Heidi. The music was written in 1941 by Hy Zaret, Joan Whitney, and Alex Kramer. Jimmy Dorsey and his orchestra recorded the music, and it was once again sung by Bob Eberly. In Britain, it was recorded by Oscar Rabin and his band.

After the Germans invaded Russia in July 1941, the song 'Russian Rose' became popular. It was composed by Hugh Charles and Sonny Miller. The music can be heard between scenes in *Dad's Army*, 'The Honourable Man' (season 6, episode 5.) It was recorded by The Joe Loss Orchestra with vocals by Sam Brown.

The music for the tune 'Little Brown Jug' was written as far back as 1869 by Joseph E. Winner of Philadelphia. It was originally a drinking song, and it became a very popular song, certainly among us boys, who delighted in changing the lyrics to our own particular version (not repeatable here).

A piece of music I never got tired of playing is 'How Deep Is My Ocean'. Another gem from the pen of Irving Berlin, it was written in 1932; and if the lyrics are anything to go by, it was a low point in his life. Indeed, the lyrics are somewhat philosophical and ask a series of questions—among them, how deep is the ocean and how high is the sky. Whatever the nuances of the lyrics suggest, the melody is out of this world. The music was played by Paul Whiteman and his orchestra as long ago as 1933. Benny Goodman recorded it in 1941, with vocals by Peggy Lee. The song is universally loved, and in the 1930s, it was also recorded by Ethel Merman and Bing Crosby. Harry James recorded the song in 1954, Ella Fitzgerald in 1958 with the Paul Weston Orchestra, Eric Clapton in 2010, and Bob Dylan in 2017.

CHAPTER 5
Choirs, Brass, and Bombs, 1941

It is said that, if you put fifty Welshmen into a room together, they would immediately form a choir. Put fifty Englishmen into a room, then they would form a club. And if you put fifty Irishmen into a room together, they would start a riot. In the late 1930s, our gang of boys ranged in age from nine to twelve. Although we enjoyed singing together, our ability to stay in tune could only be described as limited. Ken by far had the best voice, a fine baritone. Colin, or Fatty as he was then called, had some pretensions as a tenor. Perhaps in order of ability, I came next, with an under-distinguished baritone/tenor voice. Archie, or Molly as we more often called him, had a voice that had no curves. His voice, like that of David (Dai), was flat. In fact, both were so flat it would have been possible to iron shirts with them. Dill sang in a soft plaintive voice, and it was almost impossible to coax a crackle like sound out of Bryn.

Most of the gang swore at regular intervals but of course never in chapel. Molly never swore, even when all around him indulged. The daring swear words of the day were mainly 'bugger' and 'damn', mild by today's standards. With Molly the only word that approximated to a swear word was 'strewth', and he had to be sorely vexed to use such a terrible word. As a punishment for his purity, we made him sing a then popular song made popular by the Ink Spots called 'Bless You for Being an Angel'. Good sport that he was, he always obliged, while

I played the piece on the piano for him. All the gang just screamed helplessly with laughter, and this performance became a regular party piece. Perhaps it was no surprise when Molly joined the Glamorgan Police Force, and after a few years, he then joined the Metropolitan Police Force in London, where he dispensed justice as a detective in the 'drug squad'. I suppose just punishment would have been served on the accused, had they been made to listen to Molly's rendering of 'Bless You for Being an Angel'.

Almost forty years later, Molly now addressed as Arthur, still never swears and presumably still cannot sing. As a present some years ago, I presented him with a copy of the sheet music of his favourite piece of music, 'Bless You for Being an Angel'. And even that failed to drag a swear word from him. Honesty and common decency were some of the facets on the diamond of Arthur's character, which I always knew were present. In fact, he always had an old-fashioned glint of goodness and virtue in his eyes, and I for one am proud to say that he has remained a close friend to the present day.

Anybody today listening to the singing of our gang would be surprised to know that Wales is known as the 'Land of Song'. This is due largely to its wonderful male voice choirs. I remember the names of the principal choirs—the Rhos from North Wales, the Pendyrus from the Rhondda Fach (the small Rhondda), the Treorchy Choir from the Rhondda Fawr (the large Rhondda), and the Morriston Orpheus Choir from Swansea. The Treorchy is the oldest, having been formed in the 'Red Cow Hotel' Treorchy in 1883.

In Welsh culture, the National Eisteddfod of Wales is a festival of literature, music, and the performing arts, held in August of each year alternating between North and South Wales. It is the largest such festival in Europe and dates back to 1176. In 1895, The Treorchy Male Voice Choir performed for Queen Victoria at Windsor Castle, but when the South Wales Valleys suffered badly in the Great Depression and through the two world wars, they disbanded, only to restart in October 1946.

The present choir became an international institution. They gained a record of eight wins in the National Eisteddfod and won a total of twenty-two firsts out of twenty-seven appearances. The choir was heard worldwide as it made regular radio broadcasts, television appearances, and recordings. They also made two feature films and became the first male voice choir to venture into the field of popular music. It has made two visits to Canada and four tours to the United States, where it performed at the White House and in Denver, Colorado; Seattle; the Midwest; and San Francisco. It became the first Welsh choir to perform at the Sydney Opera House and also held concerts in Adelaide, Melbourne, Brisbane, and Perth. The choir has also shared the stage with some of the world's top entertainers, such as Ella Fitzgerald, Julie Andrews, Tom Jones, Katherine Jenkins, Max Boyce, Ozzy Osbourne, Jon Bon Jovi, and Andrea Bocelli. In Wales, they have become regular entertainers at the Millennium Stadium in Cardiff for Wales Rugby Union matches. The choir has also launched its own musician of the year, which has encouraged more than a thousand children per year from the Rhondda to enjoy the opportunity of performing.

The Treorchy Male Voice Choir, in its rendering of 'Myfanwy'—a women's name derived from the Welsh word annwyl (beloved), is a very popular Welsh song composed by Richard Parry first published in 1875. The music was composed to the lyrics written by Richard Davies (1833–1877). To hear gnarled and scarred miners in any Welsh choir singing 'Myfanwy' is enough to bring a tear to the eyes of most people. It certainly had that effect on my father, as the beautiful melodic singing reached deep into the soul. The Treorchy Male Voice Choir is today a registered charity and has raised many thousands of pounds for worthwhile causes.

My second favourite male voice choir is the Morriston Orpheus Choir from Swansea. The Morriston was formed in 1935 and, by 1937, had achieved its first success at the National Eisteddfod, winning on a further six occasions. It is presently in great demand and performs up to twenty-five engagements per year. It has made two tours to Taiwan, Abu Dhabi, and Oman. It has also performed in Dubai, en route to a concert tour of Australia and New Zealand. In 2008, Morriston performed a charity concert in Geneva and, whilst there, sang in the control room of the European Organisation for Nuclear Research (CERN). In previous tours, the choir has performed in the former West Berlin and also represented Wales at Expo in Seville, Spain. Morriston has also performed in all the major cities in Australia and New Zealand and received standing ovations at its appearance at the world-famous Sydney Opera House. The choir also received five standing ovations at the Carnegie Hall in New York City. It has regularly featured on radio and television, has produced over fifty recordings, and features in more than a hundred compilation albums. Like the Treorchy Male Voice Choir, the Morriston Orpheus is a registered charity and is devoted to assisting other charities, including Leukaemia Research and Save the Children Fund, among others. These choirs have brought great joy to audiences around the world and, in their way, proved that Wales is indeed 'The Land of Song'.

Another musical phenomenon from Treorchy is the Cory Brass Band, the oldest and best known in the world. It was formed in 1884 and had several name changes in its early life. Since 1920, it has carried its original name, the Cory Band. It has won the British championships six times and the European championships the same number of times. It is recognised as Wales's finest and most innovative music ensembles. In 2005, it was ranked as number one in the world (according to Braystats World Ranking). In Britain, it has won the open championships for the fifth time in eleven years. In 2016, the band undertook eight concerts in a tour of the United States and won all the British titles the same year. From its roots in the Rhondda in South Wales, the band has travelled all over the world. In 2016, it became the first band in history to win three major titles—namely, the British, the national title of Wales, and the European brass band titles. In brass band terminology, this is called the 'Banding Grand Slam'. In addition, the band has retained the title of the number one ranked brass band in the world for the tenth consecutive year.

In one of its tours of the United States, the Cory Brass Band showed its amazing talent by playing music across many genres. At one concert the bland played music from *Star Wars*, as well as celestial-themed pieces such as Hoagy Carmichael's 'Stardust' (the most recorded song in history) and highlights from Gustav Holst's *The Planets* suite.

Coupled with the remarkable singing of the Treorchy Male Voice Choir, the Cory Band, also from Treorchy, has helped to keep Wales in the forefront of world music and created memories that last a lifetime. Perhaps the title of 'Land of Song' is appropriate after all.

As, in World War I, a British expeditionary force crossed the English Channel to assist the French but nothing seemed to be happening, the Americans coined the period the 'Phoney War'. All the newspapers seemed to show were pictures of French troops entering, drinking, or sleeping and using their system inside the magnificent tunnels of the Maginot Line.

I had been breakfasting with my grandmother and the headlines in the morning paper read, 'The Inglorious Ending of the German Pocket Battleship *Graf Spee*', this on 17 December 1939. Gleeful publicity was given to this event when the *Graf Spee* was scuttled rather than continue her fight with two Royal Navy cruisers waiting for her off the River Plate. Captain Langsdorf, the captain of the *Graf Spee*, however, had little chance, being low on fuel and ammunition. Having made arrangements for his crew, he retired to his room and wrote his final letters. He then lay down on a German battle flag and shot himself in the head.

Hans Wilhelm Langsdorf was born in Bergen on the island of Rugen on 20 March 1894 and had received the Iron Cross Second Class for his bravery in the Battle of Jutland in 1916 and the Iron Cross First Class before that war ended. He was the eldest son of a family with strong legal and religious traditions, rather than naval. He died on the 12 December 1939, aged forty-five years, and is buried in the German section of La Chacarita Cemetery in Buenos Aires

Elsewhere at sea, matters began to look increasingly grim as German U-Boats sank merchant ships in ever-increasing numbers, particularly in the vital North Atlantic routes from the United States and Canada. These losses increased in winter 1940/41 after naval bases in France became available to the German Navy.

At home, the blackouts caused major irritations, as people had to grope their way around on moonless or cloudy nights with the aid of hand torches. Signposts on most roads were removed so that any German spies or Fifth Columnists would have difficulty locating their positions. Road vehicles had their headlights restricted to narrow slits, and with no street lighting, it was inevitable that death and injuries from road accidents increased.

From January 1940, radio listeners found themselves a new BBC radio station to tune into in addition to the Home Service. The

Forces Programme, originally devised for British troops in France, became popular with civilian listeners. Throughout the duration of the war, the BBC Home Service and the Forces Programme made a major contribution to keeping morale high in the civilian population. Together, the stations ensured that the general public was informed of all the war news and kept entertained by comedy shows, plays, concerts, and dance music.

A news-hungry public now saw a great increase in newspaper sales, which grew from 19 million copies in 1938 to 24 million copies by 1945. However, most newspapers were limited to four pages, simply because of the rationing of newsprint. *The Times* and *The Daily Telegraph* chose to print eight pages but decided on a smaller print run. However, these two newspapers had a scant readership in the valleys. There was no censorship of the news in Britain, but there was a system of D-Notices (Defence Notices) issued to newspaper editors requesting they not print certain news matters. Failure to comply with the D-Notice meant that the newspaper could be prosecuted.

In May 1940, when the Germans reached the Channel Coast of France, an emergency powers act was passed, giving the government unprecedented powers over the lives of British people and their property. Soon our first evacuees arrived, and our guests came from Hounslow and St Pancreas in West London. I remember the day well when, in threes, they marched into our community with their helpers, along the road leading from our railway station in complete silence. Suddenly, as if it were preordained, there began a sustained roar of cheering and clapping to welcome these poor children into our midst. Accordingly, my family grew by one with the addition of a Miss Helen Pretty.

The boys had decided and planned the previous day—we would be a dawn patrol, scouring the local mountain for German parachutists. We considered that we had a better chance of locating them in the early hours, as they would be less likely to be on their guard and, thus, easier to spot.

Dawn was breaking as I left the house to meet the gang at our favourite place in front of Bert Matthew's shop at the top end of our street. Five of the gang showed up, and we made our way to the bottom of the mountain. The hedgerow and trees were now emerging from darkness as we climbed through Ponts Woods, making use of every piece of cover in our climb to the summit of the rocks at the top of the mountain, where we had a completed den, which we called our headquarters. We were equipped with an assorted bunch of weapons, ranging from one slug gun to knives latched onto long poles. We carried enough food and drink to last all day as we searched high and low in the tall ferns, behind rocks.

Fortunately for us, no Germans were ever seen.

A few days later, we continued our search. It had been a hot sunny day, and we stretched out on the grass hot and sweaty following our exertions. It was now time to go home. We had searched high and low for Germans without success, so we took the shortest route down the mountain. The route took us past the grand imposing Glyncornel Mansion, which we knew was the new home to a number of evacuees. We discovered later that these children all came from difficult backgrounds and some had served time in prison type institutions. We descended the steep pathway in single file and approached the low stone wall that marked the mansion boundary.

Suddenly, there they were, standing around the grounds like statues. We must have seen one another at the same moment. Dai (David) sidled up to me and whispered, 'Shall we fight them?'

However, I had already taken in the scene and done a quick calculation of both their numbers and size. I had counted fifteen and quietly whispered to Dai that we were badly outnumbered. He nodded sagely as we stood in line unmoving, facing them in complete silence. Neither side moved an inch. The impasse lasted a few minutes or so, and then almost by common consent, each side went about its business.

The mountain was our patch, and we had held our ground. We felt a great sense of elation as we went on our way. It had been a victory of sorts. So as per usual, we burst into song, which signalled a wonderful feeling of togetherness. 'Home, Home on the Range' sounded through the trees as we made our way home for tea.

By this time, there was a general nervousness of the terrible consequences of aerial attack. This was brought home to many people by the newsreels shown in the local cinemas. News told of the attack on Madrid and Barcelona in the Spanish Civil War and the air attacks by the Japanese on Chinese cities like Shanghai. The Spanish nationalists under General Francisco Franco had the assistance of German and Italian aircraft, and the German Condor Legion's attacks on the ancient Basque Town of Guernica in April 1937 made a profound impression on people's minds. Such feelings had been reinforced by Pablo Picasso's painting *Guernica*, which had been put on display at the Paris Expedition in 1937.

Such was the fear of air raids that, soon after the start of the war, the government, implementing pre-war plans, began evacuating tens of thousands of children from London and the South East of England to what were considered to be safer—areas elsewhere in the country. The South Wales valleys were considered such a safe place.

The Rhondda received many thousands of evacuees, and five community centres were created to ease the distribution caused both by the evacuees and their hosts, as children were placed in local homes. Not all of them were welcoming to their uninvited guests. This constant flurry of activity made an immense impact on valley society—still reeling from the interwar depression and now having to adjust to wartime conditions. For many families, times were clearly difficult, with food shortages and queues for the first time; coupled with the absence of husbands, fathers, brothers, and sons; and, on top of that, the presence of strangers from England with different habits, accents, and attitudes.

A frightening fictional picture had been painted in many sensational novels of the 1930s, describing in vivid detail the consequences of massive air attacks on civilian populations with bombs and poison gas. Even their titles could make your spine tingle: *Europe at the Abyss* (1933) by Hanns Gobsch, *The Poison War* (1933) by Ladbroke Black, *Invasion from the Air* (1934) by Macitraeth and Connolly, and *The Day of Wrath* (1936) by Joseph O'Neill.

Mass air raids were now clearly 'on the cards', and we were not kept waiting for long. It soon became quite usual to hear German aircraft overhead as they proceeded to bomb targets further afield. The noise of their engines was quite distinct, as they seemed to fly with their propellers unsynchronised. How German aircrew could bear to fly with their engines out of synchronisation remains a mystery to me.

Yet they did night after night. And clearly, they were under orders to do so. It certainly frightened many people as well.

I remember when I flew the Vickers Viscount aircraft with its four Rolls Royce Dart engines it was almost inevitable that at least one of its engines would wander off into a rhythm of its own, even when we as a crew had thought we had it sorted. The Heinkel and the Dornier DO17 were both twin-engine aircraft, and therefore, to synchronise their engines would be quite an easy task unless the German engine designers had found a way to make engine synchronisation impossible, a thought I could hardly believe!

The attempted destruction of British cities had now begun. The late afternoon of 7 September saw over three hundred German bombers attack London, escorted by six hundred fighters. This we felt was the prelude to invasion, and the code word 'Cromwell' (invasion imminent) swept the country. In fact, Hitler had little appetite for the plan and was probably hoping that, by terrorising the civilian population, he would entice the British to ask for peace. The ploy was not successful, and unsung men and women did incredibly brave things not only in London but also in Southampton, Glasgow, Hull, Cardiff, Plymouth, and Swansea and other small towns and villages across the country. These attacks were called the Blitz from the German world 'Blitzkrieg' (lightning war).

People at large across the country certainly felt we would soon be invaded, and the word was out that such an invasion would be preceded by parachutists and sea landings. The gang joined the Local Defence Volunteers looking for them, but the excitement died when none were to be found. Most people have now forgotten the jokes about the LDVs, whose initials were given other meanings, like 'Look, Duck, and Vanish'. However, quite soon, the name was shelved, and the Home Guard was born.

In the first four days of September 1939, almost three and a half million people were transported from towns under threat of being bombed to places the government considered safe. Most of this number was schoolchildren. The evacuation order forthwith was issued at 11.07 a.m. on Thursday, 31 August 1939. Not all the bombed people were as uncomplaining as the news and newsreels would have us believe. When Churchill visited Bristol with some top local officials of the corporation, the children were given flags to wave. There, he found great hostility, particularly from women who had lost friends near John Street. When Churchill arrived, the women turned on him and became extremely hostile and started booing and shouting abuse. Movietone News resorted to a cover-up and showed in its newsreels Churchill's visit with cheering crowds. In fact, some of this uplifting footage had been filmed when Churchill had visited Swansea on a previous occasion.

During the war, Cardiff, like many other towns and cities in Britain, endured a large number of air raids by the Luftwaffe. Luftlottte 3 was stationed in Upper and Lower Normandy, as well as in Brittany. The Luftwaffe's nearest bomber station to Wales and the West of England was Maupertus near Cherbourg, and the station's main task was to concentrate its bombing on Wales and on the North and the South of England. Luftflotte 3 was led by General Feldmarschall Hugo Sperrle from his headquarters in Paris. Between 1940 and a final raid in 1944, approximately 2,100 bombs fell on Cardiff, killing 355 people and leaving about three times that numbers injured. The first raid was on 3 January 1941. That night, a full moon shone brightly, 'a bombers' moon' as it was then called. KGr 100 (a Pathfinder Unit) was based at Vannes on the Atlantic coast and operated Heinkel 111 aircraft. They were the first pathfinders and spearheaded the way. They were responsible for identifying the target, with flares and incendiaries illuminating the target area. That night, the flares drifted down, bathing the city in a beautiful green light, a beacon for the follow-up bombers crossing the channel. The attack was made over a ten-hour period by approximately one hundred aircraft.

In a conversation with an inexperienced pilot in the 1980s, I pointed out the ease of navigating at night the length of the British Isles simply by using the huge luminosity emitted by its cities. Today such observation would hardly be possible, as most of the country is so well lit that a pilot couldn't be sure where the lights of one town began and another ended. Now just imagine flying over the country during the war with a complete blackout across the land. How could one determine where the target was, complete the correct identify, and drop their bombs? German-occupied Europe, with its much greater land mass, created a much greater difficulty for RAF Bomber

Command to identify and bomb its target than that faced by the Luftwaffe bombing this country.

Early in the war, Bomber Command navigators merely drew a line on their topographical charts from the airfield of departure to the target and then measured the distance and took the track bearing. They would then apply the forecast wind speed and direction to establish a course and time. This was converted into a course magnetic by applying the average magnetic variation (in other words, the difference between true north and magnetic north). Finally, a factor for magnetic deviation would be added to establish the compass course the pilot would steer to the target. This would also provide the speed over the ground of the aircraft (groundspeed). The navigator could then complete the ETA (estimated time of arrival) over the target. This was all well and good, provided that the forecast wind was correct and remained as forecast throughout the flight. Sadly, this seldom happened, and I can well remember the sick feeling in my stomach when training, as a town that was to appear at a certain time in my flight plan had simply vanished from sight. If it were difficult by day, then one can only imagine how much more difficult it was by night in wartime conditions with blinding searchlights and guns firing at you.

Following the conquest of France, the Germans developed and invested their efforts in radio navigation systems. The code name Knickebein (meaning crooked leg) was taken from the shape of the wireless aerials attached to the aircraft. The beam from a single transmitter could guide the bombers to their target but not tell the crew when they were over it. Therefore, a second transmitter was constructed so that its beam crossed the path of the first, indicating the point at which the bombs would be released. The first Knickebein transmitter was built in 1939 at Kleve on the German Dutch border. After the fall of France, further transmitters were constructed in the Netherlands and at Stoltenberg in Norway. To improve their system the Germans now incorporated the X-Gerät system, which operated on a much higher frequency and was first installed at Cap-de-la-Hague just a few miles west of Cherbourg. KGr 100 was the first to be equipped with this system as the main pathfinder.

RAF Bomber Command followed this concept later in the war, despite the objections to it by its leader Air Vice Marshall Harris.

In a short space of time, the Luftwaffe realised that the British were deploying successful countermeasures in bending the beams away from the target cities. Consequently, they soon lost faith in the state of electronic navigation aids. Hitler now turned his attention to Russia, and the Luftwaffe was largely deployed to the east. At the same time, RAF Bomber Command continued its attacks on German cities with little success. When the Butt Report was released on 18 August 1941, the findings made horrific reading.[1] The report indicated that only 5 per cent of RAF bombers that set out dropped their bombs within five miles of the target. Even in 1942, one bomber station in Lincolnshire reported on a raid as follows:

> 25 Lancaster bombers set out on the raid. 4 aircraft thought they had bombed the target, 8 bombed on ETA (estimated time of arrival), but uncertain where they were, 6 aircraft were unable to reach the target and released their bombs on any other place, 3 aircraft jettisoned their bombs in the sea, 3 aircraft turned back early to base and 1 aircraft did not return.

The poor bombing accuracy on that raid were largely caused by the poor flight conditions encountered with multi-layered clouds enroute and embedded cumulonimbus. All pilots know from very early in their training that cumulonimbus clouds meant trouble—in the form of severe icing, lightning discharge, violent turbulence, hail, and snow. The areas on that raid had met with such conditions enroute to

---

1 The Butt Report was released on 18 August 1941 reporting the widespread failure of bombers to find and attack their targets. Indeed, the RAF had not invested very much on navigation skills needed to fly at night. Armed with a small Dalton computer and the forecast wind, it was inevitable that aircraft got lost in the dark, as during a raid, several turning points would be included in the flight plan, largely to confuse the enemy. Also, the wind would very likely change during the course of the raid. Aircrew, in those early days, were really 'on a hiding to nothing'! Consequently, as the Butt Report stated, only 5 per cent of the bombers that set out bombed within five miles of their target. There must have been many frightened cows in the German countryside, as 49 per cent of all bombs fell there.

the target; hence, the poor bombing results. Such conditions affected Luftwaffe crews just as much as RAF Bomber Command.

The Luftwaffe planned a two-city attack on 29 April 1941. The main attack that night was on the port of Plymouth in Devon, while the second attack was to be on the coal port of Cardiff in Wales. The raid on Plymouth lasted nearly four hours, and the main weight of bombs fell on Keynham and Milehouse, between Plymouth and the docks at Devonport. It proved to be the last concentrated attack on the town.

The planned attack on Cardiff did not have the usual precursory flares and incendiaries. Shortly after the sirens sounded, four parachute landmines fell on the city, killing over thirty people and injuring many more. The Parish Hall in Wyverne Road was destroyed. But remarkably, the fourth Cardiff Scout flag that had been carried to the Antarctic on Scott's fateful expedition was recovered from the rubble undamaged. The majority of Luftflotte III aircraft that had set out that night from their Normandy bases for Cardiff miscalculated both the strength and direction of the strong south-easterly wind. To add to their woes, the ground in South Wales was covered with stratocumulus cloud, ranging between 3,000 and 5,000 feet, above sea level. They, therefore, flew a few miles west of the city of Cardiff for a further four to five minutes to reach their ETA (estimated time of arrival) over the target. This put them over the small mining village of Cwm Parc at the north end of the Rhondda Fawr. The German aircrew must have been pleasantly surprised by the absence of searchlights and anti-aircraft fire. However, the people of the village of Cwm Parc were now to endure an experience that was to live with them forever.

Dr Fergus Armstrong of that little village had a late patient with him that night, and as he accompanied the patient to the door of his surgery, he noticed many coloured lights on the hillside looking down towards Maendy. These were the flares from the early visitors, and soon the hills above the village were ringed with hundreds of incendiary bombs blazing brightly and setting fire to the hillside grass. High explosive bombs then began to fall, plus a complement of landmines landing with a loud thud as the parachutes folded. The little village, hemmed in on three sides by mountains, now heard sounds the likes of which they had never heard before. In a matter of minutes, twenty-seven of the villagers had lost their lives (some of them children), and more than half of its thousand houses had been destroyed or damaged.

But Cwm Parc, if remote, was not unprepared. As soon as the incendiaries fell, in the words of an eye witness, 'They came into action the fire bomb fighters—troops of them, a whole army of them, advancing along the main road, emerging from side streets and whooping some undistinguished form of war cry as they swooped upon incendiaries with a kind of supressed fury, extinguishing them with a precision and certainty born of months of preparation for just such an emergency.'

The wardens and the rescue services got to work soon afterwards among the tumbled heaps of slate and grey stone where their friends and relatives lay. The task was not long, for the miners and their sons had little to learn about digging and tunnelling at speed. The family intimacy of village life in which I had grown up was nowhere closer than here, where every death was regarded as a personal bereavement. By lunchtime the next day, the homeless had all been billeted, in all a national record.

Among the youngest killed that night were two brothers and their eight-year-old sister, who had been evacuated from London earlier that year. Their parents doubtlessly thought that, in the narrow valley and mountains of the Rhondda, their children would find safety during the troubled years of the war. Sadly, they found only death.

Sherwood Street, where I lived a few miles away, was not exempt from tragedy that night, and George Davies in the Police War Reserve, who lived close by, was killed that night while on duty. His two daughters attended the same school as me, and I was astonished at their composure and bravery. I had great doubt that I would have behaved as well had I been in their position.

Today, there is a memorial garden in Cwm Parc on the area known locally as the 'Bomb Site'. In the local cemetery, there is a separate monument for the three young evacuees with their names suitably inscribed.

The official radio announcement the following day by the BBC simply declared that there had been a 'light' enemy activity over Wales but no casualties. Such is the fog of war! That night, all the German aircraft that had attacked us returned to their bases in Normandy and Brittany, not having been assaulted by our guns or fighters. In fact, the only German loss that night was a Focke-Wulf Condor aircraft that crashed into the sea off the Shetland Isles in the north of Scotland.

The Germans Blitz on Cardiff lasted from early 1940 to March 1944. During that period, 355 people were killed and countless more injured, 33,000 houses were destroyed, and over 2,000 bombs fell on the city. At that time, Cardiff Docks was one of the largest coal ports in the world and a strategic target for the Luftwaffe. See the weather chart for 29 April on the next page.

The Attack and Betrayal of Pearl Harbour, 7 December 1941

This short story begins and ends in Washington DC. America had, by 1941, invented and manufactured a deciphering machine called Purple, which was capable of deciphering the Japanese Diplomatic Code. Such information from these machines was named 'Magic'. America manufactured eight machines, and they were distributed as follows:

- Four were to remain in Washington, two for the army and two for the navy
- Two were sent to London, one for the decoding agency at Bletchley Park and one went to Churchill's wartime bunker
- One was sent to Manila in the Philippines
- One was to be sent to Pearl Harbor

Bletchley Park however, requested a further machine, for which the British would, in exchange, send the Americans an Enigma machine, which could break some of the German's codes.

It was Vice Admiral Kelly Turner in Naval Intelligence in Washington who made the decision to send to Britain the one machine that had been detailed for Pearl Harbour. The navy and army commanders in Pearl Harbour, however, had no idea that such a machine existed or that one had been scheduled for Pearl Harbour. It also appears that nobody in Washington considered the manufacture of an additional Purple machine, which then could have been sent to the Pearl Harbour base. However, Admiral Kimmel, commander of the Pacific Fleet and General Short, commander of the army on Oahu, had been assured by their seniors in Washington via Admiral Stark, head of Naval Operations and General Marshall, his army counterpart, that all relevant information received in Washington would be forwarded directly to Pearl Harbour. Nevertheless, the reverse occurred, and apart from some chatty, nebulous, and often contradictory letters from Stark and warnings by Marshall of potential sabotage by the sizeable Japanese population, little of consequence was received.

The army was responsible for the defence of the fleet when in port, but the navy was responsible for all reconnaissance flights in surrounding waters. In other words, there existed a lack of a central command system on Oahu. This system had been in practice for some time, arranged by their predecessors. And nobody had thought to change it. Admiral Richardson had been commander of the Pacific Fleet prior to Kimmel's appointment, and he had visited Washington on at least two occasions to plead with the president to have the Pacific Fleet moved back to San Diego on the West Coast. Richardson considered that the fleet was too exposed at Pearl Harbour. He also believed that the naval authorities, not politicians, were the best judge of policy. The net result of these meetings was that Richardson was relieved of his post, and Rear Admiral Husband E. Kimmel replaced him.

Kimmel, in fact, had served as aide to Roosevelt as early as 1915, when Roosevelt was assistant secretary to the navy. From the time of his appointment, Kimmel had requested on numerous occasions, additional equipment, particularly reconnaissance aircraft. But the only aircraft that landed on Oahu were destined for the Philippines and not for Pearl Harbour or the islands of Wake and Midway. Effectively, Pearl Harbour was unprepared for war in December 1941. However, the American nation had considered Pearl Harbour to be an impregnable fortress, much as Singapore had been so regarded in the eyes of the British people. Unfortunately, in both cases, they were only a shell of what the general public thought they were—hence, the great sense of shock when they were attacked. Jaluit Atoll in the Marshall Islands lay 2,000 miles from Oahu, far to the south-west. It was the nearest Japanese-controlled island, and Kimmel expected, in the event of war, the Japanese threat would occur from that direction. At no time did he receive any intelligence or hint that there was any threat to Pearl Harbour from any direction but the south-west.

By October/November 1941, the threat of war between Japan and America became more and more evident. Roosevelt often used the phrase, 'They must strike the first blow,' as well as saying, 'We are a democracy and have a good record.' At that time, America had a very strong isolationist movement, and the people were in no mood to accept the inevitability of war.

The commander of the Japanese fleet at that time was Admiral Isoroku Yamamoto. For some time, he had planned in secret an operational plan—a pre-emptive strike against the American fleet at Pearl Harbour as a means to give Japan time to fortify its newly conquered territories in south-east Asia. Under the command of Vice Admiral Chuichi Nagumo, the strike force or *kido butai*, left the naval base and assembled in the fog-shrouded Hitokappu Bay in the Kuril Islands. The fleet operated in complete radio silence and used signal deception to disguise the true location of their aircraft carriers. The fleet left Hitokappu Bay on 28 November 1941 and set out on its long 3,400-mile journey across the north Pacific. As this was in progress, two Japanese representatives, Admiral Kichisabarō Nomuro and Special Envoy Saburō Kuriesee, were attending talks in Washington with the American Secretary of State, Cordell Hull.

At Pearl Harbour, Admiral Kimmel and General Short had been taken fully out of the 'intelligence loop' by Admiral Stark, aided and abetted by Vice Admiral Kelly Turner and General Marshall in Washington.

The following messages were obtained in Washington by the Purple machine and its messages termed Magic. These decrypts should have been forwarded to Pearl Harbour and were not:

1. *What became known as the 'Bomb Plot' messages.* These messages sent by Tokyo to their consulate in Honolulu were frequent and asked the consulate to report the positions and nature of ships present in Pearl Harbour, based on an already

established grid system. These should surely have been sent to Pearl Harbour *but were not.*

2. *What has been described as the 'Winds Message'.* In Japanese, it read, 'Higashi no kaze ame', literally meaning 'East wind rain' and, translated, meaning, 'War with the United States'. This had been understood in Washington to mean that war with Japan was imminent. Yet again, this message was *not sent* to Pearl Harbour.

3. *The fourteenth part of a message intercepted in Washington early on 7 December, indicating that 'something was going to happen at the time of 1:00 pm Washington time', which coincided with 07.00 hours in Hawaii.* The significance of this message seemed to simply elude Admiral Stark, even after his intelligence officer pointed out its significance to him. Stark actually lifted the telephone to call Kimmel in Hawaii and then said he would instead call the president. Admiral Stark later stated that he was under the mistaken impression that Kimmel had available a Magic decrypting machine in Oahu and that any more alerts would only confuse the situation. This clearly spoke volumes regarding his relations with Turner in Washington at such a critical moment in American history. Had Kimmel and Short had just those few hours of warning, they would have had their fighter aircraft aloft and the ships fully armed and manned. Also, all the reconnaissance aircraft would have been airborne looking for the Japanese fleet. Whether they would have detected the Japanese approach is open to question, but their presence would have certainly made life difficult for the advancing fleet. It was fortuitous that Kimmel had sent his aircraft carriers to sea on separate missions; else the Battle of Midway six months later might well have ended in catastrophe for the United States.

The attack started at 06.00 hours, when the Japanese carriers and fleet were approximately 200 nautical miles north of Oahu. Two waves of attacking aircraft, around 360 in total, set out one hour apart. Yamamoto's plan had called for a third wave, this to target the oil storage tanks clearly visible from the air, which contained 4.5 million gallons of fuel oil. However, Nagumo, fearing a counter-attack by the absent American carriers, refused his airmen a third-wave attack and turned for home. Consequently, the oil tanks, the dock repair facility, and the submarine base were left untouched. This was to prove a fatal mistake in many experts' opinion. The destruction of the oil storage tanks should have been a primary target, as their destruction would have driven the United States Pacific Fleet back to the West Coast of America. This would have given the Japanese freedom of operation in the Pacific and allowed their conquest of the Pacific Islands and the South East Asian countries to proceed unhindered. Later Yamamoto considered that Nagumo's decision to withdraw before a third strike was undoubtedly a huge mistake. In the many pre-war discussions of Yamamoto's plan, Nagumo had always appeared somewhat lukewarm about the project. Consequently, it has always remained a puzzle to me why it was that, since it was so vital for the attack to succeed, Yamamoto himself did not see fit to lead the attack. After all, he was the commander of the Pacific Fleet. The answer, sadly, will always be buried in the depths of time.

As a result of the attack, Kimmel and Short were publicly and immediately pilloried for the disaster they were powerless to prevent. General MacArthur, on the other hand, not only had the Magic intelligence available to him in the Philippines but was also aware of the attack on Pearl Harbour nine hours before. Yet despite protests from his aircraft commander, he refused him permission to take off and attack the Japanese bases. Consequently, his aircraft fleet was wiped out on the ground nine hours after the first bombs had fallen on Pearl Harbour. Despite all this, General MacArthur escaped any charge of accountability and rose to the highest rank, while Kimmel and Short were both relieved of their commands, reduced in rank, and dismissed the service.

Then proceeded eight investigations held between 22 December 1941 and 15 July 1946, which contributed largely to the death of General Short. Some held that the two local commanders were derelict in their duty; others considered that they were simply guilty of errors of judgement. Both men requested court-martial, but their requests were refused by the army and navy authorities.

My interest in the story of Pearl Harbour really began following my reading of Gordon W. Prange's book *At Dawn We Slept: The*

Untold Story of Pearl Harbour, which I purchased in Miami on 1 March 1983. The very title of that book suggested at least a lack of vigilance and even negligence on the part of the two commanders.

The authorities in Washington had clearly considered the Pacific Ocean distances so great as to preclude any attack on Pearl Harbour. Hence, the attack caught everyone by surprise. The damage was so great and so unexpected that the president could not ignore it. It would have to be investigated, with any faults found and blame attached; otherwise the blame for the fiasco would fall back on Washington and its leaders. This could not be allowed to happen with a war now starting. As the news spread across America, a large part of the country closed ranks behind the President. Kimmel and Short both would have subscribed to this, as a penance for being unalert, but then they were completely unaware at the time of the information of which they had been deprived. Their superiors had been at fault and were fully responsible for the disaster. However, the war had just begun and was best dealt with by scapegoating the two commanders on the spot. Kimmel and Short were undoubtedly the martyrs of Pearl Harbour.

It was on 25 May 1999 that the United States Senate passed a non-binding resolution, exonerating both Admiral Kimmel and General Short by a 52–47 vote. It stated that both men were denied vital intelligence that was available in Washington. The resolution was attached as an amendment to the Department of Defense Spending Bill and cleared Congress as a whole in October 1999. It urged President Bill Clinton to restore Kimmel and Short to their full wartime ranks. However, neither Clinton nor his successors George W Bush or Barack Obama acted on the resolution. Admiral William Standley maintained that the two officers were martyred, and if they had been brought to trial, they would have both been cleared of any charges.

> Note 1: Admiral Husband Edward Kimmel was born on 26 February 1882 and died on 14 May 1968, aged eighty-six years. General Walter Campbell Short was born on 30 March 1880 and died on 9 March 1949 aged sixty-eight years.

Note 2: General George G. Marshall remained as head of the United States Army throughout the Second World War, reaching the highest rank in the American Army as a five-star general. Admiral Harold Rainsford Stark retained his four-star rank as a full admiral and served out the rest of the war in London with some distinction

Kimmel and Short, in contrast, were reduced in rank, retired against their wishes, and were never again employed on active duty. Stark had been godfather to Kimmel's two sons. But after Pearl Harbour, Kimmel never spoke to him again.

CHAPTER 6

America Wakes to War
(12 October–11 November 1942)

'I Left My Heart at the Stage Door Canteen' was a song composed by that master musician Irving Berlin. As a young boy, I had no idea what was meant by the lyrics, and that state of ignorance lasted until I read the book *Music of the Second World War'*, written by an American, Sheldon Winkler. The United Service Organization was set up by Roosevelt to provide entertainment and refreshments for servicemen. These stage door canteens were uniquely American; the servicemen could enjoy food and the company of film stars and other celebrities, with whom they could dance. The British had no direct equivalent. However, they did create ENSA (Entertainments National Service Association), or as the troops renamed it 'Every night something awful'. As the name suggests, the army provided entertainment most nights of dubious quality.

Another song by Irving Berlin and a favourite of us boys was 'This Is the Army'. 'This is the army, Mister Jones,' it quipped. 'No private rooms or telephones.' Even today I can remember most of the lyrics.

Earlier in the narrative, we met up with the song '(There'll be Bluebirds Over) The White Cliffs of Dover'. Another lesser-known song by the same composer and lyricist was 'When the Roses Bloom Again', which I liked and played on the piano. My mother had written my name and that of the school on the front cover. I still retain the copy today and treat it with great reverence.

The song 'Praise the Lord and Pass the Ammunition' was another great favourite of our gang of boys. I had no idea of its origin, and once more I am indebted to Sheldon Winkler and his publication *Music of the Second World War*. The song is credited to a wartime American naval chaplain, Howell Maurice Forgy, during the Japanese attack on Pearl Harbour on 7 December 1941. Chaplains in the American Navy were not permitted to handle firearms or ammunition. During the Japanese attack, he stood behind a line of sailors passing shells for the operation of the guns. As they did so, he slapped their backs shouting, 'Praise the Lord and pass the ammunition.' The music was written by Frank Loesser, the son of German immigrants. The song was first recorded by the Merry Macs in July 1942. But it was Kay Kyser and his orchestra that provided the bestselling version, which reached the number one spot in 1943. Chaplain Forgy left the United States Navy in 1946, when he returned to the civilian ministry.

The song, 'As Time Goes By', was composed by Herman Hupfeld and was a part of the story from the play originally titled *Everybody Comes to Ricks*. The film, of course, was *Casablanca* and was set in the year 1942. The music for the film was composed by that master film composer Max Steiner. Max was unhappy with this assignment, as no composer appreciates or likes having to use other composers' music. He tried very hard to replace the music with his own, but the constraints of time and the availability of some of the actors made this impossible. For these reasons, the music, 'As Time Goes By' became the central theme of the film's music, coupled with the National Anthem of Germany, 'Deutschlandlied' and 'La Marseillaise' the French National Anthem. Steiner wove these components into a wonderful composition, which was nominated for an Oscar. The film became a cult classic and remains one of the most popular films ever made, much to the surprise of all who made it. The music by Steiner played a huge part in its success, although Steiner himself had little love for it.

Herman Hupfeld was born in Montclair, New Jersey, in 1894 and composed 'As Time Goes By'. He worked as a composer, conductor, and pianist. His other successful songs included, 'Sing Something

Simple' (1930) and 'Let's Put out the Lights and Go to Sleep' (1932). 'As Time Goes By' was written in 1931. Hupfeld died in June 1951, also in Montclair, the town of his birth.

It was Walter Kent who wrote another favourite song of mine, 'I'll be Home for Christmas', which conveniently leads me on to 'White Christmas', with lyrics and music by that American genius Irving Berlin. When he had completed the writing of this song, he said 'That's the best song anybody's ever written.' Its popularity took off when Bing Crosby recorded the music in 1942. It has since become the bestselling single song in the world, with estimated sales today in excess of 160 million copies, the Crosby version accounting for 100 million of those. In the film, *Holiday Inn*, the song won the Academy Award for the best original song of 1942. It also appeared in the film *White Christmas*, which became the highest-grossing film of 1954. The Crosby version of the song also holds the distinction of being ranked number two on the Songs of the Century list, behind Judy Garland's 'Over the Rainbow'. 'White Christmas' has been recorded by Harry James and his orchestra, Frank Sinatra, Johnny Mathis, and others. The music never loses its appeal at Christmas, and I doubt that it ever will!

We boys loved nothing better than singing cowboy songs. The two best remembered were 'I've Got Spurs that Jingle Jangle Jingle (As We Ride Merrily Along)' and 'Don't Fence Me In'. The first was published and recorded in 1942, with the music and lyrics written by Frank Loesser and Joseph J Lilley. I remember Gene Autry singing it. And later, in 1944, it was recorded by Glenn Miller and his orchestra.

Loesser went on after the war to write the words and music for the Broadway hit, *Guys and Dolls*. 'Don't Fence Me In' was written by Cole Porter, which surprised me—no, amazed me—when I played the music and saw his name on the top of the music sheet. Indeed, it was almost incomprehensible! I was not surprised when I later discovered that, despite the song's great success, for Porter, it was the least loved of all his music. The song itself stretched back to 1934, written for a film that failed to materialise, only to re-emerge in 1944. Again, when sung by Bing Crosby and the Andrews Sisters, it sold over a million copies. (There's more on this song under Cole Porter in chapter 11, 'Composers of the Glory Years'.)

I was smitten and my mind enveloped by a mysterious bug late in 1942. It coincided with the arrival in the village of a beautiful girl named Joyce. She had left her parents' home in Cardiff a mere twenty-six miles away because of the air raids on that city and now resided with her aunt in an adjoining street to mine. I had not, at that time, reached my early teens. But my mind, usually tuned into the rough games of rugby and soccer, suddenly displayed all the dubious qualities and consistency of a marshmallow. The word 'sex' had, at that time, not entered my vocabulary—indeed hadn't been invented in my world. And clearly, babies arrived magically by stork. I was struck with a mystical belief that Joyce would be my princess, and it was my duty to escort and protect her, much like my then current screen idol, Errol Flynn, would do for his leading ladies in his screen roles.

It is quite extraordinary how certain songs, at times, remind one of events of long, long ago. It was the music 'Dearly Beloved' that arrived at that moment on our radios, and it was that piece that forever reminded me of Joyce. The music was composed by that virtuoso of melodic music Jerome Kern, with the lyrics supplied by Johnny Mercer.

Sadly, Joyce left as suddenly as she had arrived. And for me, the song ended. I never even knew her surname. 'Dearly Beloved' was one of three songs by Kern that were outstanding melodies in the film *You Were Never Lovelier*. The title music itself was quite wonderful. And the third piece, 'I'm Old Fashioned', was yet another gem. To play those pieces today gives me unalloyed joy.

Johnny Mercer had landed the position as lyricist for the film's music produced by Columbia Pictures. First, however, he required the approval of Jerome Kern. The latter had spent much of his song writing moving from one lyricist to another. It was a well- established fact that Kern was not the easiest person to work with. Indeed, Kern tended to regard most lyricists as somewhat lesser mortals. When he first met Mercer, he handed over a bundle of manuscripts and virtually instructed Mercer to come back with some suitable verses. Mercer later stated that he was awestruck and honoured to be working with Kern. Sometime later, when he presented Kern with the lyrics of 'I'm Old Fashioned', Kern played the piece, and his face creased into a smile. Having croaked through the music, he called Eva, his wife, and asked her to come and listen to the piece. When Kern finished playing, he stood up, hugged Mercer, and kissed him on the cheek. 'I'm Old Fashioned' was just one of the big hits of the film *You Were Never Lovelier*, and all have stood the test of time and will continue to do so with so many of Jerome Kern's other offerings.

Another American musical genius in music composition was Harold Arlen, who, in 1942, had published 'That Old Black Magic'. Here again, the lyrics were provided by Johnny Mercer. During that year, Mercer also wrote the lyrics for 'Tangerine', which featured in the film *The Fleet's In*. The music was written by Victor Schertzinger. The music 'Hit the Road to Dreamland' from the film *Star Spangled Rhythm* was also composed by Harold Arlen, with the lyrics once more provided by Johnny Mercer. This piece of music seems to have passed me by in the forties, but it re-emerged in the fifties when it became the introductory music of our college band at St Paul's College, Cheltenham, where I was in residence as a trainee teacher. It always brings back pleasant memories.

The first time I heard the song, 'Moonlight Becomes You', it was sung by Bing Crosby and, thereafter, recorded and sung by many other singers. But it was Bing who made it his own, and it became a hit (standard). It was composed by Jimmy van Heusen, and the lyrics provided by Johnny Burke. It was written for the Paramount picture *Road to Morocco* in 1942. It was also recorded by Harry James and his orchestra, with Helen Forest providing the vocals.

When Cy Feyer of Republic Pictures rang Sammy Cahn and asked him if he'd like to do a picture with Jule Styne, Sammy jumped at the idea. He later wrote that he had hit rock bottom when the call came in. In fact, he said that he'd have done a picture with Adolf Hitler if asked, such was his desperation at that time. Jule already had a score, which he played for Sammy.

'Would you play it slower?' And then Sammy said, 'I've heard that song before.'

To this, Jule said bristling, 'What the hell are you, a tune detective?'

'No,' said Sammy, 'that wasn't a criticism. It was a title for the song.'

The words then just flowed:

> I've heard that song before
> It's from an old familiar score
> I know it well that melody

Sammy considered it the best lyrics he had ever written. However, the word was that Jule thought it was one of the worst lyrics he had ever heard. When the song was recorded by Harry James and his orchestra on the B-side of a record to a Jimmy van Heusen / Johnny Burke song, the B-side became the A-side. And later, Jule called Sammy and suggested that they write some more songs together. It grew into a wonderful and fruitful partnership.

My sister Gillian remembered the time when I wished to improve my skills on the dance floor. Apparently, I sent for a correspondence course from the Victor Sylvester school of dancing. While practising at home, I held a broom in place of a partner. Working on a half turn, I managed to put the broom handle through the living room window. My parents were not amused. There ended any chance of my being the next Fred Astaire.

I remember sometime later my first hesitant steps on the local dance floor known to us as 'The Library'. The dancers moved across the floor, and they would hum or sing a song, one of which of always sticks in my memory more than any other. It was a Duke Ellington number, originally written in 1940, but the lyrics were only added by Bob Russell in 1942. The words remained with me:

> Missed the Saturday dance,
> How they crowded the floor,
> Couldn't bear it without you,
> Don't get around much anymore.

I should have been aware of Bob Russell sooner, as he had also written the lyrics of two of my favourite songs, 'Maria Elena' and 'Frenesi'. A better-known song of his was 'You Came a Long Way from St Louis'.

Finally, in 1942, I well remember a song called 'My Devotion', written by Roc Hillman and Johnny Napton, again little known in this country. Hillman was a composer and author and was educated at the University of Colorado. He directed army shows during the war. He and Irving Berlin had one thing in common, in that they both lived to be 100.

The Wannsee Conference, 20 January 1942

It is clear from Hitler's *Mein Kampf* that he was obsessed with the Jewish problem. He saw Jews as a nation within a nation, undermining its parent country from within. Clearly, he was wedded to the idea that Judaism was a world plague and had to be eradicated. From the moment he acceded to power on 30 January 1933, his attacks on German Jewry began. He purged the civil service between 1933 and 1934 and virtually denied the Jews any opportunity to make a living. He also set up special centres to facilitate Jewish emigration.

He chose two of his subordinates, Hermann Goering and Heinrich Himmler, to settle 'the Jewish Question'. Goering sent a letter in the summer of 1941 to Heydrich—to give him his correct name and rank, Reinhard Heydrich SS Obergruppenführer—empowering him to find a solution to the Jews in the German sphere of influence in Europe. Heydrich was the head of the Nazi Security Service (SD), chief of the Security Police, and deputy to Heinrich Himmler, head of and responsible for the SS Security (SD) Police and the Secret State Police, or Gestapo. Goering was also head of the Gestapo, the first-year industrial plan, and the Luftwaffe.

Such method of devolving of authority was ridiculously complicated but a direct result of Hitler's character. In modern terms, Hitler would be called a control freak. He would ensure that one, two, or more of his subordinates had responsibility for the same office or part thereof. This would result in the same subordinates complaining to him about the others. In this way, he would retain control of the agenda. What a way to run a country!

A meeting was arranged to be held at the Wannsee Villa situated in the south-west suburb of Berlin in the borough of Steglitz-Zehland located on the beautiful Wannsee Lake. Today it is very difficult to understand how fifty senior government officials could sit down with Heydrich as its chairman to implement the murder of European Jewry. Heydrich had prepared lists of Jews for the conference and outlined how the Jews would be rounded up and sent to camps in Poland, where they would be exterminated.

All this, of course, was largely unknown to the Allied authorities at that time and would have remained buried in the mists of time, had it not been for the staff of the American prosecutor at the Nuremburg Trials. They discovered a document stamped 'Herne Reich SS acte' (secret Reich matter) tucked away in a German Foreign Office folder. This document outlined the minutes of the Wannsee Protocol, which clearly showed a plan for the genocide of the Jews. The Americans had unearthed the most shameful document of modern times. It is estimated that 11 million or more people died in the Holocaust.

The 1,000-Bomber Raid, 30 and 31 May 1942

At this stage of the war, the role that was to be played by Bomber Command was still in some doubt. Then two bombshells occurred. Firstly, Chief of the Air Staff Sir Charles Portal proposed to the government that a force of 4,000 bombers over a succession of German cities would cause Germany to collapse and was the only alternative to a costly invasion and prolonged land campaign with its inevitable heavy casualties. The British government rejected this proposal, reasoning that the project was well beyond the ability of British industry to fulfil, as it would require a huge transfer of resources to provide and maintain such a force. It did agree, in part, to bomb German cities to cause mass dislocation and destruction of people's homes and, hence, destroy their morale, causing their home front to collapse.

The second bombshell took place with the appointment of Sir Arthur Harris as commander in chief of Bomber Command on 23 February 1942. At that time, Bomber Command had a mere 469 bombers available in its frontline force. Harris was to remain in charge of Bomber Command for the remainder of the war. Sometime after his appointment, Harris came up with the idea of a 1,000-bomber attack on a German city. He approached Charles Portal and the government, and they approved his idea.

The recent introduction of GEE would improve navigation.[2] And the idea of a bomber stream would be introduced, allowing aircraft to

---

2 GEE was a radio navigation system, which, by measuring the time delay between two radio signals, produced a fix for the navigator to ascertain the aircraft's position. In 1942, it had an accuracy of a few metres up to a distance of 350 miles.

fly along the same route at varying heights but at the same speed. This process would allow the stream to pass over the target in the shortest interval of time. In this attack, only 90 minutes would be allowed for the bombers to transit the target. (Two hours had been allowed for a smaller force to attack Lübeck on the night of 28/29 March.[3] Using borrowed aircraft from his conversion units and flying training commands, he managed to reach just over 1,000 aircraft for the raid. At one station in the briefing process, one flight member asked the briefing officer how many aircraft would be lost in collisions. The answer was two, which brought gales of laughter from the assembled aircrew. In fact, only two were lost in this way, which was quite extraordinary. The initial choice of target was Hamburg, but the bad weather there meant that Cologne would be the target chosen.

The Battle of El Alamein

I had not reached my teenage years when the battle started in North Africa.[4] Why we were fighting over a thousand or so miles of desert was a complete mystery to me, so I asked my father. He looked completely nonplussed but mumbled something about the importance of the Mediterranean. I was pleasantly surprised many years later to read that the North African campaign had no strategic importance and was largely a device to fight the Axis anywhere but in Germany,

---

3 It must have been the night of 28 May when the roar of aircraft roused me from my bed. I watched them fly past, all aircraft with their navigation lights on. What I was seeing was aircraft from the training airfields of West Wales, positioning to airfields in the east to refuel and ready themselves for the greatest raid to date on a German city. The attack was described in the media as a resounding success, and it became a turning point in Bomber Command's war. It raised the morale of both the public and the aircrew, also confirming Bomber Command's future as a major force. It was reported that 150,000 of Cologne's citizens fled the city in panic, and during the course of the raid, Bomber Command lost forty-one of its aircraft, which amounted to an acceptable 3.9 per cent of the attacking force. (These statistics are from an Air Ministry broadcast at the time.)

4 The war in North Africa lasted from 14 June 1940 to 13 May 1943, when the Axis powers surrendered in Tunisia.

thought up by our then Prime Minister, Winston Churchill. Looking back over the years, it is quite incredible to believe that the prime minister was stripping away our defences at home and sending men, tanks, and aircraft to the Middle East, when we at home faced an imminent threat of invasion.

To confirm this ludicrous course of action, General Sir John Dill, the Chief of the Imperial General Staff (CIGS), wrote on 6 May 1941, 'It is the United Kingdom … and not Egypt that is vital and the defence of the United Kingdom must take first place. Egypt is not even second in order of priority.'

Churchill went on to sack Dill the following November.

At this time, my family took the *Daily Express* newspaper, and generally, on its front page, it would have small pictures and maps of the North African scene. These really intrigued me, and as a result, I became familiar with most of the towns/villages on the North African coastline, viz. Tobruk, Bengazi, Mersa Matruh, Sollum, Bardia, and Sidi Barrani.

The last named, together with the Italian Army, became the butt of many jokes on the BBC at that time, most of which I failed to understand and now I fail to remember.

By summer 1940, Churchill had achieved a certain moral authority in this country, and his speeches were nothing more than trumpet calls to survive the German threat and, in the long term, to win, although that seemed totally improbable at the time. As prime minister, Churchill as war minister virtually became a dictator. It became quite clear as the war progressed that Churchill distrusted his generals. Yet he, from his early days, yearned to be a super general, where he would emulate his ancestor, Marlborough. The clear object of the war was to defeat Hitler, but just about everything that Churchill wanted was to avoid direct confrontation with the Germans. His tactics were diversionary, knowing that Britain was, by itself, not strong enough to engage the Germans on the continent of Europe.

When Operation Compass was undertaken by the Allied Army, led by General Richard O'Connor, the Italian forces were defeated. O'Connor was now in a position to continue the advance to Tripoli. It was at this stage that Churchill intervened to order General Wavell (the senior British officer in North Africa) to withdraw much of his army for operations in Greece, and so the battle, nearly won, was halted. Wavell strongly objected to the prime minister's orders but was overruled.

Wavell was correct in his assumptions and Churchill wrong, and the results were to bear him out. The Germans drove out the Allied Army from Greece and even captured the island of Crete. The remnants of the Allied force returned whence they had started. As a riposte, the Germans had sent a small blocking force through the port of Tripoli completely unopposed. However, their commander, Erwin Rommel not content with just a blocking action, attacked and drove the Allied forces back 500 miles to their start point.[5] In addition, they captured General O'Connor, who later escaped from the prisoner of war camp, returned to Britain, and took a leading part in the invasion of the continent. This clearly was the result of Churchill's decision to withdraw much of Wavell's army strength, a decision he again repeated later, transferring forces to the Far East. Accordingly, Rommel then pushed back the Allied troops a second time, so all the gains of Operation Compass were lost. Churchill's response was to sack Wavell and replace him with General Auchinleck, who he would also subsequently fire.

For almost two years, the battle in North Africa swayed backwards and forwards, monopolising the front pages of the British daily newspapers. It appeared to the ordinary citizen that it would never stop. Then, on 25 February 1942, Churchill faced a censure motion in the House of Commons, which he won, but his position was certainly weakened. More than anything else, Churchill wanted/needed a victory to cement his position as prime minister, but time and time again, Rommel had thwarted the Allied troops in the desert.

He was a thruster and a master of improvisation, always leading his men from the front. He undoubtedly had a magical effect, not only on his own men but on his enemies as well. His title as the Desert Fox was well deserved.

---

5 Note that I have called the British and Commonwealth forces in this article 'The Allies'. They comprised British troops, as well as Australian, Indian, New Zealand, and South African troops and the Sudan force.

The Allied army had now retreated to the Egyptian railway, halting at El Alamein only fifty miles east of the port of Alexandria. Here, despite his depleted and tired troops, Rommel attacked but was repulsed by Auchinleck's men at what has been described as the First Battle of El Alamein. Despite this defensive success, however, Auchinleck was removed from his post, coincident with the arrival of Churchill and Alanbrooke in the desert. Churchill then appointed General Alexander as head of the Middle East Command and Lt General Gott as the commander of the now called 8th Army. Alanbrooke felt that Gott was a tired man, having been in the Middle East from the very beginning. Gott, however, was killed when the aircraft in which he was flying was shot down. Alanbrooke now had his way, and a new face in the form of Lt General Law Bernard Montgomery was thus ordered out to take over as 8th Army commander.

Meanwhile, the Anglo-American forces had now landed in North West Africa, and the threat to Rommel now hung over his head like the sword of Damocles, poised to destroy his troops, who by this time had been driven to the extreme limit of their endurance.

His army was literally gasping for breath and had no reserves of any kind. To add to their woes, Rommel was now taken ill and flown back to Germany for treatment. The die was cast.

General Georg Stumme took over in Rommel's absence. But in an Allied attack, he died of a heart attack. In addition to his superiority in men, tanks, and aircraft, Montgomery had the distinct advantage of being able to read all the German messages through ULTRA, the information passed to him from the crypto analysts at Bletchley Park. Montgomery now knew their order of battle, its supply problems, its army's disposition, and its moves and intentions.

By day three of the battle, the 8th Army's attack had stalled, and Churchill railed, 'Is it impossible to find a general who can win a battle?'

However, by 1 November, Rommel, now back in harness, realised the battle was lost and began a retreat. By the eleventh day of the battle, the Egyptian border was clear, and the pursuit was on. The second Battle of El Alamein had been won, and Churchill ordered all the church bells to be rung in Britain to signify our first victory over the Axis forces.

The Battle of Midway, June 1942

Following the attack on Pearl Harbour, Oahu, on 7 December 1941, the Americans had received a salutary does of humility. The universal public shock that the Japanese had attacked successfully the pride of the American fleet in their great naval base at Pearl Harbour was a wake-up call to the American nation. Indeed, it was as great a shock as the attack on the Twin Towers of 11 September 2001 would be decades later. (I would be in New York at the time, enabling me to see at first-hand the shock and anger of my American friends.

Admiral Nimitz had assumed command of the Pacific Fleet on 3 December 1941 and improved morale considerably by retaining the staff already in place. His assets had been greatly depleted when the carrier, *Saratoga*, was torpedoed in January. And the carrier, *Lexington* had also been sunk in the Battle of the Coral Sea the following May. Nimitz and his staff knew that the Japanese were ready again to attack. The problem he had was to determine the where and when. He largely depended on Station HYPO based near the naval base in Pearl Harbour and the services of the cryptanalysis of its staff, led by Commander Joseph Rochefort, for his information. The latter worked very closely with Captain Edwin J Layton, the fleet intelligence officer.

By March 1942, Rochefort largely knew where the Japanese fleets were located, but at that time, he was only able to decipher 20 per cent of all messages. Naval Intelligence in Washington disagreed with Rochefort's findings, despite translating from the same decrypts. Nimitz, however, preferred to trust his own staff and not the intelligence emanating from Washington. He certainly had no wish to suffer the same fate as his predecessor, Admiral Kimmel, who had been made a scapegoat for the Hawaiian attack, due to the miscalculations of the Navy Department in Washington.

A Japanese March decrypt from Tokyo gave Rochefort the first indication that the Japanese planned an attack on one of the American islands in the Pacific. This provided an inkling that the letters 'AF' in the message could be the island of Midway. Rochefort now deciphered

'50 miles northwest of AF'. Washington thought, at this time, that the Japanese objective was the West Coast of the United States. In order to silence the sceptics in Washington, Rochefort 'cooked up' a fake message, which indicated that there was a shortage of fresh water on Midway. This was written in a code that could be easily read by the Japanese. This was done not to prove to Nimitz that he was right but, rather, to prove that Washington was wrong.

The message was sent in a code easily read by the Japanese and approved by Nimitz. Soon, the Japanese gave the game away when a careless Japanese radio operator reported that 'AF' had a freshwater shortage. So, what the Japanese hoped for and expected to be a trap for the United States Navy turned out to be a trap for themselves.

However, the results were by no means a foregone conclusion, and although forewarned by superior cryptanalysis and radio intelligence, a much inferior American naval force in numbers, brilliantly succeeded in achieving a stunning victory. The Japanese carriers, *Akagi*, *Kaga*, *Hiryu*, and *Soryu*, under the command of Vice Admiral Nagumo, all of which had attacked Pearl Harbor, were all sunk, with the loss of almost three hundred aircraft. Pearl Harbor had been avenged. Of the three American carriers in the battle, the USS *Yorktown* was lost, but the *Enterprise* and *Hornet* survived. It was the most stunning victory in naval warfare when the opposing fleets, for the first time in history, had never once seen one another.

For the Japanese, they paid the penalty for what they termed the sin of hubris. Small margins often win battles. And here, the Japanese carriers were caught while refuelling and rearming their planes with the usual umbrella of fighters being absent overhead. They had paid little attention to the art of aerial reconnaissance, as it was considered in the Japanese Navy, a defensive measure and not valued highly—like the French, early in the First World War, with their mantra to attack.

The Americans, too, made their mistakes. And Washington, by its political blunderings, repeated its blunders of Pearl Harbour, which so easily could have lost them the crucial battle of Midway.

The Russian Front, 1942

The Allies were certainly losing the war early in 1942. The drive on Moscow in July and August 1941 was favoured by all the leading German generals. It was considered by the German general staff that Russia would be paralysed by the loss of its capital city. The conditions of 1941 were vastly different from those confronting Napoleon in 1812. Moscow then was a somewhat barbaric city in the middle of a primitive state. In 1941, however, it was the nexus of Stalin's administrative Empire and a great industrial area. Most of all, it was the centre of the railway system of European Russia. In the minds of the generals, it was essential to take it. And in the summer, it was very likely they would have succeeded. It was that genius, Adolf Hitler who thought otherwise. And as the head of the German army, he veered his armies away from Moscow down towards the Ukraine.

Although a tremendous success was then achieved in the encirclement of over 600,000 Russian troops when generals Guderian and Kleist closed the trap, Hitler on the final day of the battle of Kiev ordered the opening of the battle of Moscow. Its code name was 'Typhoon' and it was to be launched on 2 October 1941. His order of the day read, 'The last great decisive battle of this year will mean the annihilation of the enemy.'

Everything was magnificently planned, only the weather could not be foreseen. By 7 October, the first snow started falling. At the same time, clouds of smoke were rising from the chimneys of the Kremlin as the members burned their secret papers. But the Germans were stuck and helpless on the roads that had turned to deep mud. Field Marshall Bock, who led the German central armies, at last conceded victory to the morass of rain and snow that had made his advance impossible.

'Hold until the frost comes' was the German order of the day.

When Stalin had been informed by his spying sources that the Japanese would be attacking the Americans and not Eastern Russia, he moved his Siberian armies to the Moscow front. By 5 December 1941, the air temperature registered between 30 to 50 degrees below zero centigrade. No man could lie in a foxhole for any length of time without a sheepskin topcoat, felt boots, and gloves. The German troops had none of these things. In a 600-mile stretch in front of

Moscow on this date, the German offensive had come to a standstill in a literal sense, frozen into inactivity. Tragically for the German troops, they were still wearing their summer uniforms and suffering frostbite and dying in droves In fact, there were more casualties through cold and frost than through enemy action.

As a consequence of the terrible weather and with its lack of reserves, the German Army was driven back but not broken. When General Model was given command of the 9th Army, he had the task of repairing the line and halting the retreat. He was a master of defensive fighting, having learned his craft in the trenches of the Western Front during the First World War. When he arrived in the 9th Army Operations, he looked at the operations map and exclaimed, 'Rather a mess.'

He then ran his fingers over the red arrows indicating the Russian penetrations and said, 'We have to turn off the supply tap of these Russian divisions—and then strike them in the flank and catch them in a stranglehold.'

His audience was amazed at his optimism. The chief of staff of the 8th Army then asked, 'And what, Herr General, have you brought us for this operation?'

Model calmly regarded him and then said, 'Myself,' and then burst out laughing.

They all joined in the laughter. They all knew that a different spirit had arrived, and this live wire general soon was everywhere and anywhere on foot or on a horse. The line was held, and all his troops knew that, when Model was in command, the good fortune of war was present.

Hitler's hubris believed, you only had to kick the door down, and the whole Russian house would collapse. Clearly, like most of his decisions, his war on Russia was a huge mistake.

CHAPTER 7
The Tide Turns, 1943

Despite the fact that the tide of war in 1943 was swinging in the favour of the Allies, only one war song of note seemed to have been written. That song was 'Coming in on a Wing and a Prayer'. It was composed by Jimmy McHugh, and the lyrics written by Harold Adamson. It was recorded by the Song Spinners and was the only war song to reach number one that year.

The song, 'You'll Never Know' became a widespread favourite that year and has remained a standard. It was composed by Harry Warren with lyrics by Mack Gordon. It was introduced in the 1943 film *Hello, Frisco, Hello.* when it was sung by Alice Faye. She also sang it in the 1944 film *Four Jills in a Jeep.* The song won the 1943 Academy Award for Best Original Song that year. It was recorded by Dick Haymes and Frank Sinatra and by Doris Day later, in 1958. It was such a popular song that it continued to be recorded, in 1965 by Shirley Bassey and by Michael Bublé in 2004. It was one of the most endearing songs to come out of the war.

'A Lovely Way to Spend an Evening' was another wonderful song from 1943. Again, it was composed by Jimmy McHugh, with the lyrics once more by Harold Adamson. Like 'You'll Never Know', the song has been recorded countless times, and both are considered to be pop standards.

I loved the way Bing Crosby sang 'Sunday Monday and Always'. It impressed itself on me as a youngster. Perhaps it was his jaunty style I liked that made me remember it. Clearly, it was very popular, and it reached the number one spot in the charts. It was also recorded by Sinatra, Nat King Cole in 1961, and Pat Boone in 1964.

Novelty songs always seemed to generate a following, and 'Maizy Doats' was one of the early ones. It was composed by Milton Drake, Al Hoffman, and Jerry Livingstone. It appears to have been based on a British nursery rhyme. I have to say, however, although it was fun to sing as a child, I never understood what it meant. Come to think of it, I still don't.

'It Can't Be Wrong' was and still remains a great favourite of mine. It was composed by that master- of- film- music, Max Steiner. He composed it as a large part of the background music and the main theme for the Warner Brothers' film *Now Voyager*, winning the Oscar and first shown in 1942. Kim Gannon provided lyrics for the music, and it was published in early 1943. It was recorded by Dick Haymes and the Song Spinners, and the song became one of the top-selling songs in sheet music sales in America that year.

I have to admit my surprise when I discovered that the song 'When the Lights Go on Again' was written in 1943. In my mind, I had always thought that the song belonged to 1944/45.

The song was written by Bennie Benjamin, Sol Marcus, and Eddy Seiler. It was first recorded by Vaughan Monroe in 1943 and reached number one in the charts that year. The title of the song alluded to the remarks made by Edward Grey, first Viscount Grey of Fallodon, a Liberal statesman and British foreign secretary in World War One. It was 3 August 1914 as he watched the lamps being lit outside the Foreign Office in London. He remarked, 'The lamps are going out all over Europe. We shall not see them lit again in our lifetime.'

It appears that, on the piano, I have a natural empathy for the rhythms and beat of South American music. The following are songs that appeared in 1943, starting with 'Poinciana' ('The Song of the Tree'). This piece of music was originally written in 1936 by Nat Simon, with words by Buddy Bernier. Recently, I purchased a book of music labelled *The Best Latin Songs Ever*. Therein I found 'Poinciana', a piece of music I hadn't heard since the war years. I must have heard it played by Glenn Miller and his orchestra (then called his Army Air Force Band) during the war. I had not heard it played since, so it was a joy to play it on the piano. It certainly brought back memories.

Similarly, 'Besame Mucho' prompted many memories. The title, literally translated, is 'Kiss me Much'. It was composed by Consuelo Velasquez. The English lyrics were provided by Sunny Skylar.

Perhaps it was the song 'Amor' that was the most popular. It was composed in 1943 by Gabriel Ruiz, and the original Spanish lyrics were by Ricardo López Méndez. The English lyrics were provided by Norman Newell. The biggest selling versions of this music were the recordings by Bing Crosby and Andy Russell.

'Tico Tico (Tico Tico no Fubá)' literally translated means, 'Sparrow in the Cornmeal'. It's a Brazilian piece of music that stretches back as far as 1917, when it was written by Zequinha Abreu. The original Portuguese lyrics were written by Aloysio Oliveira, and Ervin Drake provided the English lyrics. The piece reached its peak of popularity in 1943 in a recording by the Andrews Sisters.

Finally, in 1943, another firm favourite was 'You Belong to my Heart' ('Solamente una vez'). The words and music were written by Ray Gilbert. The words are the translation of a Mexican Bolero song. It has been performed by a whole list of artists and singers, notably Julio Iglesias, Andrea Bocelli, Placido Domingo, and Nat King Cole. Bing Crosby recorded the song with the Xavier Cugat's orchestra, and his version reached the bestseller's chart in 1945.

'Straighten Up and Fly Right' was written by Nat King Cole and Irving Mills in 1943. It became part of a film of that year entitled *Here Comes Elmer*. The words of the song were from a church sermon that Cole had once heard. In his need for money, Cole sold all the rights to the song for $50 and, consequently, never received any royalties from it. However, when it hit the jukeboxes, his moneymaking increased exponentially.

When Johnny Mercer (singer-songwriter) started Capitol Records, he asked Nat to make records for him on that label. Nat also wanted to do some vocals, and the first of these was 'Straighten Up and Fly Right'. Following that, he became a vocalist, and that song became his first recording, despite the fact that he was one of the best jazz pianists in the business.

The Nat Cole Trio made the song their own. It was also used in the 1995 HBO (Home Box Office) war drama *The Tuskegee Airmen*. The Andrews Sisters recorded it in 1944, Robbie Williams on *Swing When You're Winning* in 2001, and the King's Singers on *Swimming Over London*, 2010.

I well remember a flight instructor at Biggin Hill, Kent, in the 1960s who used those immortal words when a rookie pilot drifted off course, speed, or height. He also used some profound expletives, which are not repeatable here!

Lynn Riggs's play, *Green Grows the Lilacs* had been a flop, but Oscar Hammerstein believed it could be turned into a fine musical. He had, over the years, written many fine lyrics for Jerome Kern's music when he was then approached to write the music for the show. However, Kern was not enthusiastic about the book or the play based on the book. In the face of Kern's lack of interest, Hammerstein approached Rogers and Hart, who had written many successful musicals and more than five hundred songs. Larry Hart was physically and mentally worn out at the time, the inevitable results of drink and drugs, but Rodgers quickly saw the play's virtue. Hart could not be persuaded and showed no interest in the project. He thought his partner was backing a loser and suggested that he, Rodgers, should undertake the musical with Hammerstein. At that point, Rodgers realised that his long-enduring partnership with his friend had, sadly, reached a conclusion.

Almost everybody in show business told both Rodgers and Hammerstein that they were crazy to do a 'cowboy musical', particularly in the middle of a world war. Also, with Larry Hart, Rodgers had always written the music first, with Hart's lyrics to follow. Now he had to furnish the music to Hammerstein's already completed lyrics. Furthermore, Rodgers had never worked with Hammerstein previously. The title of the musical was now changed to *Oklahoma*, and the advance messages received on the show were universally bad.

There was a saying on Broadway about musicals. 'No tits, no legs, no hope!' The opening scene in the show depicted an old woman churning butter, sitting on the steps of a log cabin. In its New Haven debut, an unaccompanied baritone voice from off stage sang, 'There's a bright golden haze on the meadow,' and 'the corn is as high as an elephant's eye.'

In Hammerstein's words, 'It was like a light from a thousand lanterns, and you could feel the glow!'

For Rodgers and Hammerstein, it was like a renaissance, a point for which both had waited all their lives. The Broadway opening took place on 31 March 1943 and was such a smash hit that it ran for an unprecedented 2,212 performances. For Rodgers, its success was dimmed by the poor health of his former pal and partner, Larry Hart. They had been together since both were students at Columbia University, and apart from their many songs, they had put on twenty-eight stage musicals together. Larry Hart died on 22 November at the young age of forty-three years. Undoubtedly, he was a genius with words and one of the greatest of all American lyricists—a true poet of Broadway! When the show reached London, it ran for 1,502 performances at the Theatre Royal, Drury Lane, and put a smile on the faces of its many audiences.

Rodgers and Hammerstein went on to write the musicals they will always be remembered for. After *Oklahoma* in 1943, *Carousel* followed in 1945, *South Pacific* in 1949, *The King and I* in 1951, and *The Sound of Music* in 1959. These were really the 'pick of the crop'. *Oklahoma* was made into a picture in 1955 starring Gordon MacRae and Shirley Jones in the leading roles. In 1956, it won the Oscar for the best music and scoring in a musical picture. Rodgers and Hammerstein were the ones who initiated the golden age of musical theatre.

Oklahoma had followed the innovations that first appeared in *Show Boat* in 1927, where the songs and dances were integrated into the storyline—not surprising, perhaps, as Hammerstein had written both shows. The songs in *Oklahoma* were 'Oh What a Beautiful Morning ', 'Surrey with a Fringe on Top', 'People Will Say We're in Love', and 'Oklahoma' itself.

At that moment in time (1943), my Aunt Glenys had fallen in love with Tom, a handsome sergeant in the Royal Air Force. She bought me a copy of the sheet music 'People Will Say We're in Love' and insisted I played it incessantly. Sadly, later that year, Tom crossed a hangar crowded with aircraft, ducking under tail planes, wings, and propellers. Incredibly, one careless aircraft fitter had left the ignition switches on a particular engine on live, so as Tom moved under the propeller, it suddenly kicked into action and removed a part of his brain. He died shortly afterwards.

Glenys never married, but the song remained with her for the rest of her life. When she reached ninety years or more, I used to visit her, usually to find her dozing in the usual chair. I would then kneel alongside and gently sing in her ear the words of 'People Will Say We're in Love'. Soon a smile would appear on her face, and with her eyes still closed, she would begin to sing the words with me, much as she had done when a young girl during the war years. Such is the magic of music.

The Battle of Stalingrad, 23 August 1942–2 February 1943

While the battle to encircle the German 6th Army in Stalingrad was under way with Operation Uranus, the Soviet forces undertook a great effort in the area around Rzhev on the central front. This operation named Mars was conducted by Marshal Zhukov and was aimed at destabilising the German Army Group Centre and was also a ploy to draw German reserves away from the Stalingrad front. Operation Mars resulted in a major defeat of the Russian forces under Marshal Zhukov.

Fortunately for the Germans, they were led by General Walter Model, the best defensive general of the war. He had stabilised the Eastern Front in 1941 and later commanded more than one hundred divisions. He became the youngest field marshal in the German Army and one of the most able. Russian losses amounted to over 400,000 men dead and wounded, an event that has been 'airbrushed' out of Russian history and scarcely mentioned by Western historians.

Hitler had clearly realised the danger to Army Group B in pushing its way into the noose of Stalingrad, while at the same time exposing its flanks to attack. On 19 November 1942, the Russians duly obliged by launching Operation Uranus, a massive attack by the Red Army against the Romanian Front, which guarded the flank of the German 6th Army. The result was inevitable and foreseen by Hitler. By 23 November, two Russian armoured pincers had closed some twenty miles south east of Kalach, enclosing some 250,000 German and Romanian troops in the pocket.

Field Marshal Manstein was appointed Commander in Chief Army Group Don and took up his post on 27 November, with the express purpose of rescuing the 6th Army. In the meantime, the immense task of feeding the trapped army was undertaken.

The army required 750 tonnes of supplies each day to maintain its fighting ability, particularly now that winter had set in. The best the Luftwaffe managed with its limited number of fifty-two transport aircraft averaged just 150 tonnes or less. Clearly, enemy action and poor weather contributed largely to this disparity. However, it was possible to fly out of the pocket up to 40,000 wounded men.

Hitler was now micromanaging troop movement in the pocket from 1,300 miles away. He hoped and expected that Stalingrad would remain a firm base on the Volga and forbade Paulus permission to attempt a breakout of the pocket. Indeed, on 28 November, Hitler informed Manstein that Stalingrad was to be held at all costs. It is now clear that Manstein never thought that he had sufficient forces to relieve Stalingrad without the 6th Army launching its own attack to link up with the relieving force. He was also aware that Paulus, a very able staff officer, was a weak and compliant character who had little previous battlefield experience as a field commander.

Manstein commenced his attack on 8 December with the code name Winter Tempest. It reached twenty miles away from the Stalingrad pocket, but in accordance with Hitler's orders, the 6th Army was not ordered to fight its way to meet it.

In any war, the enemy also makes plans, and Manstein clearly realised that the Russians were likely to start another offensive towards Rostock on Don, which would not only cut off Manstein's Army Group but also Army Group A, which had penetrated southwards into the Caucasus and was now largely immobile. In fact, Manstein had guessed correctly, and the Russians were already planning such a move under the code name Operation Saturn.

It was on 18 December when Manstein's attack was closing on the Stalingrad pocket that he sent a request to Hitler for the beleaguered 6th Army to 'break out'. Manstein's signal remained unanswered.

Consequently, between Hitler's iron will to stand firm and Paulus's passivity, the 6th Army was doomed!

The Stalingrad battle lasted almost five and a half months, and on 2 February 1943, Paulus surrendered to the Russians. The symbolism of Stalingrad and the German defeat shattered its army's reputation of invincibility and was a devastating blow to the German people. The fault of the defeat clearly fell on Hitler's shoulders, and it marked the turning point in the war. The Germans lost 200,000 and killed almost the same number of their Russian opponents. Some 30,000 to 40,000 were airlifted to safety, and 90,000 entered captivity. Of these, only 5,000 ever lived to see their homeland again.

The Bombing of the Dams, 16/17 May 1943

Well before the Second World War, the German Ruhr Dams were listed as potential targets in the event of war. Sometime in early 1943, the Air Ministry supported the idea of such an attack. The problem the ministry confronted was how an attack could be effectively made.

They do say that cometh the hour cometh the man. In this case, the man was Barnes Wallis, who at that time, was working on aircraft design. To establish a method of attacking the dams, he first designed a bomb adequate for the purpose. Unfortunately, such a bomb was so large that no aircraft then available could carry it or reach the planned height to drop it. Consequently, he also designed a six-engine aircraft that fitted the purpose. However, the resources needed for this enterprise were far beyond the ability of the Air Ministry to provide at that time, and the idea was dropped.

I don't suppose there are many boys in the world then or now who haven't stood on a beach or alongside a large pond and not thrown small stones at the surface of the water to see how many bounces they could make. Clearly Barnes Wallis was one such boy, and probably with that in mind, he developed what was to be called the 'bouncing bomb', which was given the code name Upkeep. The theory was that such a missile would bounce on the water until it came to rest against the dam wall. Its inertia at an end, it would then sink to the base of the dam where the change in pressure would cause it to explode, causing a miniature earthquake.

Air Chief Marshall Harris was commander in chief of Bomber Command at that time and really showed little enthusiasm for the project. He always resented any efforts to use his aircraft and airmen on any targets other than what he considered to be its main purpose, which was to attack and destroy German cities. Any other projects he termed 'Panacea Targets'. However, an order was an order, and the operation code named Chastise was ordered to take place. Harris handed full responsibility for the operation to Air Vice Marshall Ralph Cochrane, who at that time, was the air officer commanding Number 5 Group. The new squadron to be formed for this operation was Number 617 and was to be commanded by Wing Commander Guy Gibson, who, following meeting with Cochrane, agreed to undertake one more trip. Gibson had already completed three tours and had amassed just over 1,000 flying hours. The new squadron was to be based at RAF Scampton in Lincolnshire.

The initial intention of Cochrane and Gibson was to select aircrew who had completed at least one tour (thirty operations) or more. In the end, however, they accepted some crews who had not even completed one tour and must have only completed some four hundred to six hundred flying hours.

Having been an airline pilot myself with over 10,000 hours in my logbook, I find it unbelievable that pilots with such limited experience could be expected to fly across Europe at night below 100 feet and then descend to 60 feet to attack their target. But this was wartime and the young pilots averaging a mere twenty-one or twenty-two years old did just that!

Following concentrated training by day but mostly at night, nineteen Lancasters were despatched on the night of 16/17 May 1943 to attack the great dams of Germany. Gibson, plus four other aircraft, bombed the Möhne Dam and successfully breached it; two other aircraft attacked the Eder Dam and breached that also. Two more attacked the Sorpe Dam, and one aircraft, the Schavelme Dam without breaching their structure. The Sorpe Dam had a different construction to the others. It was earth covered with a concrete watertight core, which remained only superficially damaged. The RAF did send several observation flights over the Sorpe, but no leaks were observed.

The operation at night, as planned, was clearly extremely arduous, and Gibson had already rejected Wallis's earlier proposal of a daylight raid. Of the nineteen aircraft with their 133 crew members that were despatched, eight were lost, with the deaths of 53 crew members; 3 of them became prisoners of war, and 2 of them were badly injured.

The raid resulted in a loss of 42 per cent of the force. In the 1,000-bomber raid on Cologne a year earlier, the loss was only 3.2 per cent. So the question that had to be asked was, was the raid worth such a loss? Sir Arthur Harris clearly thought not. He had always regarded the raid as hare-brained, with some justification. He later wrote, 'I have seen nothing ... to show that the effort was worthwhile except as a spectacular operation.'

Sir Charles Webster and Noble Frankland, who wrote the four-volume official history of the RAF Strategic Air Offensive against Germany, believed that the attack was oversold, and its achievement exaggerated! With typical German efficiency, the dams, which had taken five years to build, were repaired within just five months and were never seriously attacked again by the RAF. The raid caused the deaths of over 1,200 civilians, many of whom were foreign workers. The damage caused by the flooding was soon repaired. The German view indicated that, had the main attack been on the Sorpe Dam instead of the Eder, the effect on the Ruhr's industrial production would have been far more significant. In any event, the Sorpe Dam managed to keep the Ruhr supplied with water until the Möhne was repaired.

A film of the raid was made in 1955, with Michael Redgrave playing the part of Barnes Wallis and Richard Todd as Guy Gibson.

The film was well received, but changes were made away from the truth for dramatic licence. Some of the fake information is listed below:

1. Barnes Wallis did not encounter opposition from the bureaucracy.
2. He was not the chief designer of the Wellington bomber but did work on its design.

3. Gibson was not a popular man, and only one of his former crew members followed him to the new 617 Squadron, and that was Wireless Operator Hutchinson.

4. The dams were identified before the war as potential targets. Attacking them was not Barnes Wallis's idea.

5. The spot lamps on the aircraft to gauge height over water came from a suggestion by Benjamin Lockspeiser of the Ministry of Aircraft Production and not by Gibson following a visit to the theatre.

6. There is no historical evidence to support the idea that the idea of the bouncing bomb came from Nelson bouncing cannon balls into the sides of enemy ships during the Battle of the Nile.

7. Richard Todd played Gibson as an amiable and friendly squadron commander. From all accounts, he was anything but that and certainly never one who was at ease with other ranks.

Gibson was born in Shimla, India, his father, a civil servant. When he was six years old, his parents separated. And at eight years of age, he was sent to prep school at St Georges in Folkestone, Kent. At thirteen years of age, he continued his education at St Edwards Preparatory School in Oxford. In 1937, he joined the Royal Air Force.

When I first researched Gibson's background, I felt extremely sorry for him. Perhaps the Royal Air Force was the only real family he ever had. To meet and to talk with other ranks must have seemed to him akin to meeting Martians. Furthermore, he was only twenty-four years of age when he became commander of 617 Squadron.

If he lacked the social skills, he certainly did not lack leadership skills and courage. Indeed, after his attack on the Möhne, he then flew alongside the second and third attacking Lancaster and, in so doing, deliberately attracted the German defensive fire. He certainly deserved his Victoria Cross. (See the page from his logbook and his VC inscription below.)

SINGLE-ENGINE AIRCRAFT				MULTI-ENGINE AIRCRAFT						PASS-ENGER	INSTR/CLOUD FLYING [Incl. in cols. (1) to (10)]	
DAY		NIGHT		DAY			NIGHT				DAY	NIGHT
DUAL	PILOT	DUAL	PILOT	DUAL	1st PILOT	2nd PILOT	DUAL	1st PILOT	2nd PILOT		DUAL	PILOT
(1)	(2)	(3)	(4)	(5)	(6)	(7)	(8)	(9)	(10)	(11)	(12)	(13)
					1·50							
					1·30							
	1·00											
					1·00							
					3·00							
					1·15							
								3·05				
								6·40				
50·25	431·50	3·10	8·50	4·20	577·40	16·00	–	644·25	–	NAV. 87·45	10·55	478·30

AWARDED   V.C.   23 : 5 : 43.

8. Sadly, the film concerned itself with the officer class only, ignoring the majority of the squadron. Yet two-thirds of all the aircrew on the raid were non-commissioned airmen, in other words, sergeants and flight sergeants. The film clearly reflected the class system that existed in the country at the time and still does.

9. Eric Coates's music was not written especially for the film. Indeed, Coates had a profound dislike of writing film music, as he would have to write to a fixed time scale that he himself had not set. Shortly after writing the music, he was asked to provide a musical march for the film. With the music already written, it was named the 'The Dam Busters March', and this became his most famous piece.

Shortly after he had written the music, Coates was approached by the film producers, who told him that the film was of national importance. He considered that the music he had just completed would make a perfect overture to the film. It was performed by the Associated British Studio Orchestra and created a superb background to the film, worthy of the deeds depicted on the screen.

Gibson had completed over 170 operations by the age of twenty-six. He was then sent on a tour of the United States and Canada. On his return, he was posted to the Directorate for the Prevention of Accidents, ostensibly to write a book on his experiences, a book he named *Enemy Coast Ahead*. He became restless when, on leave, he heard about the D-Day landings. By September 1944, he wangled himself back on operations as a controller on bombing raids. On such raids, he would fly low to mark the target, assisting the bombers to bomb more accurately.

During a raid on 19 September 1944, he flew a Mosquito aircraft with Squadron Leader Warwick as his navigator. The aircraft crashed near Steenbergen in Holland, killing both crew. The exact cause of the crash remains unknown and is likely to remain unknown. Both men are buried side by side in the cemetery of the small town of Steenbergen, Holland.

The propaganda value of the raid on the dams was immense and certainly lifted the morale of Bomber Command crews and the general civilian population. It created the impression that Britain, together with its Allies, was capable of winning the war. A total of 55,573 Bomber Command aircrew was killed during World War II. Their average age was twenty-two years.

My hero from those times was Flt. Lt. Roy Milton, who flew with the Royal Canadian Air Force, based at Leeming in Yorkshire. Roy died on his twenty-sixth raid to Augsburg on 25/26 February 1944. His Halifax aircraft was shot down by a night fighter. We had lived in the same street as young boys and attended the same junior and grammar schools, albeit about ten years apart. Because of his bravery, I followed his example and became a pilot, albeit a civilian airline one.

Mohne Dam after the raid

Eder Dam after the raid

CHAPTER 8

The Americans are Coming and D-Day 1944

'It Could Happen to You' is one of the many songs written by Jimmy Van Heusen, with lyrics by Johnny Burke. It featured in a film *And the Angels Sing*, with Dorothy Lamour and Fred McMurray. Its first hit recording was by Joe Stafford with the Paul Weston Orchestra in July 1944. Many other vocalists also recorded the song—Lena Horne, Barbra Streisand, Kiri Te Kanawa, and Dave Brubeck.

Jimmy Van Heusen's real name was Edward Chester Babcock, a name adopted by Bob Hope in the film *Road to Morocco* and others. The pair also wrote the best seller 'Swinging on a Star'. Bing Crosby sang it in the film *Going my Way*, and it won the Academy Award for Best Original Song in 1944. Its first recording was with Bing Crosby and the John Scott Trotter Orchestra in 1944.

The song 'It Had to Be You' was composed by Isham Jones, and the lyrics were by Gus Kahn. It was first published in 1924and recorded again on 28 June 1944, when it reached the bestseller charts. It appeared in the film *Mr Skeffington* in 1944 and was recorded by many artists, including Dick Haymes and Dinah Shore in 1944, Frank Sinatra in 1979, Tony Bennett in 2012, and Michael Bublé with

Barbara Streisand in 2014. The song also was included in the top 100 tunes in American cinema history.

'Skyliner' was written by Charlie Barnet, who, at the time of writing, was running his own swing band. He used it to carry along with him an old foot pump portable organ. He used this to write the piece when performing at the Royal Theatre in Baltimore. It was recorded on 13 July 1944 and became one of Barnet's most exciting records. Charles Daly Barnet (1913–1991) was an American saxophonist composer and successful bandleader. He had learned to play the piano and the saxophone as a child. His permanent band lasted from 1939 to 1941. His programs always started with 'Cherokee', which was written by Ray Noble and arranged by Billy May.

Barnet certainly had a yen for life, enjoying women, drinking, and having fun, completely unlike Glenn Miller, who enforced a strict code in dress and behaviour. Barnet had a remarkable talent for assembling a band very quickly—he'd use three or four men from a previous band, find some new players, rehearse for two or three days, and that would complete another hard-drinking, hard-driving swinging band. Barnet saw no colour, and his band was a mix. If a venue turned him down because of this, he would seek another, and the show would continue.

His piece 'Skyliner' has remained through the years one of my top favourites. I seemed to have missed it in my youth, and the first time I heard it play was at the fairground in Coney Beach Porthcawl in South Wales, a seaside resort on the South Wales coast. It hit me with a bang, and it has followed me around on my life's travel ever since. I still play it on the piano, and some years ago, I was at the Bath and West Show in Somerset when I heard a band playing. I walked towards the bandstand and said, 'Can you guys play "Skyliner"?'

They went off in a roar, and my senses began soaring as I found the years unreeling. It seemed that Barnet saw the name Skyliner on the side of an aircraft, and that was it. Billy May produced the arrangement at the time when music meant music. I just loved the alto sax playing in the background. It was a new American sound even to them and a revelation to me. It has remained my favourite piece of swing music.

Away from the bandstand, there were always the ladies like Dorothy Lamour. Barnet of course was tall and very handsome, and women flocked to his concerts. His behaviour displayed the amorality of the jazz world. Although Barnet's source of inspiration was Duke Ellington's music, he was no crass imitator. He married thirteen times; some accounts say fifteen. Many of these weddings took place in Mexico, which Barnet thought of as illegal anyway. He was heir to a fortune but nevertheless had a natural empathy towards people. However, he was in the big-band business simply because he loved it. I say amen to that!

'I'll Get By (As Long As I Have You)' was a song first published in 1928. Fred E Ahlert wrote the music, with lyrics by Roy Turk. It featured in a film in 1943 called *A Guy Named Joe*. The version I remember was that of the Ink Spots, which reached the top ten in the hit parade. A 1944 poll found that the song was the third most sold sheet music among American soldiers in the United States and Europe. Connie Francis recorded it in 1950, and Shirley Bassey in 1961.

The song 'I'll Be Seeing You' was first published in 1938, but it reappeared in 1944 in a film of the same name. The music was composed by Sammy Fain, with the lyrics written by Irving Kahal. The theme of this song had a great emotional feeling and was much loved during the Second World War.

> The song climaxed with:
> And when the night is new
> I'll be looking at the moon
> But I'll be seeing you

The song really hit the heights when Bing Crosby recorded it that year. It was also recorded by Vera Lynn in 1962 on her *Hits of the Blitz* and Tony Bennett in 1992. It also featured in *Midsomer Murders* in 'Dance with the Dead' in 2006, set near an old Second World War airfield. This was sung by Anne Shelton. Many others have also recorded it.

Following the musicians strike in the United States (1942–1944), Harry James recorded this song, and it immediately became the number one hit in the country. Four men were listed as co-writers, namely, Duke Ellington, Don George (lyrics), Harry James, and

Johnny Hodges (Ellington's famous saxophonist). There are many versions of how the song received its title. One story suggests that it was the Duke's inspiration, following his joining of the Free Mason, but who really knows? The Duke often asked his audience to sing along with his music; consequently, its words remain one of the best remembered. It became a jazz standard when recorded by Ella Fitzgerald and the Ink Spots and reached number five in the American Hit Parade.

'Long Ago (and Far Away)' was composed by the master Jerome Kern and featured in the 1944 film *Cover Girl*, with stars Rita Hayworth and Gene Kelly. The lyrics for Kern's music were written by Ira Gershwin (brother of George). Many singers and orchestras have recorded this beautiful music, including Bing Crosby in 1944, Perry Como the same year, Doris Day, Pat Boone in 1964, Margaret Whiting in 1960, Rosemary Clooney in 1979, Mantovani and his orchestra, Tommy Dorsey and his orchestra, and Errol Garner, among others.

The song 'I Should Care' appeared in the film *Thrill of a Romance*. The music was written by Axel Stordahl and Paul Weston. The lyrics were provided by Sammy Cahn. I first heard it sung by Shirley Bassey, but it was also recorded by Bing Crosby, Frank Sinatra, Nat King Cole, Mel Torme, and many others. It has become a very popular standard.

'There Goes That Song Again' was written by Jule Styne, with lyrics by Sammy Cahn. It first appeared in the film *Carolina Blues* in 1944. Many vocalists and orchestras have recorded it, including Russ Morgan and his orchestra, Sammy Kay and his orchestra, Harry James and his orchestra, Bing Crosby, Frank Sinatra, Charlie Kunz, and others.

'San Fernando Valley'—I remember this piece from the war years. The last line struck in my memory, 'Make the San Fernando Valley my home.' I suppose as a small boy I would have liked that. Sadly, however, I never knew where the San Fernando Valley geographically existed. But the American troops knew exactly where it was, and many, having heard the song, dreamed of building their homes out West. Gordon Jenkins wrote the song but didn't much like it. However, when it became a success and the money rolled in, he liked it much more. There is little doubt that Crosby's dignified baritone voice resonated with the troops and sent the song on its way.

'Twilight Time' was a popular piece of music of 1944, with the music composed by the trio called the Three Nuns, namely Monty Nevins, Al Nevins, and Artie Dunn, with lyrics provided by Buck Ram (sounds like a drink). The most popular rendition was recorded in November 1944 by Les Brown and his orchestra. It became one of his most popular pieces, with soprano sax leading the reeds, the brass adding rich sounds, and a trumpet playing easily over the rhythm. This version was released in 1945 as the B-Side to 'Sentimental Journey'. Later, a very good version of the song was recorded by the Platters, which became a bestseller and number three in the United Kingdom. Bert Kaempfert and his orchestra recorded it in 1960, and Willy Nelson in 1988, among others.

'Moonlight in Vermont', as the name suggests, is about the American state of Vermont. Karl Suessdorf wrote the music, and the lyrics were written by John Blackburn. The lyrics are unusual, as they don't rhyme. The song was first introduced by Margaret Whiting in 1944, and today the song is considered the state song of Vermont and is invariably played as the first dance at Vermont wedding receptions. Many other vocalists have recorded this song, including Billie Holiday, Willie Nelson, Ella Fitzgerald, Nat King Cole, and Johnny Mathis, to name a few.

When 'Sentimental Journey' was first written by Ben Homer, the song was no more than eight bars of music and fairly humdrum and repetitive at that. Nobody came up with the lyrics until Bud Green saw its possibilities, and the phrase 'gonna take a sentimental journey' suddenly jumped out at him. Many servicemen were about to return home, and the song's title implied sentiment and romance. When Doris Day first heard it, she loved it and recorded it with the Les Brown Orchestra in 1944. With her casual-sounding and friendly voice and the saxophones playing the melody, the song became an overnight success and jumped to the top of the hit parade for sixteen weeks. The song was written in 1944, but because of the 1942 to 1944 musicians' strike, it became Doris Day's first hit in 1945, coinciding with the end of the war in Europe. The song became a favourite and was recorded by both Johnny Ray and Peggy Lee in

1958 and Bob Dylan in 2017. It also appeared in the film *My Dog Skip* in 2000, which featured the Harry James Orchestra. The music had also featured earlier (1978) in an episode of *Mash'* called 'Your Hit Parade!''Ac-Cent-Tchu-Ate the-Positive' was a song composed by Harold Arlen, with lyrics supplied by Johnny Mercer, and it appeared in the film *Here Comes the Waves*. Apparently, it stemmed from a church sermon that Mercer had previously attended. When Mercer heard the words, 'You got to accentuate the positive and eliminate the negative,' he was on his way and needed no more encouragement. The song was nominated for an Academy Award for Best Original Song. On 25 March 2015, Mercer's version would be inducted into the Library of Congress National Registry for the song's cultural, artistic, and historical significance to American society and legacy. Bing Crosby and the Andrew Sisters recorded it on 21 December 1944.

Ella Fitzgerald recorded it in an album dated July 1960, and Barry Manilow also recorded it for his studio album *Night Songs* in 2014. In the UK sitcom of World War II *Goodnight Sweetheart*, the last episode was titled 'Accentuate the Positive' in a reference to the song.

I have always remembered 'Swinging on a Star.' This was again written by the magnificent pair Jimmy Van Heusen (the music) and Johnny Burke (the lyrics). It was sung in the film *Going My Way'* by *Bing Crosby* (who else) and won the Academy Award for Best Original Song in 1944. It was recorded by Bing with the John Scott Trotter Orchestra in Los Angeles on 12 February 1944.

Johnny Mercer wrote the words and music for his song 'Dream'. He conceived the music for the Chesterfield cigarette radio show, hence the words in the song 'watch the smoke rings rise in the air'. Paul Weston, whose orchestra performed in the show, recalled Mercer's hesitancy about his music. However, when the Pied Pipers recorded it in 1944, everybody wanted to record it. It became a tremendous hit and sold over a million sheet copies.

Johnny Mercer was born in Georgia, and when I first heard him singing, I thought he was a black singer. In 1944, *Johnny Mercer's Music Shop*, his daily radio show, was taken off the air simply for that reason—Mercer sounded too 'black'! So clearly, I was not alone in thinking that!

My favourite recording of the song 'Dream' was in 1964 with Ella Fitzgerald backed by the Nelson Riddle Orchestra.

'Every Time We Say Goodbye', a song by Cole Porter straight out of the Great American Songbook, was introduced by Nan Wynn in 1944 in Billy Rose's musical revue. The lyrics from 'Major to Minor', are accompanied by Porter's adroit changing of the music from an A major chord to a minor one, matching the words to the music Ella Fitzgerald recorded in her album *Ella Fitzgerald Sings the Cole Porter Song Book* in 1956.

The year 1944 started quietly enough, with no more howling of the air raid sirens, which frightened more people than ever the Germans did. The Luftwaffe clearly had other battles in mind on that vast continent of Russia. In the early years of the war, I had been a pupil in the local junior school when the sirens sounded. We stood calmly by our desks and then marched out of the school, before running home as fast as we could. I remembered one particular day when I had almost reached home but was caught in a shower of cartridge shells falling from a dogfight above my head. I automatically stopped to watch a Spitfire chasing a Messerschmitt 109 across the valley tops, completely oblivious to any danger. My mother's shouts woke me from my daydreaming, and I made it to the house safely. This was my sole encounter with the Luftwaffe by day. My next encounter would be at night, and this time I had no recollection of the siren sounding.

I was asleep in the back bedroom of the house when I felt my body raise itself from my bed and fly across the room, coming to rest unhurt on the carpet below the rear window. The house rule then was always to leave the windows open, even in winter because of the danger of bomb blasts. A large bomb, probably a 500 kilo one, had landed near Glyncornel House on the adjacent mountain, a mere four hundred yards from the house where I lay sleeping.

It was my mother's scream that both awoke me and alarmed me at the same time. At my father's side of the bed stood a small table with a thick glass top screwed down securely at each of its four corners. Having heard the bomb exploding, he had reached out to find his glasses, not being aware that the glass top of the table had been completely fractured. When he put his glasses on he also managed to smear his face with blood from his cut fingers. My mother had raced to close the blinds so as to be able to turn on the lights; when she saw my father's face, she had screamed, causing me to wake and take notice.

On the night of 29 March 1941, a squadron of German bombers had taken off from their Normandy bases to bomb Cardiff. They had erred both in time and track and, by mistake, dropped their bombs on the small mining village of Cwm Parc in the Rhondda, a mere four miles away as the crow files. I remember standing in the garden that night with my father, feeling the ground shake as the bombs and landmines hit their target.

Note: A full story of this raid can be found in my book *Only Angels Have Wings?*

It was on 8 December 1943 that the news suddenly arrived that the American Army would be arriving in our little valley. The news was broken to the population by the Rhondda Urban District Council and its members. This exciting news spread like wildfire, and the people were determined to give them a great welcome. The valley folk were well known as a friendly and hospitable people, and they knew full well that these soldiers would face an uncertain future. Under wartime regulations, billeting troops in private homes was compulsory. And earlier in the war, the Rhondda had been home to over 1,500 children, mostly from the London area during the Blitz.

Now, however, there was a lull. The weeks passed, and still no American soldiers in sight. Nothing seemed to be happening despite the many preparations already made.

I have no memory of that moment when it did arrive. But Bryan Morse described the moment well in his book *A Moment in History: The Story of the American Army in the Rhondda in 1944*. This is what he said: 'Next morning I heard the news the Americans are up in DeWinton Field.'

'The same American troops had set up home in Glyncornel Woods behind my home, and all their trucks and jeeps were parked on DeWinton Field. We ran on to the fields, and my friend shouted up to one of the trucks, 'Got any gum, chum?' and raced on.

A voice shouted, 'Hey, kid, hang on', and the door of the truck swung open.

Invited to climb up, I mounted the metal steps and looked into a huge cab. A khaki-clad figure with his back to me was rummaging behind the canvas seats. He turned, holding a handful of sweets, and, with a broad smile, handed them to me. I was amazed. He was a black soldier and the first black man I had ever seen. He escorted me off the field, and I ran home, clutching my sweets.'

The black American truck drivers belonged to the 89th Quarter Master Mobile Battalion of the Transportation Corps. My own attempt to approach an American soldier for gum was strikingly unsuccessful. I was walking alone along Salem Terrace when an American soldier, also walking along, approached me. *This is my chance*, I thought. It was to be my first attempt at a conversation with an American. As he came closer, I looked at him, recognising him as an officer. 'Any gum, chum?' I asked in the most polite voice I could muster.

He walked past without even a glance. He couldn't have been less interested if he had passed some dog excrement on the pavement. It was to be my first and last attempt at conversation with any American soldier.

By early January 1944, small groups of American officers began arriving. And by 30 April, there were 3,300 GIs in the Rhondda. The valley had become the new home of the 186 Port Company of the 487th Port Battalion, and three port companies became resident in the Rhondda Fawr.

American officers tended to be billeted in the homes of professional people, such as lawyers, teachers, and doctors, where the homes would be suitably equipped with bathrooms and telephones. These dwellings were far removed from the more humble homes of working-class miners. My pal Molly had three soldiers lodging in his home, and whilst they were eating downstairs, he would often enter their bedrooms and take a rifle and line it up through the windows at certain passers-by. The rifle, of course, was unloaded. Molly, years later, joined the RAF and became an established marksman.

Nissan huts now became a common sight and often served as canteens. I remember the one that adjoined Zion Chapel on Llwynypia

Road. A new word entered our language, namely 'chow time'—whi
for the American soldiers, meant eating time.

The 487 Port Battalion arrived, commanded by Lt Colonel
Montgomery C. Jackson. And thanks to the advanced planning of
the civil military authorities, mostly everything ran smoothly. The
Thistle Hotel in Tonypandy became home to the headquarters of the
Battalion.

The total compliment was 33 officers and 1,406 enlisted men.
Port Battalion's crew eventually became stevedores, trained to load and
unload ships efficiently. Soon these men were sent to Slapton Sands in
Devon and Mumbles near Swansea to train in amphibian operations
while attached to the 5th and 6th Engineer Brigades. Almost a quarter
of US troops who were to be landed on Normandy beaches on 6 June
6 were to be combat engineers. By this time, much of Britain had
become an armed camp—indeed almost like an aircraft carrier, from
which a decisive jump for the conquests of the continent of Europe
would soon be made.

The Germans were fully aware that an invasion of the continent
was imminent. What they didn't know was when and where it would
occur. They had agreed, however, that the Allies would land at high
water, and the beaches were littered with steel obstacles and thousands
of mines. The Allies plan, however, was to land at low waters when the
many obstacles would be completely visible. Consequently, the combat
engineers would land first to blow up obstacles and detonate the mines
in order to clear safe passages and channels for the incoming infantry
landing craft to land safely. At least that was the plan. But like all
plans, they tended to go adrift in the 'fog of war'.

I first visited the Normandy beaches in October 1965 and
toured the museums (former German strong points), cemeteries,
and any other places of interest starting at Utah Beach in the West
to Arromanches and Pegasus in the East. I subsequently revisited the
area on at least three further occasions and availed myself of every
piece of printed matter I could find. I remember having a meal in the
small town of Barfleur and being told by the patron of the restaurant
that the Dorset Fox (General Field Marshall Erwin Rommel) had once
eaten here. Today, Barfleur is better known for being the departure
point for the Norman Invasion of England and the famous battle of

Hastings that followed. There is a large medallion fixed to a harbour rock that commemorates that departure.

I had always had the desire to see the invasion beaches from the air. Such a moment arrived in the late 1970s. I was to carry out some training with two of my new pilots. In these days, the favourite training airports for independent British carriers were Ostend or Cherbourg. Without hesitation, I chose Cherbourg Maupertus, simply because it was only a few minutes flying time from the invasion beaches.

Training completed, I flew along the beaches low and slow (below 100 feet), passing first Utah Beach and then Ponte Du Hoc, with its prominent headland and 100-foot cliff face. It was here that the American Rangers stormed ashore, using rope ladders and grappling irons as if it were medieval days of conflict to climb the cliff, wonderfully illustrated in the film *The Longest Days*.

Then came Omaha Beach, forever to be named 'Bloody Omaha' and the American cemetery at Colleville-Sur-Mer on the cliffs overlooking it. Here the white crosses of the graves—almost 9,400 of them—stood out.

Then I went across Gold, Juno, and Sword Beaches towards Ouistreham, the landing beaches of the British Canadian and Free French Troops. I marvelled once more at the bravery of those young soldiers who landed there that day. Many were still seasick after a rough crossing and having to face a resolute foe particularly on Omaha. It was here that the Americans bombed from above cloud, delayed dropping their own bombs for fear of hitting and killing their own troops. As a result, the German defences were left largely untouched.

Finally, with my little tour completed, I turned the aircraft on to a north-westerly heading and climbed into a darkening sky and back to Cornwall and home.

There is a time capsule buried in the American cemetery at Colleville-sur-Mer under a pink granite slab engraved with the words 'to be opened on June 6, 2044'. The sealed capsule contains news reports of the 6 June 1944 landings, placed there by newsmen who were there on that day.

The Battle of Hürtgen Forest, 1944

The success of the D-Day landings, the breakout from Normandy, and the winning of the so-called Battle of the Bulge have been exhaustively discussed and written about. Why not, indeed, as they were all Allied victories, and it is the victors who tend to do most of the writing? The Battle of Hürtgen Forest has been largely ignored and most certainly by American historians. Indeed, it has been carefully airbrushed out of American military history. Yet it was the longest and the most- costly battle the Americans ever fought in the Second World War. In his autobiography *Crusade in Europe*, Eisenhower gave the battle a measly single paragraph and General Omar Bradley, in his book *A Soldier's Story* gave the battle a single line. The Battle of Hürtgen became known as the American Passchendaele of World War II, where the leading generals planning it never deemed it necessary to visit the area over which the battle was to be fought. In the British Passchendaele of World War I, the British general in charge of the operation also never went close to examine the battlefield. Lloyd George, the British prime minister during that time, remarked that General Haig 'was brilliant to the top of his boots'. Lloyd George was fully aware of Haig's shortcomings but, in effect, was quite powerless to stop the slaughter. However, he did manage to slow up the transfer of troops going to France and the slaughterhouse that had become Passchendaele.

My favourite American general remains General James Gavin, or 'Slim Jim' as he was often referred to. During the war, Slim Jim parachuted four times into Sicily, Italy; Normandy; and, finally, Holland, where leading his 82ⁿᵈ Airborne division in the failed Battle of Arnhem, although his division succeeded in capturing its objective. Many years ago, while training on a pilot's course at St Antonio in Texas, I came across Gavin's book *On to Berlin!* I was so suitably impressed by his courage and intelligence that, when my son was born, I named him Gavin also. Gavin's words and views on the Hürtgen Battle were quite succinct. 'It was the most- costly most unproductive and most ill-advised battle that our army ever fought.'

So where was this Hürtgen Forest, and why did the Americans consider it so important? Well, the forest itself bordered Germany and Belgium and stretched over fifty square miles. It lies within an area outlined by the towns of Aachen, Monschau, and Duren, with the River Roer running alongside its eastern edge. The whole area is known as the Hurtgenwald. As far back as 1938, the Germans had fortified the forest as a part of the much-vaunted Siegfried Line. However, the Americans were not alone in thinking and believing that, after their victory in Normandy and their free run across France, the war was effectively won. The top American generals and the British chiefs of staff adhered to this optimism and now considered that the end was in sight. How wrong they all were!

The 1st American Army was the largest American army in Europe, and its commander was Lt. General Courtney H. Hodges, a general who had risen from the ranks. He had fought in the First World War and had won two purple hearts after being gassed. He termed these awards as excessively 'sissy', which said something about his character. At times, he appeared confused in his thinking, and his ability to create any logical plan of battle was by no means a certainty. His favourite motto was to 'keep smashing ahead', believing it to be 'safer and sounder'—an opinion much like that of Haig in the First World War. He also, like Haig, never visited the front line. After the war, the official American army historian described his campaign as lacking in imagination.

The most obvious method to make the Hürtgen Forest a danger was to send American infantry to attack into its depth so denying them of their main strength—air advantage and the mobility of its tank force by way of its superiority in aviation. The forest had been strengthened by interlocking log bunkers, concrete bunkers, and machine-gun posts. Barbed wire was organised into kill zones, in addition to the planting of thousands of mines of varying types. Deep in the forest in that winter of 1944 was a complete lack of forward visibility, particularly in the snow, rain, and sleet showers that prevailed. Darkness came early in those winter months, and German snipers were plentiful and well concealed.

There is evidence that the Germans had some doubt as to whether the Americans would be foolhardy enough to attack through the forest. However, they underestimated the stupidity and obstinacy of the American generals. Eisenhower called it in his book 'American doggedness'. It should have been clear, as I have already stated, that the Hurtgen would neutralise all American advantages—in other words, their superior armour, their air superiority, and their greater mobility. Hodges, however, was convinced that he needed to clear the forest, in order to drive his army to the River Roer and its dams. By capturing the small town of Schmitt, it would be possible to view all the approaches. No consideration was ever given to bypassing or screening the forest, and thus being able to outflank Schmitt from the south. Instead, they conceived a plan that made little operational or tactical sense. Furthermore, they completely underestimated the strength and the psyche of the German soldiers and their determination to defend their homeland.

A new German commanding officer had arrived by the name of Feldmarschall Model, whose name has already been mentioned in this book. Earlier in the war, he had been an aggressive panzer commander and had thwarted the Russians time and time again at Rzhev Orel and in Estonia when they had been totally confident of overwhelming him and his troops. He was known as the German's best defensive tactical commander and as Hitler's fireman. Here at the Hürtgen, he gave the American Army a bloody nose and their greatest defeat of the Second World War. He skilfully used his limited infantry artillery and engineers to decimate the American divisions, which had been committed to the battle piecemeal. In the three to four months of Hodges's offensive, Model's dogged defence of the German West Wall inflicted up to 57,000 casualties on the 1st and 9th American Armies. Model's defensive battles, both at Arnhem where he had defeated the British, and the Hürtgen, where he defeated the Americans, did much to restore the moral of his front-line troops.

It was on a cold misty morning on 2 November 1944 that the main American attack began. In the opening American attack, a total of 11,000 artillery shells were fired, but the appalling weather prevented any air support. Across a 170-mile front, the 20th division was the only American force attacking. Their General 'Dutch' Cota had objected to the plan, but his objections had been waved aside. He himself considered that the impending attack had but a gambler's chance of success.

By mid-November, the 28th Division was relieved, having lost up to 70 per cent of its strength, and General Cota had descended from a man known for his valour on Omaha Beach and St Lo to a defeated soldier tottering on the brink of dismissal. In less than six months, six American divisions were fed into the slaughterhouse of Hürtgen, along with other armoured units. In all, 120,000 fought there and suffered, in total, around 50,000 casualties in a battle that should never have been fought in the first place.

It proved to be the most inept battle of the war in Europe. It started on 19 September 1944 and ended on 10 February 1945, when the German offensive in the Ardennes ended the Hürtgen Battle. It proved to be a German defensive victory, and while the American generals had their eyes completely focused on the Hürtgen, they were soon faced to flee westward when the German Ardennes offensive began on 16 December, catching them completely off guard and creating a salient of almost sixty miles in their lines in what became known as the Battle of the Bulge. General Eisenhower, a political general at best, now had to forsake his golf and take control of the situation. But that, as they say, is another story.

General Model had the greatest ability to relate to his front-line soldiers, and in contrast to the Red Army generals, his American opponents Bradley and Hodges were rank amateurs, with little or no battlefield experience. Bradley's only war experience was spent as a corps commander in 1943. Hodges, like Bradley, was thrust into high-level command without adequate time spent at lower levels. Consequently, both failed to develop the kind of experience and instincts that Model had learned in two world wars. It is very clear that Model would never have sent his troops into the Hürtgen or similar without personally examining the terrain over which they would have to fight. He would have also ensured that he knew every battalion commander in his command. In other words, he was a firm believer in front-line leadership, an attitude shared by the likes of men like Guderian and Rommel. Model was the youngest field marshal in the German Army and cared about his men, never treating them as 'cannon fodder'! His troops were inspired by his presence and created the slogan, 'Where Model is present, nothing can go wrong.' Model's ability, demonstrated many times, was to overcome hopeless situations both on the Eastern and Western fronts, which sets him high in the ranks of the great commanders in World War II.

On 2 April 1945, with his army surrounded, Model dissolved his army group and sent them home. In a forest clearing between Dusseldorf and Duisburg he later shot himself. He had said that a German field marshal never surrendered. On 21 April 1945 he was eventually reburied in the Soldaten Fried Hof Vossenack, Vossenack, Durenerlandkress, Nordrhein-Westfalen Germany. His plot is grave 1074.

The church was newly consecrated after the Second World War. On the church portal, an inscription tells of the 68,000 dead in the Hürtgen Forest. It is perhaps interesting that Walter Model is buried there.

Courtney Hodges was born in Perry, Georgia. He enlisted in the United States Army in 1906 as a private soldier in the infantry. He served under Bradley as the deputy commander of the US First Army and by August 1944 succeeded Bradley as the commander of the unit when Bradley was moved to take over the 12th Army Group. The battle of the Hürtgen Forest was a part of the main American effort to breach the West Wall (Siegfried Line). The overall cost of this offensive against the Siegfried Line cost the lives of close to 140,000 soldiers.

Eisenhower referred to Hodges as 'fearless' and 'the scintillating star' of the American advance into Germany. I think it is rather doubtful that his men saw it that way. However, Hodges was promoted to the rank of a four-star general on 15 April 15 1945, and he became only the second soldier in American army history to achieve the climb from private to four-star general.

Hodges died in San Antonio, Texas, on 16 January 1960, age seventy-nine. He is buried at Arlington National Cemetery, Section 2, Grave 890-A.

The Baby or Little Blitz, 1944

The V-1s and the V-2s—*Vergeltungswaffe*— were the German revenge or vengeance weapons. The first of these was used against London and the South East of England on 20 June 1944. Both types of weapons were built and developed at Peenemunde on the Baltic by the Luftwaffe under General Walter Dornberger. The V-1s were launched from the Pas-De-Calais area of France and Holland. The attack began just one week after the D-Day landings in Normandy had taken place. More than one hundred were launched per day against London, and such attacks would continue against the city until March 1945. To Londoners, they became known as Blitz bombs or 'doodlebugs', and these attacks became known as 'Baby Blitz' or 'Little Blitz'.

The speed at which these missiles flew varied. The slowest flew at around 300 miles per hour, and the fastest, 440 miles per hour at heights that varied from 2,000 feet to 3,000 feet. They flew straight and level and were driven by a pulsejet engine pulsing at fifty times per second. The engine used 75-octane fuel. To some people under their flight path, they sounded just like a two-stroke motorbike engine. It was when the engine stopped that you needed to run for cover. The worst incident occurred on the 25 July, when one flying bomb fell on the main shopping centre at Lewisham in London. It penetrated an airfield shelter, causing fifty-one deaths, with more injured.

The missiles crossed Kent, which became known as Doodlebug Alley, and it was that area that contained the largest number of anti-aircraft guns. The V-1s were pilotless aircraft that had a guidance system consisting of a simple autopilot, which regulated its speed and altitude. It also had a rudder that controlled its steering. It possessed no ailerons and, consequently, it was vulnerable to any interference in the rolling plane.

There were four established methods of destroying them, hopefully short of their intended target. The first method was to shoot it down by conventional anti-aircraft fire. The second method was to shoot it down by fighter aircraft. This operation, however, had to be finely judged, else much damage could be caused to the fighters if it exploded the flying bomb at too close a distance. The third method was a more delicate operation, in which the fighter pilot had to fly with his wing slightly under the wing of the flying bomb and then tilt it upwards. As one can imagine, this was an extremely hazardous operation, as the V-1s were skinned in rolled steel, whereas the fighter's wing was made of weaker light alloy. A fourth and far neater method was, therefore, planned.

This method was simply to make use of simple aerodynamics without the necessity of making physical contact with the flying bomb at all. The fighter pilot would fly his aircraft with, for example, his port (left) wing slightly above the starboard (right) wing of the flying bomb. In effect, this would destroy the lift over the bomb until its wing (losing lift) began to drop. As the angle of the bank increased, the rather crude stabilisation system could no longer cope, and the flying bomb would commence a spiral dive and explode well short of its intended target, which was London and its suburbs. At the same time, the fighter would, of necessity, also roll his aircraft to the right and then watch the flying bomb, hopefully, explode in open country.

The V-1s caused over 6,000 deaths in London. But soon the capital would be faced with a new type of attack—against which there was no defence.

The V-2s were rockets and were the first to cross the boundary of space on 20 June 1944. Three thousand were launched against London and, later, against Antwerp and Liege. But strangely, none were launched at any Russian city. The missile was propelled using 74 per cent ethanol/water mixture plus liquid oxygen. The rocket could climb to a height between 50 to 100 miles at a specifically set angle until the engine shut down at the top of its parabolic curve. Then the rocket would continue on a ballistic free fall trajectory at a speed approximately two and a half times the speed of sound.

General Walter Dornberger, who was in charge of this German rocket programme, announced to his colleagues that a new era of transportation had arrival—namely space travel—when one of his V-2s reached an altitude of 52.5 miles above the earth's surface. In fact, after further testing, a height of 108.5 miles was attained.

The V-2 was the world's first long-range ballistic missile. It carried a warhead of 910 kilos or (2,010 pounds) of explosive. The missile could be launched from practically anywhere, including off roads running through forests, which became their favourite launch sites. Like the V-1s, the V-2s were designed at Peenemunde on the Baltic Coast, and more than 6,800 V-2s were built. In London alone, they killed 2,754 civilians and injured a further 6,523.

At first, the British attempted to conceal the explosions and deaths caused by the V-2s and ineptly blamed defective gas mains. The public were not fooled, however, and renamed the explosions flying gas pipes. It was eventually on 11 November 1944 that the government finally announced the truth of the V-2s.

However, the government had been aware that the missiles construction site was at Peenemunde and, on 17/18 August 1943, ordered Bomber Command to launch an attack against the research establishment and other installations there. The raid involved almost six hundred bombers, and they attacked in moonlight conditions in order to increase the chances of success. The pathfinder aircraft leading the raid found the target without much difficulty, and the raid proved a great success, having destroyed the V-2 assembly hall and the workers' housing blocks. Almost 1,800 tons of bombs were dropped, and it was estimated that the raid set back the V-2 programme by at least two months. Following the attack, the Germans moved the whole installation underground and safe from any further air attacks. The raid cost Bomber Command, the loss of forty aircraft, which represented 6.7 per cent of the attacking force dispatched. At that moment in time and considering the importance of the target, it was considered an acceptable cost.

The most- costly V-2 strike on London occurred on 25 November 1944, when a Woolworth store in New Cross was hit, killing 160 people and injuring a further 100.

A scientific reconstruction on the devastation of a V-2 was carried out in 2010. This experiment discovered that a V-2 explosion created a crater twenty metres wide and eight metres deep. The explosion would eject some 3,000 tons of debris into the air.

The final V-2 attacks took place against London on 27 March 1945.

No V-1s or V-2s were launched against Wales or the North of England, largely due to the weapons restricted range. The V-2s were launched by the Germans in retaliation for RAF Bomber Command's relentless attacks on German cities. I find it rather strange that Hitler did not use the weapons against the advancing Russians or even Moscow or the Allies invasion ports. It is a frightening thought to end on, but had Hitler put more resources into the V-2s programme, those weapons would have been used a few years earlier. Perhaps it is a thought and a conclusion best not contemplated.

As mentioned earlier, the leader of Germany's V-1 and V-2 rocket programme was Major General Doctor Walter Dornberger based at Peenemunde. At the end of the war, he was captured by the Americans and detained for two years at the prisoner of war camp at Island Farm, Bridgend, in South Wales. Along with other scientists, he was taken to the United States, where he eventually rose to be the vice president of the Bell Corporation. He played a leading role in the creation of the supersonic BellX-15 aircraft and, later, in the development of the space shuttle. He eventually returned to Germany and died there at Baden-Wurttemberg in 1980 at the age of eighty-four years.

Werner von Braun worked with General Dornberger and was also captured by the Americans. He was one of the leading scientists credited with inventing the V-2 rocket. He was taken to America, along with 1,600 other scientists as part of operation Paperclip. He worked and developed America's first space shuttle explorer and later the Apollo manned flights and moon landing. He never returned to Germany and died in Alexandria, Virginia, in 1977 at the age of sixty-five years.

The Disaster of the UK State System of Education after World War II

The Education Act of 1944 and its Aftermath

The R. A. Butler Education Act of 1944 was planned through the years of the Second World War. It aimed to create a tripartite system of education in Britain, which in theory would implement education for all children free of charge, regardless of their background and that would be appropriate to their needs and abilities. It's interesting now to read how the then Ministry of Education described the tripartite system at the time as per their pamphlet London / Her Majesty's Stationery Office (HMSO) 1947. In short:

- *Secondary grammar schools.* These would 'educate' a minority of intellectual able pupils.

- *Secondary technical schools.* These would 'cater for' those who displayed a technical or vocational bias (all this at the tender age of eleven years?).
- *Secondary modern schools.* These would 'cater for' around three-quarters of the eleven- to fifteen-years range. The modern school would provide a balanced training of mind and body and correlated approach to the humanities, natural science, and the arts not with any specific job or occupation in view, but in order to make a direct appeal to interests, which it would awaken by a practical touch with affairs.

Thus, the secondary modern schools were to be the protagonists in a great adventure, part of the boldest investment that any war-crippled nation had ever made in its children, the citizens of the future.

Furthermore, these schools would be shielded from the stultifying effects of external examinations (all of this Ministry of Education words). Note the choice of words above—the grammar schools *educate* the children whilst the children in the technical and modern schools would be *catered for.*

Despite the hubris at the time resulting from being on the winning side in the war, the secondary modern school became the Cinderella of the secondary school system. These schools would be neglected and inadequately funded, despite being responsible for the education of around 80 per cent of the country's children. The grammar schools received most of the available funding!

In the post-war period, the implementation of secondary technical schools barely took place and, at their peak, only catered for 2 to 3 per cent of available children. This was largely due to lack of money in the system after the war and also to the fact that there were insufficiently and inadequately trained teachers available to fill the would-be job vacancies. In 1947, there were 300 technical schools in the country, a number that dwindled to 100 by 1970. The Crowther Report of 1958 sharply concluded, 'We do not now have and never have had a tripartite system.' Perhaps this was not surprising, as Chairman Baron Crowther had studied languages and economics at Cambridge and, like most of his contemporaries, had little time or sympathy for the technical side of education. To add to the government's woes, the expected baby boom took place, rising to a peak in 1946. These children reached the secondary schools in the 1950s. To increase teacher numbers, an emergency scheme was devised, largely aimed at ex-service personnel, with training to be concentrated into one year. By 1950, almost 25,000 students were in training, and by 1951 one in six of all teachers were emergency trained.

In general terms, 20 per cent of all children would attend the state grammar schools, whilst 80 per cent would attend the secondary modern—a division of the country's children based on a solitary examination at the age of eleven years (known thereafter as the eleven-plus examination.

To describe this examination as discriminatory would be an understatement. To achieve a place in the grammar schools was not random. It depended on a number of parameters, including the personal circumstances of the parents, the ability of the child, and one's geographical location, among other criteria. Eleven-plus successes in one area would allow a mere 10 per cent pass rate, whilst others were over 30 per cent.

In the early 1950s, East Sussex had the lowest number of grammar schools per head of school population in Britain, whilst Merthyr Tydfil had the highest. It was a countrywide lottery!

Further, only 4 to 6 per cent of grammar children progressed to the sixth form and only 4 per cent went to university. The findings of the Crowther Report, published in 1959, indicated that most grammar school children tended to come from the better-off homes, where parents were able to provide additional help for their children. Indeed, there was a huge clamour of such families to get their children into grammar school. However, most children left these schools before or following their school certificate examination at the age of fifteen or sixteen years. Almost 80 per cent of the grammar school intake was thrown onto the job market with a mere scratch of a liberal education, virtually valueless as realistic equipment to begin a career—perhaps only suitable to show prospective employers who were taking on low-paid clerks. Secondary modern children left school at the age of fifteen years without even an examination certificate to their credit and no organised further training in sight. Here was an education system largely turning out untrained serfs.

The much-heralded tripartite system, planned by the Conservative-led wartime coalition government and put into action by the Labour government post 1945, proved to be a failure for the reasons listed above. It quickly turned into a bipartite system with technical schools almost disappearing into oblivion.

The eleven-plus examination and its consequences caused great damage to the self-esteem of many children and divided whole communities and even families. Certainly, there was no parity of esteem between the grammar and secondary modern school. They even played different games—rugby at the grammar school (like the private schools) and soccer at the secondary modern. Such a ridiculous separation fostered the notion that secondary modern (meaning the working-class children) were of lower intelligence than their grammar school counterparts. Prevalent at the time was a saying, 'Rugby is a rough game played by gentlemen, whilst soccer is a gentlemen's game played by roughs.' Only a few secondary modern schools in the country at that time played both games.

The interview was often a part of the eleven-plus examination. In it, the candidate was often asked, 'What job does your father do?' This question appeared to many as a vehicle for working class children to be shunted off to a secondary modern school, while those deemed middle class were sent to grammar.

As an aside, I was amused when I read the story of a Canadian airman in World War II who faced the air marshal during a commission interview. The air marshal asked him, 'What does your father do?'

The airman replied, 'My father doesn't want a f – – – ing commission. I do!'

I hope that the airman in question was commissioned—he deserved to be!

The eleven-plus examination was clearly more about social policy than education. Every school financed by the state should be socially integrated, not divided. Grammar schools were and the few that remain are socially divisive.

However, change was afoot, as many parents increasingly revolted against the eleven-plus examination. There was now particular concern about the reliability of such an examination as a method for categorising children at eleven. There was also a growing consciousness regarding the enormous wastage of talent among working-class children in the school system. The fundamental question had to be answered: Can we have a cohesive society where that society's children are separated at so early an age? The answer was clearly *no*! Therefore, we should plan our education system accordingly—to recognise the wide range of talent, aptitude, and intelligence in our school society. In politics, the change was rapid when virtually all state secondary schools in England and Wales eventually moved to a comprehensive system. The bipartite system lasted till 1965 and was finally abolished completely by 1976. Note that, as of this writing, a few grammar schools still exist in England, mostly in the county of Kent. However, on the positive side, the grammar schools did have a profound effect on social mobility. As a consequence, many children were lifted from their working-class backgrounds and found influential positions in society. In some measure, this challenged the public school hierarchy.

Vocational Training

Education in England and Wales even after World War II showed a complete lack of appreciation of vocational training. A look at the pre-war records (1937/38) would have shown that only one in five children received any further education. The remainder were simply pushed off the plank into the job market. It is clear now why that was the case.

Since the eighteenth century, the public schools and Oxbridge had taught the governing elite to despise trade as something beneath the activity of a gentleman. They deemed it necessary to raise their children with a liberal education as suitable for the future rulers of the British Empire. The emphasis was, therefore, on mathematics, religious knowledge, and the classics. Consequently, any activity deemed vocational—in other words, engineering, science, and technology—was simply beneath their calling and suitable only for the lower classes of society.

This was intellectual snobbery of the worst kind, and such nonsense was to permeate the educational system for many years, with dire consequences for our state schools, which educated most of the country's children. Such was the legacy of being influenced and governed by an upper-class public school and Oxbridge-dominated governing elite. Consequently, vocational training was largely ignored over a long period, exacerbated by the demise of the secondary technical schools after World War II. Is it any wonder, therefore, that today we lack trained engineers, plumbers, and carpenters—a list to which we can also now add doctors and nurses? As a result, this country's position in the world league became the lowest on record.

The answer surely is to take politics out of education or, if you will, take education out of politics. Now that's a thought to conjure with!

Social Mobility

When it comes to social mobility, it is very difficult to be politically neutral. The Conservative Party have always paid 'lip service' to the concept of social mobility, despite enthusing about creating 'the big society' whatever that might mean. The party really aspires to a small state, tax cuts, and acquisitive wealth. Public schools, now called independent or private schools, are all citadels of immobility. Just 7 per cent of the school population attend them, but they make up half of all students at Oxbridge and 25 per cent of places in other UK universities. Today 37 per cent of conservative politicians have attended private schools, and fifty British prime ministers had attended just one private school, namely Eton.

The 1944 Educational Act was, in reality, a classic piece of 'one-nation conservatism', which embodied upper-class paternalism towards the working class. Today, the public schools in Britain are all listed as charities, which all taxpayers in Britain subscribe to. What a nonsense that is!

The dawn of meritocratic society was supposed to have started in the 1960s, when working-class children would break the barriers into politics, the arts, media, the judiciary, and so on. This simply did not happen, and the class system still dominates the United Kingdom today.

The Public Schools: An Opportunity Lost

After the end of World War II, the Labour government, led by Clement Atlee, had a once-in-a-lifetime opportunity to change this country forever by integrating the public schools (so called because the public at large could not afford to send their children there) into the state system. This, at a stroke, would have removed a central plank of the class system of this country, still very evident. At that time, roughly only 6 per cent of the country's children attended such schools. With his large majority in parliament and the hubris of the population at being on the winning side in the war, such a change would have easily won the vote of parliament and almost passed unnoticed by the general population. However, despite the fact Atlee did great things for the country, including the creation of the National Health Service, he ducked this challenge. Perhaps it was not surprising, as he was himself a public-school boy, who had attended Haileybury College.

Few Labour prime ministers since have even seriously considered tackling this issue, and the United Kingdome remains that much poorer for it!

CHAPTER 9

Victory at Last

'Let It Snow! Let It Snow! Let It Snow!' is a piece of music composed by Jule Styne, who was largely a Broadway songwriter, with lyrics by Sammy Cahn in 1945. It was first recorded by Vaughn Monroe and reached number one in the charts and has since become a standard. Sammy Cahn said it was written in a California heat wave, and he said to Styne, 'Why don't we go down to the beach and cool off?'

Styne replied, 'Why don't we stay here and write a Christmas song?'

They stayed and wrote, 'Let It Snow!'

The song reached number one in the charts when recorded by Rod Stewart in 2012. But my favourite version was recorded by Dean Martin in 1959. Crosby also recorded it in 1962. The Monroe recording plays at the end of the film *Die Hard* and its sequel *Die Hard 2*.

'There! I've Said It Again' was a piece sung by Monroe, who made this song very popular the same year. It was composed by Redd Evans and David Mann, and the Monroe version reached the number one position on the *Billboard* charts of 'records most played on air'. Jimmy Dorsey and his orchestra also recorded the song, as did Nat King Cole in 1945 and, again, Bert Kaemfert and his orchestra in 1960. But perhaps the most popular version was recorded by Bobby Vinton in 1963.

'It's Been a Long, Long Time' was another major hit for Jule Styne and Sammy Cahn. It was appropriate that the name of the song coincided with the year the war ended. It was recorded by Harry James and his orchestra, with a vocal by Kitty Kallen. The song reached number one on the *Billboard* charts. By 1945, it had become standard practice in the Unites States record industry to release competing versions of hit songs. This song became a popular standard and was recorded by Perry Como in 1956, Peggy Lee in 1959, Louise Armstrong in 1964, and Tom Jones in 1966. The song was also included on the soundtrack of *Captain America*, and the film's subtitle was *The Winter Soldier*.

'It Might as Well Be Spring' was a Rodgers and Hammerstein song that was used in the film *State Fair* in 1945. The song won the Academy Award for Best Original Song that year. Dick Haymes made the first hit recording, which lasted twelve weeks in the hit parade. Harry James recorded the song in 1952, with Rosemary Clooney supplying the vocals. Peggy Lee provided a swinging version of the music in 1967, while Shirley Bassey recorded it in 2013 in her album *Hold Me Tight*.

'Along the Navajo Trail' was a song all my pals loved, only because it was a cowboy song and Bing sang it. It was written by Dick Charles, Larry Markes, and Edgar Lange. It was the title song for the film of the same name that starred Roy Rodgers. It was listed as one of the top one hundred Western songs of all time. My favourite rendition of this song was by Bing Crosby and the Andrew Sisters. Dinah Shore and Frankie Lane also recorded the music, as did the Hot Club of Cowtown in 2011.

'If I Loved You' was another wonderful piece of music from those American maestros of song, Rogers and Hammerstein, this time from their musical *Carousel*. The song was introduced on stage by John Rait and Jan Clayton. The work was originally adapted from Feronc Molnair's play *Liliom*. It ran for 890 performances on Broadway and had a similar success in the West End of London. In 1956, a film of *Carousel* was made by Twentieth Century Fox, starring Gordon MacRae and Shirley Jones but was not as well received as the play had been. The New York Philharmonic presented a staged concert version in 2013 to huge acclaim, and it was broadcast live from the Lincoln

Centre in April 2013. Time Magazine voted Carousel the best musical of the twentieth century. It was recorded in New York by Bryn Terfel in 1996.

'The More I See You' was yet another marvel of a song by Harry Warren. It seems that, much like Richard Rodger, he had a bottomless reservoir of songs at his disposal. This song is a strong major-scale ballad with fine lyrics by Mack Gordon. The song appeared in the film *Diamond Horseshoe* and was sung by Dick Haymes. The music has been recorded many times—by Nat King Cole in 1958, Nancy Wilson in 1960, Bing Crosby in 1977, Peggy Lee in 1972, Bert Kaemfert and his orchestra in 1975, and Michael Bublé in 2005.

'Love Letters' was a song composed by Victor Young with lyrics by Edward Heyman. Young was a composer, an arranger, and a fine violinist. The song appeared without lyrics in a film of the same name. It was nominated by the Academy for the best song of 1945. It was recorded by Dick Haymes in 1945 and Elvis Presley in 1966.

'I Can't Begin to Tell You' was composed by James V. Monaco, with lyrics by Mack Gordon. It was introduced in the film *The Dolly Sisters* by John Payne, Betty Grable, and June Haver. The most popular version was recorded by Bing Crosby, with the backing of Carmen Cavallaro's orchestra. It reached the number one position in the *Best Sellers* chart. It was also recorded by Perry Como and John Morgan in 1956 and, finally, by Willie Nelson in a country version in 2000.

'I Wish I Knew' was another timeless piece of music by that genius Harry Warren. The lyrics were provided by Mack Gordon. The song was sung by Dick Haymes and Betty Grable, with the orchestra conducted by Victor Young in the film *Diamond Horseshoe* in 1945. It has been recorded by countless artists over the years.

'Rum and Coca Cola' was a huge hit for the Andrew Sisters, reaching the top of the US Pop Singles Chart. The music was composed by Rupert Grant, who went by the name Lord Invader, and Lionel Belasco. Grant was a calypso musician from Trinadad. Chubby Checker also recorded the music, but it was the Andrew Sisters' version that was by far the most popular.

Laura was an American film noir produced and directed by Otto Preminger in 1944. It has been described as the most elegant murder mystery ever made. I was a young boy in 1944, and it was my habit to catch the bus back to school after lunch. The bus stop happened to be opposite the paper shop by the name of Timms. As I was early for once, I dropped into the shop to look at the magazines. On the counter immediately in front of me was a picture on the front page of the magazine *Picture Goer*, a now defunct publication. Staring at me was a goddess, the most beautiful girl I had ever seen. I drooled all the way back to school and was somewhat late as I entered my classroom.

The teacher said, 'You're late,' followed by, 'The bell has gone.'

Still in my dreamy state, I replied that I hadn't taken it.

As a result, I was sent to the headmaster, who used me as a punch bag and whacked me up and down the corridor.

The afternoon lessons passed in a dream. The goddess was the beautiful Gene Tierney, and the film she was in was called *Laura*. In 1999, *Laura* was selected for preservation in the United Sates National Film Registry by the Library of Congress as being 'culturally, historically and aesthetically significant'.

David Raksin had been hired to score the film but was having difficulty finding the musical formula for it. Preminger suggested he use Gershwin's 'Summertime', but legal reasons prevented the use of that music. His next suggestion was 'Sophisticated Lady', a piece that had been composed by Duke Ellington.

Raksin, like most composers, hated the idea of using other people's music. The weekend was the deadline, and Raksin had been given until the Monday morning to write suitable music. At home, he found a 'Dear John' letter from his wife. Normally, he said, melodies flowed from him, but now no! He took the unopened letter and placed it on the piano and started playing. The beautiful melody now known as 'Laura' emerged. It was a work of art, and Preminger was so pleased with it that he and Raksin collaborated on four further films. Johnny Mercer was asked to provide the lyrics.

Mercer had the ability to hear what the music was saying. In this instance, he wrote the lyrics without ever seeing the film. The film had made the music popular, and Mercer's lines evoked the mood and imagery of the film, adding to its popularity. 'Laura' became a jazz standard and has been recorded more than four hundred times. Cole Porter's favourite song was 'Laura'—of those he didn't write himself of course.

The song 'Day by Day' was recorded by Frank Sinatra on 22 August 1945, with the orchestra conducted by Axel Stordahl, who wrote the music with Paul Weston. The lyrics were by Sammy Cahn.

We boys were in the local chapel one evening waiting in vain for the speaker to appear. As he didn't show, we adjourned to the chapel vestry and entertained ourselves. The church organist David Bevan, a rather serious individual and a few years older than the rest of us, was with us. Suddenly, he began to play the piano. And there in the middle of winter, I first heard the song 'Day by Day'. I was somewhat astonished later when he gave the sheet music to me as a gift. I still have the sheet music, and every time I play it, I can see all the boys once again that night in Salem. David the organist (no longer with us) went on to become a newscaster on TWW television and later became a programme producer for the Independent Television Network.

Franklin Delano Roosevelt (FDR) died on 12 April 1945 at the age of sixty-three. I first heard his name when I was a young boy staying with my grandparents in Maerdy (known forever as Little Moscow). Grandad Alfred Evans (my father's father) had arrived in the Rhondda in 1891 as a young man from his native Pembrokeshire. He became a successful shop owner, and soon he was persuaded to join the Labour Party as the party's elected representative in order to fight the Communists in the local elections that year (1938). Having won the election, he remained as a councillor, eventually becoming the council's chairman, a position he stayed in until his death in 1952. His great political hero was Franklin Delano Roosevelt, and I clearly remember his pleasure when he heard of Roosevelt's 1940 victory over Wendell Wilkie the Republican candidate.

Roosevelt's motivation was always to help Britain in any way he could, short of declaring war. In any event, only Congress could do that. At that time, however, America was a strongly isolationist nation. I clearly remember the food we received, especially the spam and powdered eggs. The first guns our LDV / Home Guard received were old rifles when Roosevelt stripped his weapon stock to help us. In 1940 and 1941, he made it possible through the Arnold Scheme (and other similar schemes) to train RAF aircrew volunteers to be pilots in Georgia, Florida, and Texas. Many people in Britain today still hold the view that America only helped us after they themselves were attacked by the Japanese at Pearl Harbour on 7 December 1941. Such an opinion can now be seen to be completely untrue.

It was on 9 December 2001 when I flew into New York. A room cancellation at the hotel in Queens allowed me to fly out to Buffalo the next morning. The terrorist attack on the Twin Towers took place on 11 September, and had it not been for that room cancellation, I would have been in Manhattan on that very morning. Three days later, having concluded my business, I made my way back to New York. The airlines were all on stand down, so I took the Amtrak train service for a more leisurely and slower journey back to New York. The route took me through the towns of Rochester, Syracuse, and Utica to Albany and then down alongside the Hudson River to New York. However, I decided to leave the train at Poughkeepsie (named after a native Indian tribe), the nearest station to the home of Franklin Delano Roosevelt. I stayed at a motel directly opposite his estate and his house named Springwood.

Having dropped off my bag at the hotel, I crossed the road, jumped the fence, and crossed the field towards the house. Roosevelt had been born at Springwood on 30 January 1882, and my excitement grew as I walked around the great man's house, museum, and library. However, I was surprised at the lack of any sort of security, particularly as it was late evening and only days after the attack on New York.

The following morning, I stood in the museum, apparently alone with just a ceremonial rope separating me from Roosevelt's specially built car with its hand controls. A picture adorned the nearby wall of Roosevelt in the same car with his black Scottish Setter dog called Falla. Now I had the overwhelming urge to step over the rope and sit in the car as the great man had done so often in past years. In that split second of doubt before action, a security guard materialised out of thin air and walked towards me. I did my best to persuade him to allow me that favour but in vain. Such things were just not permissible, so I contented myself by sitting on a bench on the south lawn, much as Eleanor and FDR had done many times in the past.

Roosevelt had won four terms (a record) as America's president. Yet strangely, he had never won Duchess County, his home patch. All this and more he had accomplished, despite having been struck down in the summer of 1921 at the age of forty with poliomyelitis.

From that moment, a man who emanated animation and vitality had to crawl around his home like a baby and be pushed around in a wheelchair. He trained himself to walk with leg braces he himself designed but could only stay upright with another person's support. He had a stubborn refusal to be pitied and he presented a bright confident face to the world. A cripple then who brought his country through the greatest depression in world history saved it from the threat of communism and then stayed on as the leader and main driving force to defeat world Fascism.

I spent three days absorbing the atmosphere of Springwood in Hyde Park, and I knew that the world I grew up in was Franklin Roosevelt's world. Manifestly, it was not the world of Adolf Hitler, whose 1,000-year Reich lasted a mere 12 years; neither was it the world of Joseph Stalin, whose communist regime imploded before our eyes. Nor was it the world of Winston Churchill, who glorified monarchy and empire, concepts now largely outdated and vanishing into history.

I stood alone on my final evening in the Rose Garden, where Franklin and his wife, Eleanor, are buried with their two dogs. I knew that my grandfather would have been well pleased and proud of my efforts. I stood in the gathering darkness and paid homage to a man of the loftiest ideals. He had faced life with great courage and good humour, surely the finest and truest test for any man. In April 1945, a future president of the United States, Lyndon B. Johnson, said of him, 'He was the only person I ever knew anywhere who was never afraid. God, how he could take it for us all.'

The news of his death sent shock waves across the world. America was awash in tears. He did not see the end of the war or the formation of the United Nations, which he had done so much to create. His death affected many people worldwide. It was said that Joseph Stalin had Roosevelt's picture printed on all the Russian national newspapers, normally reserved for national news only. Franklin Delano Roosevelt will always be remembered as a man of the people and for the many great things he accomplished while in office.

Churchill did not attend Roosevelt's funeral for reasons that have never been fully explained. When Churchill died, President Lyndon B. Johnson and his vice president were conspicuous by their absence at his funeral. Read into that what you will!

It was a little more than half an hour after Harry S. Truman had been sworn in as the new president of the United States that he was informed that Roosevelt had authorised the making of a superbomb. It was 26 April that Truman had a meeting with Harry L. Stimson (who had remained as secretary of war after Roosevelt's death) and General Leslie Groves, who was in charge of the Manhattan Project. The meeting was so secret that Groves was admitted to the White House through the back door. At that stage, Truman now found that that the United States had a bomb that, alone, could destroy a large city. Groves indicated that the first bomb would be made by July and have a strength of 500 tons of TNT, and a second bomb would be ready by August with a strength of 1,200 tons of TNT.

General Marshal was chief of staff of the United States Army and secretary of defence under Truman. He advised the president that to invade Japan would end in a 'bloodbath' for both sides and would cost at least 500,000 American lives and even more Japanese troops and civilians. Truman had set up a committee to advise him on this subject that included politicians and scientists, such as Enrico Fermi and J Robert Oppenheimer.

When he took office, Truman had had little or no foreign policy experience, but he was a capable administrator and a skilled politician who had served as a state senator for some years. Following the German unconditional surrender on 8 May, Truman pleaded with the Japanese to follow the German example but was not surprised when they refused. As a result, Truman's decision to bomb the Japanese was the only decision he said he knew how to make. He did what he thought was correct, and his decision was final.

The chosen date was 4 April. A B-29 bomber named the *Enola Gay* (named after the pilot's mother) dropped a 12-kiloton bomb of TNT on Hiroshima. The code name of the uranium-based bomb was Little Boy. When it exploded that day on Hiroshima, it instantly killed 80,000 people, indeed vaporised many of them. The death toll eventually reached 200,000 by burns and the effect of radiation. Three days later, a second bomb was dropped on Nagasaki, this time a B-29 carried the bomb code named Fat Man. The power of this deadly plutonium bomb was estimated to be as powerful as 20 kilotons of TNT. A further 70,000 Japanese died instantly when the bomb exploded, and many more died as before of burns and radiation sickness.

Archival records now show that a third bomb was under assembly at Tinian in the Marianas Islands. In fact, the United States planned to drop up to twelve atom bombs had the Japanese not surrendered.

Emperor Hirohito announced three days following the Nagasaki attack that Japan would accept the Potsdam Declaration of unconditional surrender bringing to an end the Second World War, the greatest war in the history of humankind, which had witnessed over 60 million deaths across the world.

In summary, President Truman led his country through the most difficult final stages of the war and throughout the early years of the Cold War. He vigorously opposed Russian expansion in Europe and sent United States forces to South Korea to keep back the communist invasion.

Truman was born on 8 May 1884 in Lamar, Missouri. He died 29 December 1972 in Kansas City, also in Missouri. He became the thirty-third president of the United States from 1945 to 1953. In my humble opinion, he ranked second only to Franklin Delano Roosevelt in the twentieth century as leader of his country.

'It Could Happen to You' is one of the many songs written by Jimmy Van Heusen with lyrics by Johnny Burke. It featured in a film, *And the Angels Sing*, with Dorothy Lamour and Fred McMurray. Its first hit recording was by Joe Stafford with the Paul Weston Orchestra in July 1944. Many other vocalists also recorded the song, among them Lena Horne, Barbara Streisand, Kiri Te Kanawa and Dave Brubeck. Jimmy Van Heusen's real name was Edward Chester Babcock, and it was he who wrote the music for the road films. Chester Babcock's name was adopted by Bob Hope in the film *Road to Morocco* and others road films. The pair also wrote the best seller 'Swinging on a Star'. Bing Crosby sang it in the film *Going My Way*, which won the Academy Award for Best Original Song in 1944. Its first recording was with Crosby and the John Scott Trotter Orchestra in 1944.

The song 'It Had to be You' was composed by Isham Jones, with lyrics by Gus Kahn. It was first published in 1924 and recorded again in 1944 on 28 June, when it reached the bestseller charts. It appeared in the film *Mr. Skeffington* in 1944 and was recorded by many artists, including Dick Haymes and Dinah Shore, also in 1944; Frank Sinatra in 1979; Tony Bennett in 2012' and Michael Bublé with Barbara Streisand in 2014. The song was also included in the top 100 tunes in American Cinema History.

Away from the bandstand there were always the ladies like Dorothy Lamour. Barnet, of course, was tall and very handsome, and women flocked to his concerts. His behaviour displayed the amorality of the big band world. Although Barnet's source of inspiration was Duke Ellington's music, he was no crass imitator. He married thirteen times; other accounts said fifteen. Many of these weddings took place in Mexico, which Barnet thought of as illegal anyway. He was heir to a fortune but, nevertheless, had a natural empathy towards people. Barnett was in the big-band business simply because he loved it. And I say amen to that!

'I'll Get By (As Long as I Have You)' was first published in 1938 but reappeared in 1944 in a film of the same name. The music was composed by Sammy Fain, with the lyrics written by Irving Kahal. The theme of this song had a great emotional feeling and was much loved during the Second World War. The song climaxed with:

> And when the night is new
> I'll be looking at the moon
> But I'll be seeing you

The song really hit the heights when Bing Crosby recorded it that year. It was also recorded by Vera Lynn in 1962 in her *Hits of the Blitz* and Tony Bennett in 1992. It also featured in *Midsomer Murders'* in the episode 'Dance with the Dead', filmed near an old Second World War airfield. This was sung by Ann Shelton and many others.

'I'll Walk Alone' was featured in the film *Follow the Boys* in 1944 and recorded by Dinah Shore. The music was composed by Jule Styne and the lyrics by Sammy Cahn. Ricky Nelson recorded his version in 1958, followed by Cliff Richard in 1965 and Jane Freeman in 1998.

'Into Each Life Some Rain Must Fall' was a 1944 song that made its way to the Hit Parade. It was written by Doris Fisher, with lyrics by Allan Roberts. It was performed by the Ink Spots and featured the tenor Bill Kenny and the great Ella Fitzgerald. The song was played in the 2005 documentary *Why We Fight* and also in the BBC series *The Singing Detective*. The name of the song originates from a line in a poem by Henry Wadsworth Longfellow (1807–1882) called 'Rainy Day'. The last verse is as follows:

> Be still, sad heart and cease repining;
> Behind the clouds is the sun still shining;
> Thy fate is the common fate of all,
> Into each life some rain must fall,
> Some days must be dark and dreary.

'Till Then' was a war-themed song. It was written by Eddy Seiler Sol Marcus and Lyny Woodid. It was sung by the Mills Brothers with Les Brown and his orchestra and dominated the charts. Other artists who recorded it were Sammy Davis Jr. in 1960 and Michael Bublé in 2012.

A song by Cole Porter straight out of the Great American Songbook was 'Every Time We Say Goodbye'. It was introduced by Nan Wyman in 1944 in Billy Rose's musical revue. The lyrics 'From Major to Minor' are accompanied by Porter's adroit changing of the music from an A major chord to a A minor chord matching the words to the music. Ella Fitzgerald also recorded it.

CHAPTER 10
Swinging with The Big Bands

I believe it was my mother who first recognised that I was swinging a piece of music. I must have heard the beat, the rhythm, and syncopation on the radio and, having a good ear for music, clearly copied the mood on the piano. Nobody taught me how to play like that, and there was no way I could explain it any more than I could explain Einstein's theory of relativity, although I knew the formula $E=MC^2$. In defining Swing, I can only once more quote Einstein when he once said, "Imagination is more important than knowledge", and the musicians who invented/discovered 'swing music' were people who clearly used their imaginations. Thankfully, nobody ever asked me to explain swing music, and I lacked sufficient courage to play it in front of my music teacher, let alone ask him to explain it.

The dictionary definition of 'swing' stated that it was a kind of jazz played by a big band, characterised by a lively rhythm suitable for dancing. This was developed in the United States sometime in the 1920s. Benny Goodman described the phenomena of swing as 'free speech in music', a saying I consider brilliant. When Edward R. Murrow, the famous newspaper and radio correspondent, asked Louis Armstrong to define swing, Louis replied, 'Oh, Mr Murrow, if you have to ask, you ain't never gonna know.' Jimmy Lunceford described swing in a tune called, 'Tain't Whatcha Do (It's the Way Thatcha Do It)'.

Swing certainly is a driving propulsive rhythm that creates a visceral response from the dancers. Just watch Bennie Goodman on YouTube and see the smiling faces of the dancers and the various foot movements. Technically, it involves shortening or lengthening the pulse divisions in a rhythm. The word 'groovy' or the phrase 'in the groove' aptly describe music that really swings, and that is as technical as I'm ever likely to get. Let me just be happy with calling swing jazz music performed with a swing. When you see it and love it, you'll know it!

Swing music dominated through the 1930s and the 1940s and well into the 1950s. It saw a revival in the 1950s and 1960s with orchestras like Count Basie and Duke Ellington, who used popular vocalists like Nat King Cole, Sinatra, and Ella Fitzgerald. Such music holds a prominent place in musical history, and it developed into a new and significant art form that swept the world and provided great relief to many people on both sides of the Atlantic during World War II.

So how did swing music come about and who were the people and bands central to its development?

It was sometime during the early 1920's that big band swing music developed as another branch on the tree of jazz. It developed through the big black bands that moved north from their roots in New Orleans to Kansas City, Chicago, St Louis, and beyond. Their music began to swing, and the arrangers of this music featured a bandleader called Fletcher Henderson. There were other bands of course who developed this music, including Jimmy Lunceford, Sy Oliver, and Duke Ellington.

The popularity of swing music coincided with the development of radio, and it was the big bands who were the vehicles for this new creation, as it swept across the world. Disc jockeys became a large support player of the big band swing music, particularly in the 1940s. In fact, it was Walter Winchell, a popular news commentator and columnist who was credited as the first person who coined the phrase disc jockey, or DJ, a term that has lived on ever since.

Following the first Carnegie Hall jazz concert on 16 January 1938, big band swing music was no longer just a fad of young people. In fact, it became the American nation's leading form of popular music. It was the generation who had witnessed the Great Depression, fought, and helped win World War II. And when they returned home, it was America who paid for the rebuilding of Europe through the Truman Doctrine and the Marshall Plan. It was these people who became known as America's Greatest Generation.

Just one year before his death, Benny Goodman played a concert at the Marriott Marquis Hotel, Times Square, New York on 7 October 1985. Before the concert began, Goodman made a short speech, which went as follows:

Among the many things I wanted to do in my musical career, I think one of the first ones in mind was to be able to arrange and orchestrate like Fletcher Henderson. Fletcher, if you don't know about him was one of the great orchestras of the 1920's and early 1930's and the fascination with his arrangements was endless. What I mean is you heard it the first time and you heard it again and you would always hear something different and that's why I thought he was a genius and that's the reason I'm really dedicating this programme to Fletcher Henderson.

It was a pleasure for me just to see and watch the dancers moving across the dance floor, thoroughly immersed in the music.

Fletcher Henderson

Swing was one of the most important innovations in the development of early jazz, and the band that exhibited this best was the band led by Fletcher Henderson. It was he above others who paved the way for the swinging style of the 1930s and 1940s. Henderson was born Fletcher Hamilton Henderson Jr on 22 November 1904, and he grew up in a well-off African American family. His mother taught him and his brother, Horace, to play the piano. It was Horace who proved to be the better pianist. Both boys studied at Atlanta University, and Fletcher graduated with a degree in chemistry. He moved to New York in 1920, hoping to carry out postgraduate work as a chemist. However, he soon found that he was confronted with racism, which was prevalent at that time. Fortunately, for the music world, he took up music and accepted a job as a pianist demonstrating sheet music.

Between 1900 and 1920, people left the backward area of the Southern states and moved to the large cities in the north, like

New York and Chicago. It was here that they met up with the new technologies, as America became an industrialised nation. It was in the north that new strong industries were developing, including a new entertainment industry. It was here in those early days that Scott Joplin became associated with ragtime, Louis Armstrong with jazz, and W.C. Handy became recognised as the 'Father of the Blues'.

When Harry Herbert Pace, also born in Georgia set up his own record-making company, it was he who employed Fletcher Henderson. The White record companies went to great lengths to keep Pace out of business, even to the point of buying up local pressing companies who had been willing to press Pace's records.

In summer 1921, a change in fortune occurred when Henderson heard Ethel Waters singing in a Harlem basement. Her first record sold 500,000 copies in a six-month period for Pace's record label, Black Swan Records, and their two top stars were Ethel Waters and Fletcher Henderson. In 1925, radio broadcasting burst upon the scene, and this new development led to the end of Black Swan Records. Henderson left the company, and by January 1924, he formed his own big band.

In July 1924, Henderson invited twenty-three-year-old cornetist Louis Armstrong to join his band, and soon it became known as the best African American band in New York. The band also included the formidable talents of Don Redman, who became the band's arranger. At this stage, Henderson split up his band into several distinct sections. He also gave more emphasis to the rhythm section, which helped develop the swing style and gave it the necessary kick. Henderson, by this time, was a leader of a superb set of musicians. But he was always reluctant to impose discipline on his band members.

When the Depression hit America, it took a toll on his band members, and by this time, other bands had begun to copy the Henderson swing sound. Indeed, the Henderson band provided a large and significant influence on many other bands, as Duke Ellington confirmed. He credited the Henderson band as being an early influence when he was developing an early sound for his own band. The pianist Earl Hines had a similar effect on the styles of other swing era pianists, like Teddy Wilson, Nat King Cole, Errol Garner, and Art Tatum.

Fletcher Henderson, with his new big band swinging music, paved the way for the new swing style that was to become ever popular. Henderson had a great ability not just in his arrangement for the new music but also to attract and guide many generations of exceptional jazz musicians during their careers. It was ironic, therefore, that, when the swing era was at its peak, it was the white bands, such as Benny Goodman, Tommy Dorsey and others, who stole the limelight. Yet they used the musicality of Fletcher Henderson in their many hits in a manner befitting this exceptional arranger and musician.

It was the bad economics of the period that saw Henderson begin working for Benny Goodman as an arranger, and it was Henderson who made a major contribution to establishing the typical sound that Goodman would be renowned for. Indeed, many of the Goodman classics originated with Fletcher Henderson, including among others, 'King Porter Stomp', 'Down South Camp Meeting', and 'Sometimes I'm Happy'. Henderson's arrangements were often quite sparse, leaving significant room in the music for improvisation. In this, Henderson was different from other arrangers, who consequently denied the musicians the chance of a spontaneous 'hot' solo.

If Benny Goodman grew to be the 'King of Swing', then it was Fletcher Henderson who was the power behind the throne. He not only arranged the music that powered Goodman's meteoric rise to fame, he also helped to launch the careers of Louis Armstrong and Coleman Hawkins, among many others. In the American segregated world of music, both black and white musicians worked together to establish this new form of music. It was John Hammond who brought Fletcher Henderson and Benny Goodman together to form a new fabulous combination that helped change American music into a new art form.

In 1950, Henderson was part of a sextet with that excellent tenor saxophonist Lucky Thompson.

Sadly, Henderson suffered a stroke and never played again. He never fully recovered and died on 29 December 1952 in New York, at just fifty-five years old.

Benny Goodman

Benjamin David Goodman was born on 30 May 1909 in Chicago, Illinois. He was raised in poverty in a family of twelve children. His parents had escaped from Russia to free themselves from the anti-Semitism that then prevailed. He began to study music at the Kehelah Jacob Synagogue in Chicago at the age of ten and found that he had a special aptitude for the clarinet. He left school when he was fourteen in order to pursue a career in music. And by the age of sixteen, he had joined the Ben Pollack band and remained there until the age of twenty.

Goodman led his first band in 1934, largely playing Fletcher Henderson's musical arrangements. However, when the band first played in May 1935, the hotel's manager thought the music 'appalling' and the band got two weeks' notice. In the early summer of that year, Goodman recorded some of his best songs, including the 'King Porter Stomp' and 'Blue Skies'. These were essentially swinging scores, which identified the band's style. Fletcher Henderson, in his arrangement, would set off one section of the band against the crisp sound of the brass, a quite different sound from some of the other lethargic American bands.

The first time the band scored a resounding success was at the Hollywood Palomar, the most famous of all the West Coast ballrooms. At first, the band played quietly to an almost negative reaction. It was a Goodman plan after their previous experience in New York. It was a stick-or-bust situation, and it was. Goodman 'went for broke'. He led his band into his swing mood with his 'King Porter Stomp', and the kids went wild and gathered around the bandstand. The swinging music went coast to coast in a series of broadcasts. And *swing* was really in!

It was in Chicago at that time that Goodman contributed on important breakthrough in race relations. Without any fanfare, he presented Teddy Wilson on piano. Goodman was quoted as saying, 'If a guy's got it, let him give it. I'm selling music not prejudice.' He was also quoted as saying that swing music was 'free speech in music'.

Now Benny Goodman was hardly an adventurous person, and racial integration was never a personal cause with him, as it was with

Charlie Barnet who used black and white musicians sharing the same bandstand. Wilson was a well-educated highly cultured man, and some years later, he said, Playing, in public with Benny was a breakthrough. Guys in the music business were telling Benny that he'd ruin his career if he hired me. 'They weren't anti-black, they were just businessmen.'

In 1937 also, Goodman was attracted to Hollywood to make the first of his films, *The Big Band Broadcast of 1937*. It was also at this time that Harry James joined the band and was added to the trumpet section, and one of the great trumpet sections of all time was born. Also, when Goodman's vocalist left the band to get married, Goodman borrowed an exciting new signer by the name of Ella Fitzgerald to take her place.

It was on 12 December 1940 that Benny Goodman appeared as a guest soloist with the New York Philharmonic Orchestra in a performance of Mozart Clarinet Concerto and Debussy's First Rhapsody at Carnegie Hall. In the following months, he also appeared with other notable orchestras, like the Pittsburgh Symphony and the Cleveland Orchestra.

Two years earlier, Benny Goodman had made history by playing a swing concert in New York's prestigious Carnegie Hall. And in this venture, he'd been joined by musicians from the Count Basie and Duke Ellington bands. However, that night the Duke sat out the proceedings, taking his place in the audience.

In 1955, Goodman's life was depicted in a Hollywood film, *The Benny Goodman Story*, an inaccurate version of his life. However, his band did play the music for the soundtrack of the film, and it did much to expose his music to a younger audience.

Benny Goodman and his band made many overseas trips. When he performed in the USSR, one writer observed that the swing music almost blew down the Iron Curtain. In 1978, the band once more appeared at Carnegie Hall to mark the thirtieth anniversary of its first concert there. All the seats in the hall were sold out on the first day.

In 1982, Goodman was honoured by the Kennedy Centre for his lifetime achievements in swing music. In 1986, he received an honorary degree in music from Columbia University and the Grammy Award for lifetime achievement. Goodman records, however, were not restricted to swing. He also established the clarinet as a respectable instrument for a bandleader. He helped to breakdown the colour bar that existed in music, first as noted with Teddy Wilson a but also with Cootie Williams, Roy Eldridge, and Lionel Hampton.

Benny Goodman also remained semi-active at the time of his death on 13 June 1986.

Benny Goodman started his first band in 1934, as I have already stated; the location was in New York at the Billy Rose Music Hall. He couldn't take the credit for starting the swing craze. However, it was his band that made the genre universally popular. Throughout his amazing professional career, he never changed his style of playing to conform to the latest and changing trends. He always retained the original sound that defines the swing era, and consequently the world crowned him 'King of Swing'.

In the period following the swing era, Goodman still blew his clarinet, and it was outside the American continent that he made his greatest musical contribution. In winter 1956/57, he travelled to the Far East. In 1958, he took his band to the World's Fair in Brussels, where sadly I missed him. And in 1962, as mentioned, he took his band to the USSR, the first American band to do so.

If you tune into a video of Benny Goodman's band playing at the Marquis Hotel in New York on 7 October 1985, just watch the sheer joy on the faces of the dancers as they sweep across the dance floor in complete unison with the beat of the band. I suppose it could be argued that dancing was the prerequisite of the dating and mating ritual. George Bernard Shaw once described it as a perpendicular expression of a horizontal desire. Be that as it may, whatever they did or did not feel, they certainly loved the programme of 'Anything for You', 'Blue Room', 'You Brought a New Kind of Love to Me', 'King Porter Stomp', and 'Down South Camp Meeting'.

In an interview in 1975, Goodman said, 'Playing music was a great escape for me from poverty. I wanted to do something with myself and music was a great form for me. I was absolutely fascinated by it, so I set out at an early age to do what I could and devote my efforts to it and enjoy it'. Well he certainly did that and a great deal more.

Benny Goodman was buried on 15 June 1986 at Long Ridge Cemetery in Stamford Connecticut.

Time magazine called him the King of Swing in 1937 and 1938, and he now topped the Metronome's National Poll, beating the Casa Loma band by a ratio of two to one.

Charlie Barnet

I first heard 'Skyliner' being played at Coney Beach Fairground, Porthcawl, a seaside resort on the south coast of Wales. The music set my pulse racing, although at that time, in 1944 or later, I had no indication what the music was called; nor did I know the name of the band playing it. That information came later when I heard it being played on the radio, I believe by the Scottish Variety Orchestra. Charles Barnet had been born in New York City on 26 October 1913. He was born into a wealthy family and learned both the piano and saxophone as a child. His mother wanted him to become a lawyer, but he loved music and wanted above all to be a musician.

He started his first band in 1933 at the Paramount Grill, Hotel Paramount, New York City. His band became known for a hard-swinging style, with Barnet playing the tenor saxophone. In the late thirties, he added the alto saxophone to his repertoire. When he attempted to premiere his swing music style in New Orleans at the Roosevelt Hotel, Governor Huey Long disliked the sound. He, therefore, lured the band to a bordello and had them run out of town.

Charlie Barnet was an heir to his family fortune, as Barnet's grandfather was both vice president of the New York Central Railroad and also a banker. As a result, Barnet was in the enviable position of not having the financial problems that often plagued many of his contemporaries. It was from this comfortable position that he was able to maintain a fine musical organisation, both in the staff he employed and also in musical style. Perhaps because of this security, Barnet's band became a notorious party band, with drinking, drug taking, vandalism, and various exploits as a part of the game. Indeed, Barnet was married eleven times during his career, although, in his view, many of those weddings in Mexico were illegal. As he said later, 'I managed to roll up an impressive record of nuptial failures.'

On the positive side, Barnet's band was among the first in America to be racially integrated. He hired many black musicians, not, as he said, with any thoughts of being a crusader but simply to hire the best for his band.

Certainly, his band had great fun. A boat ride to Buffalo was typical. His drummer and his wife were celebrating their anniversary on the rear deck. They drank copious amounts of champagne and then, in their inebriated state, threw their glasses overboard, followed by the ice buckets. This was in turn followed by a stack of wicker chairs.

An irate purser now appeared on the scene and shouted, 'What band is this?'

Barnet shouted out, 'Jimmy Dorsey.'

I have no knowledge of how it all ended.

By 1930, the big band scene was only a shadow of what it would be a decade later. But already, there were some famous orchestras around, like those of Fletcher Henderson, Duke Ellington, Paul Whiteman, and Guy Lombardo, among others. Barnet had been attracted not first to the music but to the life that surrounded it. The first time he heard Duke Ellington playing, he recognised the music as being different and interesting, and he was an outspoken admirer of both Count Basie and Duke Ellington. Barnet wanted to form a band that incorporated the Duke's harmonic approach and tone colours and Count Basie's rhythmic drive.

Barnet's first success was at the Famous Door in New York. By this time, the band was in great shape and was an instant hit on the first night. Barnet now excelled on both the alto and tenor saxophone, and with Billy May now on board as an arranger, the band began to 'go- places'.

To keep current in the jazz and swing scene, Barnet had watched and listened to Jimmie Lunsford's superb band, who had Cy Oliver writing them arrangements. By 1935, Barnet was back in New York playing at the Glen Island Casino. At this time, he used to maintain that there were four sexes—male, female, homosexuals, and girl singers. Barnet had a rule that stated that no hanky-panky was alloyed with the girl singer, provided she could sing. However, off the bandstand there were always the ladies—at times irresistible beauties like Dorothy Lamour. It was just a part of the amoral scene of the big band age.

Barnet and his band were soon booked into the Paramount Theatre, the number one theatre in the USA. Dorothy Lamour was on the bill. At that time, she had the top following. Lamour had started out as a band singer in Chicago, and now she started a big romance with Barnet. Paramount disapproved of the relationship and made no bones about it. However, Barnet was, as he said, severely stricken.

When a stranger offered him a piece of music, Barnet played it without any satisfaction. The song was later offered to Glenn Miller, and it became one of his greatest hits. The song of course was called 'In the Mood'.

However, he had better luck a year or so later with a tune he wrote himself on an old foot-pump organ that he carried around with him. It was at the Royal Theatre in Baltimore where he first played 'Skyliner.' Billy May wrote the arrangement, and the music became a great hit.

When Lena Horne became a permanent member of the band, Barnet had no real trouble getting her accepted into hotels. The desk clerk would be told, 'Our Cuban singer would like a single room with bath.' This tended to work every time. With May's arrangement of 'Cherokee', a great hit, it moved to be a smash hit through jukeboxes and airtime. 'Redskin Rumba', with no recognisable melody, also became a hit, as did 'Pompton Turnpike', with Barnet on the soprano saxophone. At the time, critics wrote that Barnet's playing exhibited an 'astonishing verve of feeling and imagination' and said he played 'the most forceful driving reed instrument in the world.'

The relationship with Dorothy Lamour had now ended, and Barnet had moved on. Now he was recording for Decca. But with the draft, he began to assemble a new band on the West Coast. In 1948, MGM made a film called *A Song Is Born*, which had the bands of Tommy Dorsey, Louis Armstrong, Lionel Hampton, and of course Charlie Barnet. Danny Kaye played the lead in the film. Barnet had now composed a number of songs in addition to 'Skyliner' and 'Cherokee'. They were 'Swing Street Strut', 'The Right Idea', 'The Wrong Idea', 'Growlin'', 'Scotch and Soda', 'I Kind of Like You', 'Lazy Bag', and the 'Last Jump'.

The Big Band scene was now breaking up, and by the early 1950s, bookings were hard to come by. It now became evident that rock and roll wasn't going to be a fad and would not disappear overnight.

Barnet, among many others, couldn't believe what was happening. In his own words, 'The inmates had taken over the asylum.' Far from widening the harmonic and the rhythmic patterns, the music that came forth destroyed them. As a result, the musical sounds and lyrics became, for the sake of a better word, just gibberish. Perhaps in time, the young would soon get tired of the junk thrown at them, and this phase too would pass!

'Skyliner' became one of Charlie Barnet's most exciting hit records. It has always remained one of my favourites. It was arranged by Billy May and was first recorded as a V-disc in July 1944. Some say it was written as the theme music for the late 1940s United States Armed Forces Network programme, *Moonlight in Munich*.

It was said that Charlie Barnet led 'the blackest white band' of them all. He was a free-spirited bandleader, and this was reflected in the colour and looseness of his music.

His final marriage was to Betty Thompson, and it lasted for thirty-three, years. He died at the Hillside Hospital San Diego from a combination of Alzheimer's disease and pneumonia on 4 September 1991.

Artie Shaw

Artie Shaw was born with the name Arthur Jacob Arshawsky on 23 May 1910 in New York City. His father came from a Jewish family in Russia, and his mother was Austrian. When he was young, his mother bought him a C melody saxophone for forty dollars, which he learned to play with the help of a shop employee. He was shown some basic fingering, but when told he should first learn the scales, Shaw became angry. He said, 'I wanted to run ... I guess I was in a hurry.'

At school, he was bullied because of his name. And later in life, he said, 'I wouldn't get to first base with such a name, as in those days in the 1920s you had to be a Gentile in America to work.'

As he grew up, he said he didn't have a Jew's religion, didn't belong to any Zionist movement, indeed didn't subscribe to anything that had to do with being Jewish. He remained like that for the rest of his life.

Shaw was brought up in poverty like Benny Goodman, and while Arthur Arshawsky was a shy child, Art Shaw became a brash and confident person. He later described it like assuming a new identity. And at the age of fifteen, he went forth into the world as his own man. His first music job was in the band of Cavallaro, who insisted that Shaw doubled on clarinet (an instrument he had yet to play) and the alto sax. Playing the clarinet called for a different style, and the way you held it to your mouth and applied lip pressure was different too. Shaw soon became the star of the band.

When he moved to Cleveland to play for the Joe Cantor band, he now started arranging songs like 'Wabash Blues'. At night, he would stay up late listening to Holst—*The Planets* played by the London Symphony Orchestra—and also works by Beethoven. Having listened to the records, he would then play the music with his clarinet, interoperating the tune in his own way. The boys in the band called him 'Little Beethoven'.

Liquor was very much part of the music scene in the early days. Shaw was credited with the saying that jazz was born in a whiskey barrel, was reared on marijuana, and was currently expiring on heroin. (In those days, marijuana was not classed as a narcotic drug.)

During the Depression, Shaw took refuge in books. By 1931, he was almost down and out, when he was pushed to play in the Tommy Dorsey band. Shaw considered that moment a turning point in his life. By that time, he was about the best saxophonist in town.

Shaw was in the orchestra for Bing Crosby's CBS broadcast on 2 September 1931. Shaw said that Bing was an enormous influence and described him as a jazz singer who could sing the words and make you hear the notes; Bing could swing.

In 1934, Shaw was back in New York where he met up with Benny Goodman, a person in whose path he had been following one way or another all his young life. Goodman had been born one year earlier than Shaw, and it appeared to Shaw that Goodman always seemed to be one step ahead of him. They would continue to joust as pros for decades. Both were talented and ambitious players, and their clashes certainly benefited popular culture. America was fortunate to have them both. In fact, Shaw admitted what Goodman had achieved by opening a musical gate through which many would follow.

By autumn 1936, Shaw's energies were concentrated on his own orchestra. He composed his own theme music and quickly orchestrated it. It was called 'Nightmare'. With his new band, he would use the best songs by the best songwriters, and they were Kern, Gershwin, Berlin, Porter, and Rodgers.

Although it was Benny Goodman who first employed Billie Holiday as a vocalist, it was Shaw who stole her away. Her first appearance with the Shaw orchestra was a spectacular success at Madison Square Garden, drawing 20,00 spectators.

However, what Shaw was chasing in 1938 was a major hit.

'Begin the Beguine' had first been recorded by Xavier Cugat's band and, at 108 bars, was probably the longest popular song ever written. When Shaw recorded it, he played it in 4/4 time. They then played on the other side of the disc 'Indian Love Call'. Shaw and all his colleagues believed that the latter song would be the hit the band was seeking. However, it was 'Begin the Beguine' that became an overnight hit sensation and swept the nation. In 1990 and later, the record was still being purchased. Shaw described it as a real melody played with a jazz beat / swing rhythm and a Latin American tempo. It had been composed by Cole Porter, and the song made Artie Shaw a household name across America overnight.

In a period of three days in January 1939, Shaw cut sixteen sides for the Blue Bird label including 'Rosalie', 'The Man I Love', and 'The Donkey Serenade'. His new vocalist, Helen Forest, sang all the romantic standards, such as 'Deep Purple' and Kern's 'All the Things You Are'. The latter piece became a popular classic. With its enchanting melody and chord change, it was a favourite with jazz musicians for the next fifty years or so.

Shaw often voiced his criticism of other bands and their leaders, especially the bland music of Glenn Miller. By November 1939, Shaw told his band he'd had enough of the music business, despite having over a million dollars' worth of advanced bookings. However, he made his comeback on 3 March 1941, with a thirty-two-piece orchestra. His first recording and a favourite of mine was 'Frenesi'. The record sold over and over again, and Shaw was back in business.

A recording session with some of his friends saw the beginning of 'Gramercy 5', a winning sextet named after a New York telephone exchange. But when he recorded Hoagy Carmichael's 'Stardust', it became one of his all-time biggest records and the most popular recording of Carmichael's song.

Like Benny Goodman, Shaw had made many band appearances for the Russian War Relief Fund, but from 7 December 1941, America itself was at war. Shaw had what was termed a 3-A deferment, as he was the sole provider for his mother.

However, by January 1942 everything changed when he enlisted in the United States Navy. Unhappy with his treatment in camp, he went AWOL (absent without leave) and talked his way into the office of the US secretary of the navy, one James Forrestal, who he'd met previously. Shaw wanted to create a great navy band and said that he wanted to play where the fighting took place. Forrestal agreed to this proposal, and soon Chief Petty Officer Shaw received authority to find enough 1-A men in one month to make up an orchestra. The orchestra would be called Shaw's Rangers.

By July 1942, Shaw and his orchestra were on the island of Guadalcanal, where the fighting had barely stopped. Japanese bombing occurred almost every night, and much of his time was spent in foxholes. During the next two years, Shaw and his fellow musicians played concerts for the troops almost continuously. By 1944, he was physically exhausted and was sent home for treatment and rest. In 1953, Shaw told a congressional committee that both Admirals Nimitz and Halsey had congratulated him on doing a great job in the Pacific.

In 1945, Shaw's playing was described as perfection, and his recordings were superb. His recordings of 'They Can't Take That Away from Me', 'Someone to Watch Over Me', and 'Dancing on the Ceiling' all became classics. In the summer of that year, Shaw recorded 'Night and Day', 'I've Got You Under My Skin', and 'In the Still of the Night'—all by Cole Porter.

Shaw now turned to the classics, which he loved. Benny Goodman had preceded him in this, and now it was Shaw's turn. In 1949, he played at Ebbets Field, a benefit concert for the State of Israel in front of an audience of 31,000 people. This concert was conducted by Leonard Bernstein, with eighty-five members of the New York Philharmonic Orchestra. Shaw played Mozart's clarinet concerto brilliantly, and the concert was a great success.

Shaw now turned his attention to writing a book. He had been warned that, if you write a book, you'll never finish it. If you do, it won't get published. And if it is published, then nobody will read it. The best critique of the book came from the *New York Herald Tribune* saying no book is as unpredictable as its author, a conflicted man who came to realise that the thing Shaw wanted was tormenting Arshawsky and the thing that Arshawsky wanted was murdering Artie. Shaw was very proud of that.

It was on 21 April 1954 that Shaw's new Gramercy Five opened a four-week stint at the newly built Sahara Hotel in Las Vegas. It was to be the last year for Shaw in the music business. Or was it? He had a near thirty-year time span in which he had worked from obscurity to the pinnacle of success. However, the new music did not please him. He described it as hateful and political crap and black dislike of white.

The swing era, by 1968, like jazz before it, was now receding into history—although, up to 1985, Benny Goodman was still regularly filling ballrooms with his swing band. Shaw's jealousy of Goodman persisted well into the 1980s, and the jealously was fully reciprocated. Yet their music was so different. Shaw now used interviews to settle scores with his departed contemporaries. He said, 'I can say that Glenn Miller should have lived and "Chattanooga Choo Choo" should have died.'

In 1996, Shaw was voted into the American Hall of Fame. His remarks on this were, 'It's about time.' In 1989, he donated his music library, with more than seven hundred scores, to Boston University—which transferred them to the School of Music of Arizona in Tucson. In 2004, he was awarded a Grammy Lifetime Achievement Award.

In addition to his wonderful musical ability, Shaw was an expert precision marksman, ranked number four in the United States in 1962, as well as being an expert fly fisherman. He had helped make the talents of Billie Holiday, Lena Horne, Mel Torme, and trombonist arranger Ray Conniff known. With his good looks, he played in a number of films but admitted he was no actor. He played himself in *Second Chorus* in 1940, with Fred Astaire featuring Shaw and his orchestra playing a concerto for clarinets. His 1940 recording of 'Stardust' was used in its entirety in the closing credits of the film *The Man Who Fell to Earth*. Martin Scorsese also used Shaw's theme song

'Nightmare' in the Academy Award-winning Howard Hughes biopic *The Aviator*. Late in his career, he made an explosive return to play at the Royal Festival Hall in London. Shaw was touched by the huge standing ovation that he received and left the stage in tears.

Shaw, in old age, became a brilliant polymath and wrote a number of books. However, in terms of human relationships, which, after all, are the hallmarks of human maturity, Shaw was completely unable to take that pathway. Perhaps it was a relationship he had suffered in his early family life? He had a sense of humour to the end. His helper, after making his bed, asked him if he was comfortable. He looked up, grinned and said, 'I make a living.'

He died suddenly on a Thursday morning on 30 December 2004. Artie Shaw, king of the clarinet, was dead. He was ninety-four years of age.

Harry James

I knew little of Harry James until I marked my early teens in the 1940s. James had been born in 1911 in Albany, Georgia, and, at the age of eight years old, was introduced to the trumpet by this father. He became, in all probability, the greatest band trumpeter of the late 1930s and 1940s. Technically, he was flawless. And following his playing for local bands, he was soon picked out by Ben Pollack and then played in the Benny Goodman band for several years, joining the band on 5 January 1937. There he completed a renowned trumpet section with Ziggy Elman and Chris Griffin. James could play first trumpet or jazz trumpet as required. Many musicians thought he had previously played with African Americans in order to achieve such virtuosity, but that was not the case. However, he was different from any other white trumpeter of his day and one of the greatest of his generation.

Playing with Benny Goodman gave him instant recognition, and it was said by many that it was James and Gene Krupa on drums who made the band. In 1939, he formed his own band with financial help from Benny Goodman and employed a little-known male vocalist by the name of Frank Sinatra to join him. His girl vocalist was Helen Forest.

What cemented his status as a famous personality was his marriage to Betty Grable in 1945. They became the new American royalty at a time when Grable was at the peak of her career. In 1939, she had appeared in a film *Million Dollar Legs*. Indeed, she would become the American Forces pinup during World War II, and her legs were insured for US$1 million, at least so said her studio. She admitted that she became a star for two reasons, 'And I'm standing on them.' In 1943, she had become the number one box office draw in the world, and at that time she had become the highest paid actor in the United States.

Elizabeth Ruth Grable was born in St Louis, Missouri, on 18 December 1916. She was an actress, a singer, and a dancer and better at all three than many of the artists who followed her. At the same time, Harry James was playing his trumpet with an exhilarating, powerful, disciplined sound in a band that consisted of between thirteen and eighteen musicians, who were dominant in the popular music scene from the late 1930s to the end of the 1940s. This spirited music was a welcome respite during a dire period in American history, recovering as it were from an economic crisis and who soon would be plunged into World War II.

Sadly, however, Harry James ruined his own life with drink, gambling, and a perpetual attraction to women, who were in plentiful supply.

By early 1941, James's band recorded the song 'You Made Me Love You', which became the most successful and familiar record of his entire career, selling one million records. By this time, his band had adapted a sweeter style, more suited to the popular vein than that which had emerged from his jazz roots. This move did not please everybody, and he suffered significant criticism. However, the move was a success commercially, and his band continued in the style, creating musical hits throughout the 1940s. He never forgot his jazz roots, and he was much under the influence of Count Basie. James also enjoyed success with semi-classical pieces, for example, 'Concerto for Trumpet', 'Flight of the Bumble Bee', 'Carnival of Venice', and 'Trumpet Rhapsody'. All of these pieces were played and arranged in a swing flavour. His playing of popular music pieces met with a certain amount of criticism. Many people preferred jazz to the schmaltzy sobbing like phrases he included whilst playing ballad-type pieces. ('Schmaltzy' derives from German, meaning 'sentimental'.)

His introductory piece was 'Ciribiribin', a Neapolitan folk song. James played it as a rising jet-propelled version for his fiery trumpet playing. He also arranged it, and it was a perfect showcase for his trumpet playing. It should be remembered that, by the summer of 1939, there was great competition among the big bands, especially from Benny Goodman, Tommy Dorsey, and Glenn Miller.

When James, Sinatra, and Helen Forest started playing and singing ballad-type music, the plan fitted perfectly into the changing times. From that moment through 1945, romantic ballads took pride of place in popular music, certainly in America. James and Sinatra were on their way up, their recording of 'All or Nothing at All' perhaps helped lead the way, followed by 'Don't Sit Under the Apple Tree'.

Count Basie was a great influence on James's career. And in 1955, he signed a record deal with Capital Records, releasing many of his old recorded pieces as new versions representative of the Basie style. He also appeared in a number of Hollywood films, playing himself in most of them, the first was in 1937 and the last in 1983. He appeared in many radio shows, too, succeeding Glenn Miller in the programme sponsored by Chesterfield cigarettes when Miller joined the Unites States Army. In 1941, his recording of 'You Made Me Love You' was included into the Grammy Hall of Fame.

The band always respected James as a great musician, but there the respect ended. He was never one to read books and lacked education. He could only talk about baseball and, of course, music.

Harry James was active as a musician for over fifty years and, despite being diagnosed with lymphatic cancer, continued to work. His last concert was on 26 June 1983 leading his own orchestra. He died just nine days later in Las Vegas Nevada at sixty-seven years old. However, his band continued to operate until July 2018, led by Radke.

Some of his recorded music includes 'Ciribirbin', 'Harry Suckle Rose', 'Where or When', 'Trumpet Blues and Cantabile', 'Sleepy Lagoon', 'I'll Get By', 'Manhattan', 'You Made Me Love You', and 'I've Heard That Song Before'.

At James's funeral in July 1983, it was Frank Sinatra who read the eulogy. They had been friends for over forty years. Harry James had an astounding technique with the trumpet, and like the other big band leaders, his life is deeply woven into American life and culture and will remain ever so.

Betty Ruth Grable was placed in the list of the top ten moneymaking stars every year from 1940 for a number of years. She married Harry James in 1943, and they were divorced in 1965. She died on 2 July 1973 at the age of fifty-six from lung cancer. Harry James attended her funeral.

Tommy Dorsey

Tommy Dorsey was born on 19 November 1905, the youngest of four children. His father was an Irishman, Francis Dorsey, a former coal miner, then a music teacher in Shenandoah Penny Crania, a poor coal mining area. Brothers Tommy and Jimmy were taught to play the trombone and trumpet by their father when they were very young, but sadly, their two siblings died as young children. Tommy developed a huge technical skill on the trombone, and later, both brothers went their own ways in the 1930s and formed their own bands. Earlier, however, they worked together and, in 1928, broke into the charts when they recorded 'Coquette'. In 1929, they recorded 'Let's Do It (Let's Fall in Love)' with vocalist Bing Crosby, breaking into the top ten.

No bands I remember evoked the period of the 1930s and 1940s more than Tommy Dorsey and Glenn Miller. In fact, Dorsey loaned money to Miller in 1938 to assist him in setting up his own band. Tommy saw this gesture as an investment and, around that time, also purchased two music-publishing companies. It was Dorsey whose magnificent trombone playing, and smash hits influenced popular music for many years to come. I well remember his recordings of 'Marie', 'Song of India', and his great hit 'I'll Never Smile Again'.

Tommy worked in a number of bands before joining Paul Whiteman in 1927. Soon he formed his own band and developed a long-running practice of raiding other bands for talent. He thought nothing of paying musicians more money to join him, even to the point of taking over their contracts if he admired them. Among his music arrangers were Axel Stordahl and Nelson Riddle, the latter at a later date with his own orchestra giving a new lease on life to the flagging career of Frank Sinatra. Dorsey had stolen Sinatra away from the Harry James band by paying him an extra fifty dollars per week, forcing Sinatra's hand

In 1939, Dorsey was aware that his band was playing popular and vocal tunes. To spice up his music, he hired Cy Oliver away from the Jimmy Lunceford band, and it was his arrangements of 'On the Sunny Side of the Street' and 'Opus One' that helped keep the band in the forefront of big band music at that time. Indeed, Dorsey eventually gained 286 *Billboard* hits, and of those, seventeen reached the number one spot, among them 'The Music Goes Round and Round', 'Marie', 'Once in a While', 'All The Things You Are', and 'Indian Summer'. His biggest hit was 'I'll Never Smile Again', with Sinatra as the vocalist. It was clear that Nelson Riddle learned to write dynamic arrangements through the influence of Cy Oliver. And as mentioned earlier, it was this experience that allowed Riddle to compose his brilliant arrangements for a resurgent Sinatra later in his career.

The Dorsey band also appeared in a number of films for Paramount, Metro Goldwyn Mayer, and United Artists. These included *Girl Crazy* in 1943, *A Song is Born*, and *The Fabulous Dorseys* in 1947.

Although there was a strong competitive spirit between the big bands, there was also a real fraternity between jazz musicians. There was one occasion when a Glenn Miller concert was in jeopardy because Miller was too ill to make the theatre. When Dorsey heard, he sped to the theatre and led the band and also played all the Miller trombone parts. When Dorsey was ill with a virus, Victor Young joined the band and conducted it brilliantly, as he was well able to do.

Jack Leonard, Sinatra, and Ella Fitzgerald were among a number of vocalists who learned the words of a song by listening to Dorsey playing the trombone. He was now called the sentimental gentleman of swing because of his smooth playing technique. He was also a tough leader and was quoted as saying 'Nobody leaves my band. I only fire people.' Louis Bellison, that wonderful drummer, put a softer touch on it, saying that Tommy only wanted you to play your best every night.

By January 1941, Franklin Delano Roosevelt was inaugurated as president for an unprecedented third term, but the war that followed brought many changes to the life of the bands. Fewer places were now available, as the number of bands around the circuit had increased. Also, many bands had lost key personnel or were about to lose more to the military call-up. However, the swing music of the 1930s played on during the war and for a long time after it ended. It was in the thirties that dance music entered into jazz that we refer to as swing. It's interesting to note that George Gershwin was commissioned by Paul Whiteman early in February 1924 to write a piece of music for his jazz concert, in what was termed an experiment in modern music, a 'jazz concerto'. Gershwin wrote a piece he named *Rhapsody in Blue* that combined elements of classical music, jazz, and blues and inspirational melodies. It could in retrospect be seen as a catalyst of swing music, which came to light some years later.

Tommy Dorsey married at the young age of seventeen in 1922 to a sixteen-year-old girl with whom he eloped. The marriage produced two children, and the divorce took place in 1943. He married a movie actress later the same year, divorcing her in 1947. He married again in 1948, adding two more children to his tally.

Tommy Dorsey died on 26 November 1956, having just reached his fifty-first birthday. Both Tommy and his brother, Jimmy, are buried together in Kensico Cemetery in Valhalla, New York.

Glenn Miller

Glenn Miller was born on 1 March 1904. His first name was Alton, which he hated. And from his early years, he became known as Glenn. His brother played the cornet, and Glenn learned to play this in his school band but with little recognition. His mother was the driving force in the family, and she always expected her children to work hard. The young Miller always remained close to his mother, inheriting from her a demand for perfection in himself and the musicians he worked with. As a result, he was later regarded as a cold fish by many, although at times he could show a generosity and warmth of character, as well as a good sense of humour.

In the early 1920s, Miller worked with a number of small bands across America, but the breakthrough he was seeking occurred when Ben Pollack hired him to play the trombone and also arrange the music for the band. Pollock was one of the first bands in America to play big band jazz. At that time, everyone in the music business was talking about this little lad called Benny Goodman, who would show up for rehearsal in short pants. However, a pair of trousers was kept in a locker for him to wear to fit in with the rest of the band. During this period, Miller and Goodman roomed together and became good friends.

Although Miller contributed a great deal to the band, he could not reach the level of skill of Jack Teagarden when he appeared on the scene. His rendition of the blues was quite brilliant, and Miller realised that he would never be able to reach such a standard. So he left the Pollack Band and, sometime later, joined the Benny Goodman band, again both as an arranger and a trombone player. It was this move that brought him to the attention of the American public.

His next move was to join the Dorsey band, but his stay was short, owing to internal squabbling. So he soon left and set up a band for the British-born Ray Noble. Al Bowlly was the band's South African vocalist, with his warm voice and tender phrasing. Miller had arranged a song written by Johnny Green called 'Body and Soul', with lyrics by Eddie Heyman. Miller also composed 'Moonlight Serenade' around that time.

By early 1937, Miller, with financial help from Benny Goodman, had formed his own band. However, he was still seeking a unique sound for his band. Most of the other big bands were eminently recognisable, among them Goodman and Shaw with their clarinets and Tommy Dorsey with his trombone. Miller's once promising career now deteriorated into a series of one-nighters, and the winter weather with its ice and snow made life intolerable. He soon realised that his band was going nowhere, either musically or commercially. When he returned to New York, he felt depressed, as now he was financially almost broke, and he strongly felt that the chances of leading a band again were remote.

By 1938, things had turned his fortunes around. With great support, he started what was to be his final civilian big band. By this time, he featured his new sound, using a unique style of one clarinet and four saxophones that produced a mellow rich reed sound. Miller had now made Tex Beneke a star by using him as the vocalist, sometimes accompanied by Marion Hutton and also the modernaires singers. 'I've Got a Girl in Kalamazoo', 'Chattanooga Choo Choo', and Don't Sit under the Apple Tree' were all great hits.

Miller's emphasis was on discipline, and the band knew it. Indeed, some of his band called him the General MacArthur of the music business.

It was 1 March 1939 when Miller's manager, Michael Nidorf, closed the deal for the band to play at the Glenn Island Casino. Most of the other big bands had made their initial impact there. The venue also offered coast-to-coast radio coverage amounting to six broadcasts every week. Now Miller's song 'Moonlight Serenade' became the band's theme song. 'In the Mood' became one of Miller's great hit records. The dancers, largely young kids, loved to jitterbug to the music. Perhaps it was Miller's arrangement that got them going, with the saxophone reflecting the opening melody and then battering his audience with repeated fade-outs until the band roared into its screaming finale.

Not everyone liked it of course, including Artie Shaw. Sometime later, he was heard to say, 'Miller should have lived, and Chattanooga Choo Choo should have died.'

The band closed at the casino on 23 August before a packed hall. Afterwards, the kids laid on a special party for them, something no other band had received. Neither did any other band in the future enjoy the same adulation. Glenn Miller had certainly arrived!

When Miller and the band finished their stint at the Glen Island Casino, they returned to the theatre circuit and broke all records in a three-week stand shared with the Ink Spots, grossing more than US$150,000. In October that year the Miller band shared the stage at Carnegie Hall with Benny Goodman and Paul Whiteman.

Jerry Gray now became Miller's chief arranger, as he became available when the Artie Shaw band broke up. It was one of the smartest moves Miller ever made, as Gray's contribution to the band was huge. His list of arrangements included 'I've Got a Girl in Kalamazoo'; 'Adios'; and, of course, 'Chattanooga Choo Choo'. Later, with the American Army Band, he arranged their greatest hit 'St. Louis Blues March'. In late 1941, 'Chattanooga Choo Choo' became the first million-record sale in almost fifteen years. RCA Victor produced and presented Miller with a gold record.

By spring 1941, tensions had grown between the Empire of Japan and the United States, culminating in the attack on the American Pacific Fleet in Pearl Harbour. Despite his great success, Miller was getting restless, and above all, he wanted to get involved in the war effort, despite the fact that he was married and, at thirty-seven, too old for the military draft. So, at the peak of his career in 1942, Miller submitted a formal application to join the United States Navy Reserve, using Bing Crosby as his reference.

His application was turned down. It was a decision that the navy was soon to regret. In August, Miller wrote to the Army Air Force and received the most welcoming of replies, telling him to report in October and offering him congratulations and good wishes. Miller soon became a captain in the United States Army Air Force. His effort to modernise military music was resisted in certain army quarters, but the senior serving officer supported him. As a result, he took a fifty-piece Army Air Force Band across the Atlantic to Britain in summer 1943. There, the orchestra played 800 concerts, many of which were broadcast by the BBC.

Whether in the United States or Britain, the reaction to the Glenn Miller band was much the same. It appears that Miller was able to penetrate people's collective awareness in a way that few other musical sounds ever did. Miller certainly was aware of what would please the listener, and he kept his finger firstly on that pulse. In just four years, Glenn Miller and his band had scored sixteen number one hits and had sixty-nine top ten hits. These were more than Elvis Presley had achieved with his ten number one hits and thirty-three top ten hits throughout his career. Miller had reached the pinnacle of big band success. To listen today to 'Moonlight Serenade' evokes the war years and still lifts the spirit as it did through those momentous times.

The Disappearance and Death of Glenn Miller

The weather was appalling on Friday, 15 December 1944, and even the birds were walking. An occluded front stretched down the centre of England (see bottom left weather map). Such a front is formed when a cold front catches up with a warm front. The outside air temperature and the dew from temperature were the same, causing fog to form' and the freezing level was between ground level and 1,000 feet.

Miller had grown impatient and had waited for days for the weather to improve; it hadn't! It was this impatience that caused Miller to accept an offer of an early flight to Paris, where he planned to take his US Army Band for a series of concerts following that city's liberation from the Nazis. The aircraft for that day's flight to Paris was a single engine C-64A Norseman. And please note, it was only equipped with carburettor de-icing for the engine and electric de-icing for the pitot head. It was the ram air entering the pitot head measured against the static air that would provide the pilot with his airspeed. The aircraft was not equipped with any air frame de-icing, yet that day it would have to fly in freezing conditions for most, if not all, of its journey.

The pilot, John RS Morgan, started his flight that morning from his base at Alconbury (see map) and had some difficulty finding Twin Wood Farm. Ground taxiing that morning was very difficult, so Morgan taxied the aircraft to the end of its runway and left it there with the engine still running. Lieutenant Colonel Norman F. Buessell and Glenn Miller were the only two passengers. Buessell climbed into the co-pilot's seat, and Miller sat in a bucket seat behind the pilot. At 13.55 hours the aircraft took off and disappeared into the low cloud.

The distance to Paris from Twin Farm Airfield was approximately 260 nautical miles and a journey time of around three hours. It was later reported that Morgan was inexperienced in instrument flying. Yet that day, the flight he undertook would be in limited visibility in dire conditions of icing at a low altitude—a lethal combination. Stratocumulus clouds would have formed over the seas, probably by convection, the air being unstable. In such a case, the liquid water content would be higher, and a severity of icing was likely to have occurred.

Flying Office Morgan, with fewer than five hundred hours flying experience and little time on instruments, would have been very lucky indeed to make this journey safely. Adding to his woes would have been the presence of two senior officers. Who knows the pressure they put on the pilot? It's interesting to note that, on the same day, thirteen Lancasters of No. 3 Group set out on a raid to Siegen but were recalled, the weather having prevented their escort fighters from taking off. It seems a sensible deduction that Morgan flying low and slow, with severe air frame icing and no visible horizon, flew into the sea.

In 1996, the United States Postal Service issued a Glenn Miller postage stamp, and his birthplace is now part of the Glenn Miller Birthplace Museum.

Glenn Miller will always be remembered for creating a unique musical sound and for this quotation: 'America means freedom, and there's no expression of freedom quite so sincere as music.'

Glenn Miller was posthumously awarded the Bronze Star. His wife Helen accepted the award in New York on 23 March 1945.

Route taken by Glenn Miller en route to Paris.

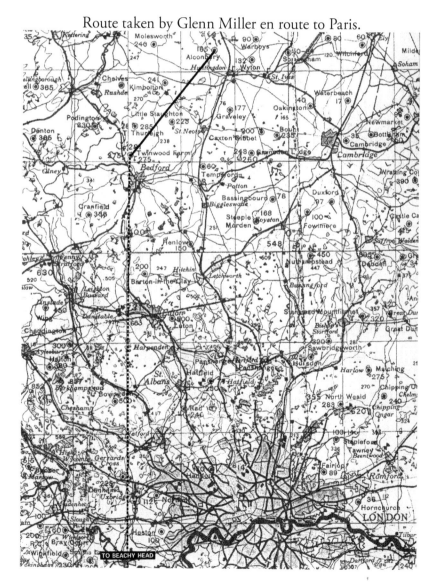

REF NO. 605

Supreme Headquarters
ALLIED EXPEDITIONARY FORCE
Public Relations Division

FOR RELEASE AT   24 December 1944
1800 HOURS

     Major Alton Glenn Miller, director of the famous United States Army Air Force band which has been playing in Paris is reported missing while on a flight from England to Paris. The plane in which he was a passenger left England on December 15 and no trace of it has been found since its take-off.

     Major Miller, one of the outstanding orchestra leaders in the United States, lived at Tenafly, New Jersey, where his wife presently resides.

     No members of Major Miller's band were with him on the missing plane.

AG 201-AGF-Miller, Alton Glenn (Off)   MAIN, APO 757
     22 December 1944

SUBJECT: Report of Missing Personnel.

TO   : Commanding General, European Theater of Operations, U. S. Army, APO 887.

  1. It is reported that on 15 December 1944 Major Alton Glenn Miller, 0-505273, AC, Army Air Force Band (Special), Headquarters Command, Supreme Headquarters AEF, departed from an airport in England enroute to Paris, France, in an Eighth Air Force Service Command airplane (C-64) piloted by a Flight Officer Morgan. There was one (1) additional passenger on this plane - a Lieutenant Colonel Baessel of the Eighth Air Force. Major Miller was taken to the air field by an officer of the Army Air Force Band who witnessed the take-off. No trace of this plane can be found and this headquarters has been advised by the Eighth Air Force Service Command that this airplane is considered missing. Likewise, Major Miller is considered to be missing.

  2. It is requested that an immediate radio casualty report be rendered to the War Department on Major Miller, and the War Department be advised that in view of the circumstances set forth in paragraph 4 below, it is considered highly desirable that this information be released to the press here at 1800A hours, 24 December, and that the War Department should confirm to your headquarters the next of kin has been notified prior to that time.

  3. The next of kin of Major Miller is Mrs. Helen D. Miller (wife), Cotswold Apartments, Byrne Lane, Tonafly, New Jersey, telephone, Englewood 3-7311.

  4. A Christmas Day broadcast has been scheduled which will be released to the United States. Major Miller was to have participated in this program. It is thought considerable publicity has been given to this broadcast in the United States.

For the Supreme Commander:

T. J. DAVIS,
Brigadier General, U.S.A.,
Adjutant General.

CONFIDENTIAL

154

CHAPTER 11
Composers of the Glory Years

The American composers I have chosen in this chapter are renowned for their music, in a body of work that transcends time and will be enjoyed by many generations in the future. Their music is rich in sophisticated melodies, harmonies, and rhythms, and their eloquent lyrics speak of love and hope and romance, which cannot be expressed in any other way. I think I can say, without fear of contradiction, that this music helped to sustain us throughout the dark days of the Second World War. They also reflect not just the era in which they were written but speak to us of something timeless, a feeling that continues to resonate in us humans as long as we remain on this planet.

The songs they have written, and I have listened to most of them, represent the golden age of the American Song Book, to which these composers have made a huge contribution. Five of them were born into Jewish families and grew up in the melting pot that was the United States of America. Here in the media explosion of the early twentieth century, they had opportunities often denied them in other businesses and professions. The invention and development of the radio, phonograph, and microphone and, later, the magnetic tape was like a blood bank to this growing and developing industry. In this market development of the popular song, a significant contribution was also made by the American black population, with their rhythm patterns of song, dance, and syncopation, which became known as jazz.

I have no favourites among the seven composers I have chosen. They all have contributed to a wonderful musical heritage that many others have enjoyed during their lifetime. I have listed them by their birthdates, starting from the oldest and moving down to the youngest. What really amazes me is the short period of time in which they were all born, with the oldest born in 1885 and the youngest, in 1905, a mere twenty years later.

I play their music as the mood dictates—from the melodic music of Jerome Kern to the simplicity of music and lyrics of Irving Berlin and the excitement and brilliance of Gershwin, from the tender music of Harry Warren and the songs of Richard Rodgers described by Cole Porter as holy to the youthfulness of Porter's own music. Finally, there's Harold Arlen, a name, like Warren, completely unknown to me in my youth. Yet his music fuels the idioms of African music with his Jewish melodies, which were his birthright.

Many books have been written about each and all of these composers, and I have attempted to include the most important features of their lives and their music in the following short accounts. It's inevitable that I have missed some out, and I apologise in advance for this.

The songs these men wrote were all American songs, which enjoyed the native characteristics of melody, harmony, rhythmic, and verbal qualities that set them apart from the composers and songs of other countries. The two texts—words and music—cannot be separated, and later in this narrative the lyricists will be discussed. These American lyricists and their texts, just like the music, are different in structure, rhetoric dictation, and rhythmic patterns from the lyrics of songs from other countries.

I have a strong belief as a pianist of long standing that the unique qualities synthesised in the American popular song arise from the genius and innovation of these few outstanding composers and lyricists. Their music has given me a delight and satisfaction that no words can effectively describe. I live in hope that the youth of today and tomorrow will avail themselves of this music and remember the genius of these people.

Jerome Kern

Jerome Kern was born in New York in June 1885, the son of a German Jewish family. As a baby he was wheeled around Jerome Park in New York, and as a consequence, his parents decided to name him Jerome. The park was owned by the Jerome family, and the daughter of that family, Jennifer Jerome, married Lord Randolph Churchill and became the mother of Winston Churchill, the future prime minister of Great Britain.

In his youth, Jerome (later known to all and sundry as Jerry), showed a great love and appetite for music and it was his mother who taught him to play the piano. Yet it was his father's view—that the young Jerome should follow him into his business—that prevailed. As a sales executive, Jerome was sent one day to purchase two pianos for his father's store from the Italian manufacturer in the Bronx. He was greeted by the head of the family who owned the piano factory. After an excellent lunch followed by copious amounts of wine, Jerome signed a purchase order for two hundred pianos, rather than the two expected and agreed on with his father. His father was certainly exasperated and decided there and then that Jerome should be released to seek his fortune in the hard-nosed music business.

Between 1903 and 1905, Kern was sent to Germany, and in Heidelberg, he continued his musical training work with private tutors. Later in London, Kern began collaborating with a certain P. G. Wodehouse, then an unknown author. At that time, Kern wrote an outstanding song, 'Mr Chamberlin', which was sung by Seymour Hicks, an outstanding actor and a long-lasting favourite of mine. It was Hicks who said in his later years that he read the obituary columns daily in *The London Times*, and if his name wasn't listed, he went to work.

In 1909, whilst introducing his music to the London stage, Kern took a boat trip on the River Thames stopping at Waltham-on-Thames. There he fell in love with the daughter of the Swan public house. They were married in St Mary's in Walton on 25 October 1910. Back in America, Kern wrote a song called 'They Didn't Believe Me' for his musical show *The Girl from Utah*. This opened in New York's Knickerbocker Theatre on 24 August 1914. The critics were unimpressed, but audiences loved it. The song spread across the world, and it was one of the first songs I heard my father sing.

In 1916, Kern wrote the music for the show *Century Girl* in conjunction with Victor Herbert. The rehearsal pianist for that show was none other than the young George Gershwin, who was in awe of working with his idol Jerome Kern and was seemingly determined to compose music similar to Kern's offerings.

In 1917, he had a great success with the musical *Oh Boy*. The book was written by Guy Bolton, and the lyrics, by P. G. Wodehouse, who also collaborated in the production of *Oh Lady, Oh Lady* in 1918. Further musical comedies were *Sally* in 1920 and *Sunny* in 1925. The best songs were 'Look for the Silver Lining' in *Sally* and 'Who' in *Sunny*.

In 1926, Kern bought the dramatic and musical rights for Edna Ferber's bestselling novel *Show Boat*. The music redefined American musical theatre by dealing with social themes like racial oppression and interracial marriage. Up to this moment, the Broadway Musicals could hardly be called serious in their content. The highlight in *Show Boat* of course was the song 'Old Man River', a majestic melody with Oscar Hammerstein II's lyrics having the eloquence of a spiritual.

The book and the lyrics were both written by Hammerstein and saw for the first time a complete integration of music and lyrics, a feat that Hammerstein repeated sixteen years later when he and Richard Rodgers produced the marvellous musical *Oklahoma*. Kern had been approached by Hammerstein to write the music for what became *Oklahoma*, but Kern could not see how an ostensible cowboy musical could be a success in the middle of a war. Lorenz Hart, long-time friend and lyricist of Rodgers shared the same conviction. Rodgers, however, saw the possibilities, and the rest, as they say, is history.

There were several movie versions of *Show Boat*, but Universal Studios 1936 version was the closest representation of the first Broadway production. The role of Joe in the film was written in for the wonderful bass baritone voice of Paul Robson singing 'Old Man River'. It was a song that thereafter he would always be associated with.

After *Show Boat*, Kern returned to writing music in the Viennese style, with Hammerstein and Otto Harbach providing the lyrics. The music, however, was as grand as ever in 'The Touch of Your Hand',

'I've Told Every Little Star', 'Lovely to Look At', and 'Smoke Gets in Your Eyes'. The latter piece came from the musical *Roberta*, released in 1935 when his Hollywood career began. A television version of *Roberta* was filmed in 1969.

In 1936, Kern wrote *Swing Time*, a marvellous score, for Fred Astaire and Ginger Rogers. The outstanding songs were 'A Fine Romance' and 'The Way You Look Tonight'. The lyrics for these songs were written by Dorothy Fields.

Kern's last Broadway musical was *Very Warm for May*, again with Hammerstein. It was to be their last show together on Broadway, and out of it came one of their greatest songs 'All the Things You Are'.

Two more songs that are fresh today as the day they were written are 'Dearly Beloved' and 'I'm Old Fashioned' and, in the film *Cover Girl* in 1944, the famous piece 'Long Ago and Far Away'. In 1941, Kern wrote 'The Last Time I Saw Paris', the only popular song Kern ever wrote. It won the Academy Award that year.

Although Kern moved his music away from the European style, he never could have been called a 'swinging' composer, in the style say, of Duke Ellington. Kern also stayed clear of symphonic music, although his background and training could well have allowed him to write such music. He knew instinctively what type of music he loved and stayed on that track. I was a young boy when I first heard and played Kern's melodies. They were unlike any other music I played, and to this day, they remain as fresh and memorable as ever.

How could anyone confuse Kern's music with any other? Just listen to 'Smoke Gets in Your Eyes' or 'The Way You Look Tonight', and you will instantly recognise the music as being Jerome Kern's. He did indeed have a kind of magic and a feeling of wonderment that has never left me. Kern wrote all his music beforehand and used a variety of lyricists to provide the words. In terms of theatre music, he provided a greater inspiration than any other composer of that genre and today is regarded as America's greatest melodist and the most significant figure in the history of the musical stage.

Kern's music became increasingly American in style, despite the fact that he revered the Viennese tradition. But now a unique style of music was bursting out of America from its multicultural roots, leaving behind the music of Friml, Herbert, and Romberg and leaving Jerome Kern in the forefront of the new music.

Kern wrote more than seven hundred published songs and also created dozens of Broadway musicals and Hollywood films, in a career that spanned more than four decades. In his music, he used such innovations as 4/4 dance rhythms, jazz progressions, and syncopation that were distinctly American.

Irving Berlin

Irving Berlin was born as Israel Beilin on 11 May 1888 in the town of Tyhem, which became the largest city east of the Ural Mountains in Siberia's Russia. The Baline family must have moved westwards into the 'Pale of Settlement', which had been created by Catherine the Great in 1791 and ended in 1917. This was a resident area set aside for Jews, from which they were forbidden to leave on penalty of death (hence the derived term 'beyond the Pale').

Pogroms, meaning the mass slaughter of Jews, were commonplace in Russia at that time. And in 1882, the Beilin family escaped one such pogrom, which saw them somehow escape the Pale, travel across Europe and then on to America.

Irving was five years of age when the Beilin family settled in Manhattan's Lower East Side. Irving's father died when Irving was three years old, so he was compelled to find work, rather than attend school. To make money, he sang on street corners and, later, was employed as a singing waiter at the Pelham Café. Having a facility for writing lyrics, his first published tune was 'Marie from Sunny Italy'. When he received the sheet music, he saw that his name had been misspelt as Irving Berlin, a name he kept to the end of his life.

His first major hit was in 1911, when he wrote both the music and lyrics for 'Alexander's Ragtime Band', which, although a catchy tune, was not syncopated and certainly not ragtime. Berlin never learned to play the piano in the conventional manner and, being self-taught, played only the black notes in the key of F-sharp. 'Alexander's Ragtime Band' sold over a million copies and made Berlin a household name across the world. The song clearly showed that Berlin had an immigrant's ear for the rhythm of his adopted country, as well as the vernacular of its streets. It was these new sounds he put in his writing and composing that became the basis of the new American popular music.

Without doubt, Berlin's gift as a lyricist and American composer is a mystery. He was unlike any of the other American greats, like Kern, Gershwin, Porter, or Rodgers. His melodies belonged to everybody, and one must ask, where did they come from? His lyrics too are simple and artless. All the other wonderful lyricists, like Lorenz Hart, Ira Gershwin, and Yip Harburg had studied poetry and light verse. Yet none of them were significantly better than Berlin, who had received the scantiest education.

He also set standards in Hollywood musicals, standards that Kern and Gershwin felt challenged to match. It seems that Berlin simply couldn't stop writing musical hits, some of which include 'How Deep is the Ocean', 'Blue Skies', 'Always', 'Say It Isn't So', 'Putting on the Ritz', 'A Pretty Girl Is Like a Melody', and 'Cheek to Cheek'. He scored dozens of musicals, including *Putting on the Ritz* in 1929, *Alexander's Ragtime Band* in 1938, *Top Hat* in 1935, *Follow the Fleet* in 1936, and *Holiday Inn* in 1942, which featured Bing Crosby singing 'White Christmas', the highest-selling piece of music in history.

As a long-term pianist, I still find myself surprised, perhaps amazed at the ability of some people to play the piano from memory without any formal training. They merely have to hear a song sung or played to repeat it almost flawlessly on the piano. Deane Kincaide, a musical arranger with the Dorsey Band, used his time to write arrangements for each of the band instruments for songs he could only hear in his head, without even a piano to help. Berlin used a transposing keyboard in order to produce songs in different keys. Later in his life, he bought a piano with a lever attached to the keyboard, which, when moved, changed the key signature to his choice. Whatever the method he used to produce music, the words and notes were clearly his own.

During both world wars, his songs became a rallying cry for Americans. In the First World War, he served in the army and wrote patriotic songs for his show, *Yip Yip Yaphank* in 1918 and *This Is the Army* in 1942. Earlier, in 1938, he wrote 'God Bless America', which remains to this day the country's unofficial national anthem.

By the 1920s, Berlin had become the most successful songwriter in America and probably the world. In 1921, he opened the Music Box Theatre, a joint venture with Joseph N. Schenk and Sam Harris.

In the 1929 Great Depression, he lost his fortune, as did many others, but nevertheless began his recovery with the show *Face the Music* in 1932.

Following the Second World War came the musical *Annie Get Your Gun* in 1946. By this time, Richard Rodgers and Oscar Hammerstein had set up their own production company. And when Dorothy Fields approached them and suggested a musical with Ethel Merman playing the part of Annie Oakley, the plot was set. Jerome Kern was approached to write the score. Sadly, however he died. And so, it was that Irving Berlin was approached to take his place. The musical opened at the Imperial Theatre in the summer of 1946, and it ran for 1,147 performances.

The show had been Berlin's first post-war Broadway show and proved a smash hit, particularly for Ethel Merman. But when MGM bought the movie rights off Berlin for US$700,000, Merman was not chosen on account of her age. Judy Garland replaced her but soon, on the verge of a breakdown, was also replaced, this time by Betty Hutton. So, what could have turned out to be a great movie turned out to be just a good one!

The songs from that film have stayed with me to the present day. They were 'They Say That Falling in Love Is Wonderful', 'Doin' What Comes Naturally', 'The Girl That I Marry', 'I've Got the Sun in the Morning (And the Moon at Night)', and 'There's No Business Like Show Business'. This last piece of music became the unofficial anthem of popular entertainment.

Call Me Madam (1952) was another of Berlin's Broadway hits faithfully transferred to the screen, this time by Twentieth Century Fox. My favourite songs from the film include 'It's a Lovely Day Today', 'Marrying for Love', and 'The Best Thing for You Would Be Me'. The most memorable song, however, was 'You're Just in Love', a wonderful duet sung by Ethel Merman and Donald O'Connor, which is one of Berlin's finest.

Irving Berlin wrote well over 3,000 songs, and his career in American and world music is clearly without precedent. George

Gershwin considered him the American 'Franz Schubert', and Jerome Kern said, 'Irving Berlin has no place in American music, he is American music.' Cole Porter put it rather aptly in one of his hit songs, 'You're the Tops' (from *Anything Goes*): 'You're the top. You're a Berlin ballad.'

For a man who could neither read nor write music, Irving Berlin can only be classed as a genius. There is no other word than can possibly describe him. Isaac Stern said on Berlin's hundredth birthday that American music was born on his piano, and it spread that popular culture throughout the world.

Berlin was born on 11 May 1888, and he died in New York on 22 September 1989. He was 101 years of age. He had arrived in New York in 1893 when he was just five years old. His long life seemed to illustrate that the American dream was achievable for anyone who had the vision and perseverance.

Cole Porter

Cole Porter was born on 9 June 1891 in Peru (pronounced [Pee/ ru]), Indiana, United States of America. His mother was the daughter of James Omar Cole, the wealthiest man in Indiana. Porter learned the violin when he was just six years old and then the piano two years later. After private school, the young rich boy entered Yale. And whilst attending, he wrote 300 songs, including the college song 'Bingo Eli Yale', which remains the university's anthem to this day.

Yale was a Welshman, and his ancestry has been traced back to his family estate at Plas Yn Lal ('Lal' translated means 'Yale'), near the village of Llandegla in Denbighshire, Wales. Elvin Yale made a substantial financial contribution in the eighteenth century to the funding of Yale College, which later became the University of Yale.

Porter was classically trained, and he and his music were drawn to the musical theatre. Although he has been described as a 'homosexual dandy', Porter joined the French Foreign Legion. His portrait is today displayed at the legion's museum in Au Bagne, a commune in a region of Southern France. He served in North Africa and was then transferred to the French officer's school at Fontainebleau and taught gunnery to his fellow Americans when they entered the war in 1917.

In 1919, he married Linda Lee Thomas, a Louisville, Kentucky-born divorcee who was eight years his senior and remained married to her until her death in 1954.

Porter, like Irving Berlin, wrote both the words and music to his songs. Indeed, there is a certain irony in the fact that Porter today is better known in some quarters for his lyrics than his music, although I do not share that view. Perhaps this is the result of his lyrics, which bordered on the vulgar, suggestive, and sophisticated all in one and were probably written for the special amusement of his own social set.

It was his show *Paris* (1928) that became the turning point in his career, with the song 'Let's Do It (Let's Fall in Love)'. Continuing the French theme, his next show was *Fifty Million Frenchmen*, with the outstanding songs 'You Do Something to Me' and 'Wake Up and Dream', following with a lovely melodious song, 'Every Time We Say Goodbye', and 'What is This Thing Called Love?' both brilliant pieces. By this time, Porter had been accepted into the upper echelons of Broadway songwriters.

In 1932, in Porter's stage show *The Gay Divorcee*, which was Fred Astaire's last performance on stage, the song that was probably Porter's best, 'Night and Day', an absolute cracker of a song, was featured. In 1934 emerged 'Anything Goes', and 'I Get A Kick Out of You', which are some of Porter's most performed songs. I like them because they lend themselves to piano improvisation. However, it was the song 'You're the Top' that became one of his greatest hit songs. The show featured Ethel Merman, who Porter loved for her huge, loud, and brassy voice.

Now I hope you will forgive me for straying from the narrative. My recently departed friend of many years, John Gilbert May, was an exceedingly clever and witty writer who loved singing with me songs from the American Song Book. He had also written short stories, broadcast by the BBC and several books. He was a thoroughbred Welshman, and when we were both young, I used to call him Metro Goldwyn May on account of his love of American films and music. In 2005, he sent me his Welsh lyrics version of 'You're the Top', a piece of music he loved singing and I enjoyed playing. To show my great respect to my friend, I include them here:

Porter's 'You're the Top' (Welsh lyrics written by John G. May in fun)

You're the top!
You're the Dragon's Fire.
You're the top!
You're a Welsh Male Choir.
You're a bardic chair;
You don't have to share at all.
You're a song by Bryn.
You're Sian Lloyd's grin.
You're a rugby ball.
You're the top.
You're the Celtic Manor.
You're the top,
Gower's panorama.
You're the top,
Snowdon summit I could plummet from non-stop,
But, baby, if I'm at the bottom, you're the top.

You're the top!
You're Caerphilly cheeses.
You're the top!
Lava bread that pleases.
You're chapel preachers, Zeta Jones's features, a Triple
Crown.
You're Tom Jones' voice, a song by Boyce, a Bassey gown.
You're the top!
You're Llandudno's Great Orme.
You're the top!
Llanfair PG's platform.
Your Brains SA I could put away till I drop,
But that leaves me at the bottom, and you're the top.

You're the top!
Cader Idris peak.
You're the top!
A gigantic leek.
You're Offa's Dyke, the miners' strike, you're Tiger Bay.
You're Penderyn malt, which has no fault.
You're St David's Day.

You're the top!
You're a daffodil.
You're the top, stirring hymns to thrill.
You're the books at Hay, where I'd spend all day at each shop.
But while I'm at the bottom, you're the top.

You're the top!
You're hand-carved love spoons.
You're the top!
Cefn Sidan sand dunes.
You're the Swansea Grand, the Cory Band, best Gwynedd slate.
You're Welsh lamb whose mint we do not stint on our dinner plate.
You're the top!
The Preseli blue stones.
You're the top!
Katherine Jenkin's high tones. etc

In 1935, Porter's musical show *Jubilee* included the longest popular song on record (108 bars). This was, of course, the beautiful 'Begin the Beguine', a piece largely ignored until it was recorded by Artie Shaw.

Another Porter hit was 'Just One of Those Things'. A year later, he wrote 'I've Got You under My Skin', a lovely piece with a beguine tempo, which appeared in the film *Born to Dance*. It was another elongated song (with 56 bars). He followed this with another hit, 'In the Still of the Night'.

In 1938, in the musical *Leave It to Me*, there were two memorable songs, 'Get Out of Town' and 'My Heart Belongs to Daddy', with its brilliant lyrics. At the end of 1941, Porter wrote a beautiful song called 'Every Time We Say Goodbye', which, when sang by Ella Fitzgerald, brings out the goosebumps. For many years, I always considered this music to be a Gershwin song. I am thus always surprised when I sit to play it and see that it was written by Porter.

In the 1970s, I lived in the small hamlet of Cowbridge in Wales. In order to keep fit, I ran around the countryside in an anti-circular pattern, which took me past a house with the name of Rundstedt. As I was a massive reader of military history, the name immediately struck a chord. It transpired that, in the closing period of the Second World War, Field Marshall Rundstedt had been delivered to a prisoner of war camp in the nearby town of Bridgend, together with a number of other high-ranking German officers. They had been sent to various villages on a weekly basis to indulge in the fine art of gardening. Sometime before the Second World War, Karl Rudolf Gert Von Rundstedt, to give him his full name, apparently made a cash offer for a German version of 'Don't Fence Me In', a piece of music written by Cole Porter. In my view, this story is as unlikely as Cole Porter having written it. In fact, Lebensraum, the German concept of territorial expansion of Germany, especially into Eastern Europe (in other words, living space) was Hitler's excuse for the war and well might, in song, be the equivalent of Porter's 'Don't Fence Me In'. In any event, it would have provided the German Army with a fine marching song.

The song had been written by Porter in 1935 for a film *Adios Argentina*, which never saw the light of day. It was ten years later that the song re-emerged from the Porter trunk for the film *Holiday Canteen*, sung by Roy Rodgers. It was a wow of a success, and it sold over a million records and copies of sheet music. It held the number one spot in the hit parade for several weeks. I remember the song well, particularly the version by Bing Crosby and the Andrew Sisters. We boys sang it with gusto on the way to football matches, and even if it were Porter's least favourite piece of music, we certainly enjoyed it.

Many years later, I discovered the story behind the title. It was 1935 when Porter, his wife, and friend Monty Woolly were on a cruise to South America and approaching the harbour of Rio de Janeiro. At dawn Porter and his wife arose early. But Monty had stayed up all night to see the sights, reinforced with a succession of whisky and sodas. As the group stood on the bow of the boat, Porter's exclamation was, 'It's delightful.' His wife followed with, 'It's delicious!' And Monty, in his happy state, cried, 'It's de-lovely!' The last exclamation gave Porter the title for a song that we all know today.

In 1937, Porter had a riding accident that shattered both his legs and damaged the nerves. Thereafter, he was in constant pain and, despite thirty-five operations, ended with one of his legs being amputated. Despite these setbacks, Porter continued to write his musicals and, in 1948, wrote his most successful show to date, *Kiss Me, Kate*. Among the most brilliant songs were 'So in Love', 'Wunderbar', 'Why Can't You Behave?' and 'Too Darn Hot'. The opening number to the show was the optimistic and lively 'Another, Openin', Another Show'.

The song 'I Love Paris' and 'C'est Magnifique' came from his show *Can-Can* in 1953, and from *Silk Stockings* in 1955 came 'All of You', with its wonderful but suggestive lyric line, 'The east, west, north, and the south of you'—dubious but quite brilliant.

In 1956, he wrote three real crackers in the musical *High Society*. They were 'You're Sensational'; 'True Love'; and, my favourite, 'I Love You, Samantha'.

Despite the pain he suffered, which monopolised his later life, Porter could have merely lived a life of luxury, which in most cases is a deterrent to any creative accomplishment. It is a credit to him as a man that he didn't. For the last thirty years or so of his life, Porter lived in New York Waldorf-Astoria Hotel in a luxurious suite.

In June 1960, Yale University conferred on him an honorary degree and shattered convention by bestowing the degree in a private ceremony in Porter's own apartment. Today his piano rests in the foyer of the Waldorf-Astoria Hotel, New York. Oh! What I would give to play Cole Porter's music on his own piano!

Cole Porter had been asked to write a cowboy song in 1934 for a Twentieth Century Studios. Sometime earlier, Porter had bought a poem from an associate for $250. Porter reworked the words and was credited with sole ownership. Porter had wanted to give Fletcher, the original author, co-authorship credit, but his publisher would not allow this. The song 'Don't Fence Me In' became a hit, as already described, and made Porter very rich. Fletcher soon took legal action and established co-ownership of the lyric (the only lyric that Porter did not write himself). Although one of the most popular songs of its time, Porter said that it was one of his least favourite compositions. Perhaps, as the money royalties rolled in, he thought better of the music.

Harry Warren

Harry Warren was born Salvatore Antonio Guaragna in Brooklyn, New York, to an impoverished family on 24 December 1893. He left school at sixteen and learned to play his father's accordion and then his snare drums. He was also self-taught on the piano. He joined the navy during World War I and became a song plugger and a rehearsal pianist.

His first published song in 1922 was 'The Rose of the Rio Grande', and in 1923, his first published collection included 'Back Home in Pasadena.'

In 1932, he signed a contract with Warner Brothers and moved to Hollywood. He partnered with Al Dubin, the lyricist, and wrote songs for the musical *42nd Street*. With Dubin, Warren would write the melody and then pass it to Dubin to write the words. The pair became known as the odd couple of the 1930s. Whereas Warren was well dressed and of medium height, Dubin was a large burly man, sloppily attired. He would often disappear for hours into a restaurant many miles from the studio. But on his return, he would have written the song lyrics on the back of a menu.

After the success of *42nd Street* in late 1932 for Warner Brothers, a sequel was made in 1933, which proved an even greater success. This was called *Gold Diggers of 1933*.

In 1934, Warren worked on an assembly line schedule. In the film *Dames*, Warren produced one of his best-loved ballads, 'I Only Have Eyes for You.' This song spent eighteen weeks on the top ten hit list. In 1935, Warren wrote twenty-seven songs for eight films. And in 1937, for the film *Melody for Two*, he composed the great 'Remember Me' and 'September in the Rain', which remained in the hit parade for eleven weeks. The Warren and Dubin team broke up in 1938, and Warren was partnered with Mack Gordon at 20th Century Fox. There, his output was no less astonishing as it had been at Warner Brothers.

Warren spent four years at the Fox Studios and won the Academy Award for Best Original Song for 'Chattanooga Choo Choo' in 1941. Another wonderful song, 'I Know Why and So Do You', appeared in the same film *Sun Valley Serenade*, and both were played by Glenn Miller and his orchestra. The hit songs continued with that lovely ballad, 'There Will Never Be Another You' out of the film *Iceland* and, in 1943, 'You'll Never Know (How Much I love You)', which became their biggest sheet music success and spent twenty-five weeks in the hit parade. In the film *Diamond Horseshoe*, Warren and Gordon then wrote two absolute cracking pieces in 'I Wish I Knew' and 'The

More I See You', both spending many weeks in the hit parade. In 1946 Warren wrote 'On the Atchison, Topeka and the Santa Fe'—this time, with lyrics by Johnny Mercer. This song spent fourteen weeks on the hit parade and won an Academy Award for the year's best song (Warren's third).

Just for You was Warren's last original musical of the 1950s. This time, the lyrics were provided by Leo Robin. However, the last song he wrote, which was nominated for an Oscar was 'That's Amore' in the film *The Caddy*. It was a song sung by Dean Martin that lost in the Oscars ratings that year, 1953, to 'Secret Love' from the film *Calamity Jane* sung by Doris Day. No popular music composer for films came close to matching Warren's durability. In fact, he wrote songs for 300 films for all the major studios in Hollywood. Yet he was a composer of songs that are better known and more famous than he was himself.

In 1941, Warren wrote 'At Last' with Mack Gordon. In the 2009 inauguration ball for Barack and Michelle Obama's first dance, Beyoncé sang that song.

During the Second World War and through the war-torn 1940s Harry Warren's songs were sung and hummed and even whistled by many people across the globe. We have much to be grateful for!

He is buried in Los Angeles, and the plaque bearing his epitaph displays the first notes of 'You'll Never Know'. His song 'I Only Have Eyes for You' has been recorded by more than a hundred artists, hence becoming a standard.

George Gershwin

George Gershwin was born in Brooklyn, New York, on 26 September 1898. He was not born into poverty as his film biography suggests, as his father was a middle-class businessman who provided sufficiently for his family.

Ira, George's brother, had been born on 6 December 1896, and both were complimentary figures in the evolution of American music, quite apart from the merits of their own separate talents. Indeed, the Gershwin legacy remains a huge force in popular music and still, after so many years, resonates with millions of people all around the world.

Their names first appeared to me on the top of a copy of sheet music I had bought in the local music shop. The name George was common and self-evident, but Ira I took to be George's sister. After all, the female name Eirwen was a common enough name in Wales, so I took the name Ira to be a shortened version of the same. In that, I was no exception, as a reporter in California unable to obtain an entrance to a Gershwin reception in Hollywood wrote in her paper rather confidently that George Gershwin and his beautiful wife, Ira, had arrived in Hollywood to make their first musical. Perhaps I could be forgiven for making my mistake, as I was only thirteen years of age at that time. However, I have often wondered what happened to that reporter.

When George was twelve years of age, a piano arrived in the Gershwin home intended for Ira. George, however, soon appropriated it for his own use, amazing his family with his ability to play simple pieces. Charles Hambitzer soon became his piano teacher and not only improved George's piano technique but also introduced him to the masters, such as Ravel, Liszt, and Debussy. He was employed at Remick's, the music publishers, and soon became their finest pianist. Max Dreyfus, the dean of American music publishers, engaged Gershwin as a staff composer simply to write his own compositions, some of which were interpolated into Broadway shows. Then Gershwin composed 'Swanee', and Al Jolson heard it. The lyrics were written by Irving Caesar, and it became a worldwide hit.

Despite this fame, George was always trying to improve his piano technique and knowledge of harmony, counterpoint, and orchestration. He developed a skill that allowed him to fashion a piece of music with an ease that would have annoyed many of his contemporaries. It was said that he could produce up to thirteen songs in a day. He once said that this allowed him to get the bad ones out of his system.

He was only seventeen years of age when his first song was published and was always inspired by the music of Jerome Kern, whom he thought a class above the music that emanated from Tin Pan Alley.

Without George's influence, it would have been unlikely that Ira would have become a lyricist, and the latter would have, rather, been happy writing poetry and short stories. It was said that Ira could struggle all night for just one word of a song. He was an absolute perfectionist, while George worked his music quickly and often and easily found his melody line. Ira accepted over his lifetime the title of a 'proud procrastinator'. He may have been slow and deliberate, but his lyrics became some of the best in the business.

In 1919, Gershwin composed his first Broadway score for *La La Lucille*, with a modest hit, 'Nobody but You,' the lyrics by Buddy De Sylva. However, it was *George White's Scandals*, which ran from 1920 to 1924, that propelled Gershwin into the front rank of composers in the 1920s, with such songs as 'Somebody Loves Me' and 'I'll Build a Stairway to Paradise.'

The latter, 1924, was a momentous year for Gershwin. Paul Whiteman had invited Gershwin to write a composition for piano and orchestra based on a jazz theme, for his 'Experiment in Modern Music'. This concert was to be held at the Aeolian Hall in New York on 24 February 1924, with Gershwin the composer of the music and also the soloist. It had been completed in a mere three weeks, despite his other commitments. To assist in the preparation, Gershwin wrote the music, and Freddie Grofe completed the orchestration.

The drunken whoop of an introduction with its seventeen-note clarinet glissando electrified the audience, who could hardly believe what they were hearing. The premier was a tremendous success. While some of the critics were less impressed, the public enthusiastically responded—and led Whiteman to hold two more concerts in the next two months, the first again at the Aeolian Hall and then at the larger Carnegie Hall.

The title *Rhapsody in Blue* was borrowed by Ira from a Whistler painting.

Another major event occurred in 1924, when Ira became his brother's lyricist. Previously, he had written lyrics for other composers but, not wanting to ride on George's fame, had used the pen name Arthur Francis. He used the wit and literacy of light verse, combined with American colloquial speech, which created a new era of song writing—one that only Johnny Mercer and Lorenz Hart would equal. Gershwin had found instant celebrity and fame with *Rhapsody in Blue*, which had landed him on the cover of *Time* magazine at the young age of twenty-six. Now, George and Ira were commissioned to write

Lady Be Good, their first Broadway score together. The songs—like 'Oh, Lady be Good' and 'Fascinating Rhythm'—with their rhythmic virtuosity, made the production a success.

The song 'Embraceable You' was written in 1928 and included in the Broadway Musical *Girl Crazy* in 1930. The song is unusual in that some of the rhythms are four syllables—for example, embraceable you, irreplaceable you and tipsy in me, gypsy in me. George would be asked by his father to play the song, as it was one of his favourites. When the line 'Come to Papa, Come to Papa do' was sung, his father would thump his chest, look around the room, and beam!

In the mid, 1920s, Gershwin went to Paris, ostensibly to study musical composition with Nadia Boulanger and Maurice Ravel. He was rejected by both in their belief that classical study would ruin his jazz-influenced style. Ravel wrote him a letter that said, 'Why become a second-rate Ravel when you're already a first-rate Gershwin.'

While in Paris, Gershwin began the composition titled 'An American in Paris'. He completed the piece on return to the States, and it was performed for the first time at Carnegie Hall on 13 December 1928, to mixed reviews. Soon, however, it became a part of the standard classical repertoire in America and Europe.

In 1931, the Gershwins produced their longest-running musical *Of Thee I Sing*. It became the first musical to be awarded the Pulitzer Prize.

Looking back over the late twenties and early thirties, the Gershwin brothers wrote songs for successful shows, such as *Funny Face* in 1927, *Strike up the Band* in 1930, and also *Girl Crazy* the same year. The musical riches that emerged from their shows included, 'Swonderful', 'I Got Rhythm', 'Embraceable You', and 'But Not for Me!'

Gershwin, having read the novel *Porgy* by DuBose Heyward, decided that he could convert it into the first American folk opera. Gershwin and Heyward met briefly in collaboration over the next two years and created a masterpiece of music. Heyward was an interesting person, having an ancestor who had been a signatory of the American Constitution. He began writing poetry and eventually founded the Poetry Society of South Carolina.

Gershwin now moved to Folly Beach, South Carolina, where he was able to steep himself in the culture of the large population of the primitive Gullah blacks. He attended their church services, where there were no musical instruments, merely a complicated rhythmic pattern beaten out using their feet and hands. When he began creating the music, he was amazed in wonder at the music he had created. It was quite unlike anything he had written before.

Gershwin was greatly moved, during the period of the creation of *Porgy and Bess*, to be invited to attend a party at the White House by President Franklin D. Roosevelt on 29 December 1934.

Porgy and Bess opened at the Alvin Theatre New York on 10 October 1935 to great acclaim by the audience but somewhat less praise by the critics, and it was the reviews that made the difference at the box office. Neither Gershwin nor Heyward would live to see the eventual recognition of *Porgy and Bess* worldwide. However, Gershwin had been certain that he had created a work of lasting value, and he had!

I was in Gothenburg, Sweden, during the last months of 1998 and found, to my pleasure, that the hundredth anniversary of George Gershwin's birth was being celebrated both in a concert at the university and the next evening at the Gothenburg Concert Hall. The university students sang and danced many of the Gershwin tunes I knew and loved, and on the following night, the Gothenburg Symphony Orchestra and chorus put on a fabulous show of *Porgy and Bess*. I had purchased the score of the music in the 1950s and had found some difficulty in replicating some of the more complicated rhythms. His genius, of course, was in blending vastly different musical styles in almost revolutionary ways. Without doubt, that concert that evening helped me to understand some of the rhythmic sequences that had troubled me for a considerable time. I have much to thank Gothenburg for!

After *Porgy and Bess*, Gershwin wrote music exclusively for films and took residence in Hollywood. In 1937 came *Damsel in Distress* and *Shall We Dance*, both with Fred Astaire, and in 1938 came *The Goldwyn Follies*. The songs included 'Let's Call the Whole Thing Off', 'They Can't Take That Away from Me', 'Love Walked In', and 'Love Is Here to Stay'.

It was while he was working on *The Goldwyn Follies* that Gershwin suffered a physical collapse. 'Love Is Here to Stay' proved to be the last song that Gershwin wrote. He was then at the heights of his musical power. He died at the Cedars of Lebanon Hospital following a brain operation to remove a cystic tumour. His death was recorded as 11 July 1937.

Gershwin's screen biography *Rhapsody in Blue* was made and distributed in 1945, with Robert Alda playing the composer. In 1946, with the musical help of Kay Swift, a number of Gershwin's unpublished songs were fashioned into a fine film score for *The Shocking Miss Pilgrim*, including a beautiful song called 'For You, For Me, For Evermore'. Three years later *An American in Paris* was filmed starring Gene Kelly, with many Gershwin favourites. The background music to the film gave the film its name. The film received the Academy Award for Best Picture of 1951, a fitting climax to the life of an extraordinary man.

Today, George Gershwin's music is played, sung, and recorded perhaps even more than when he was alive. What a tribute to an American great!

Richard Rodgers

Richard Rodgers was born into a prosperous German Jewish family at Hammels station, near Averne, Long Island, New York on 28 June 1902. His father was a prominent doctor, and his mother, a competent pianist. Rodgers started learning the piano at the age of six from his mother, Marnie Rodgers. From a young age Rodgers showed a great love and aptitude for music, matched only by his enthusiasm for the musical theatre stimulated by the music of Jerome Kern.

He wrote songs for a number of amateur productions, but his life changed when he was introduced to Lorenz Hart, who was then twenty-three years of age and had dropped out of Columbia College. Hart made the most of having descended from the great German poet Heinrich Heine. Rodgers and Hart became friends, and in Rodgers words, 'It was a case of love at first sight.' He added, 'In one afternoon I acquired a career, a partner, a best friend, and a source of permanent irritation.'

When *Garrick Gaieties* opened in May 1925, one of their songs, 'Manhattan', quickly became a hit and set them on a pathway to fame and fortune. Their 1920 shows produced such standards as 'Mountain Greenery'; 'Blue Room'; and, a great favourite of mine, 'My Heart Stood Still' from the musical show *A Connecticut Yankee* (3 November 1927), bringing to this Mark Twain story some of the best lines and infectious melodies the theatre had ever witnessed. This was followed, in *Spring is Here* on 11 March 1929 by one of Rodgers and Hart's classics, 'With a Song in My Heart'. I have always rated these two songs among the best ever written. The song 'Blue Moon' followed, a song that never reached the Hollywood screen. Yet it proved to be a bestseller, and the sheet music sale was the greatest number yet achieved, with over a million copies sold.

In 1935, the pair returned to Broadway and created a number of musical shows—*Jumbo* in 1935; *Slaughter on 10th Avenue*, 1936; *Boys from Syracuse* in 1938; *Pal Joey*, 1940; and their last original work *By Jupiter* in 1942. Some of their songs from these shows were 'There's a Small Hotel', 'Where and When', 'The Lady Is a Tramp', 'Falling in Love with Love', 'Bewitched, Bothered and Bewildered', 'My Funny Valentine', and 'Have You Met Miss Jones' from *I'd Rather Be Lucky* (the partners' first venture into potential satire).

Lorenz Hart had always been a difficult person to work with. At just under five feet tall, he had an almost freakish way with words and was housed in an equally freakish body. Combined, the two men made up a kind of genius with their contradictory chemistry. Rodgers was a romantic, a workaholic, and a serial womaniser, whilst Hart, in his alcoholism and drugs, was ashamed of his own body and seemed to invite death.

Oscar Hammerstein II had sought Jerome Kern to bring to life as a musical a play by Lynn Riggs called *Green Grow the Lilacs*. Kern had turned down the offer. When he offered it to Rodgers and Hart, Rodgers saw the possibilities, but Hart, now in the depths of dependency and ill health, did not. Rodgers now required a new collaborator and approached Ira Gershwin unsuccessfully.

When Hart died on 22 November 1943, Rodgers took up with Hammerstein. Indeed, their stage musical based on Lynn Riggs's book became a red letter for the American theatre, renamed *Oklahoma*. It proved to be a phenomenal success and achieved the longest run of any musical in Broadway history up to that time—2,248 performances with a profit of $7 million and selling over a million albums. I remember it for just one song, 'People Will Say We're in Love', the last great hit song of 1944. It seems strange on reflection that although *Oklahoma* proved a great success on both sides of the Atlantic neither partner had never visited the state.

Oklahoma was succeeded on 19 April 1945 by *Carousel*, probably the best of their musicals, with songs that will live long in the memory. Among these were 'If I Loved You'; 'June is Bustin' Out All Over'; and, the anthem of Liverpool City Football Club, 'You'll Never Walk Alone'.

South Pacific followed on 7 April 1949, based on James A. Michener's Pulitzer Prize-winning book. Its run of 1,925 performances made a profit of $9 million and stage history. The music of that show resonates with me, as I was in the Royal Air Force at the time, undergoing my national service and in love with a girl back home. How can one forget 'Some Enchanted Evening' and 'I'm in Love with a Wonderful Guy!'?

Their next musical opened on Broadway on 29 March 1951. It was called *The King and I*, featuring Yule Brynner as the king and Gertrude Lawrence as the Welsh schoolmistress. Again, the music was superb, with songs like 'Getting to Know You', 'Shall We Dance?' and 'Hello, Young Lovers'.

The historic partnership of Rodgers and Hammerstein ended with the show *The Sound of Music*. Sadly, Hammerstein died of cancer at his home in Doylestown, Pennsylvania, on 23 August 1960. The songs from their last show, however, are remembered to this day—'My Favourite Things'; 'Do Re Mi'; and, probably the best of them, 'Climb Every Mountain'.

The music of Richard Rogers continues to resonate and flourish. His music first appeared on Broadway in 1920, and his last contribution in 1979 nearly sixty years later. He was among the most eloquent, influential, longest living, and hardest working composers ever to make his mark on American musicals. He was aided and abetted by two of the most skilful of lyricists in Lorenz Hart and Oscar Hammerstein II.

Rodgers was undoubtedly a musical prodigy. He grew up watching the shows on Broadway and, from the age of seventeen, began writing them. Composing animated him much like George Gershwin.

Sadly, however, he couldn't survive the change in American culture and consciousness brought about largely by the Vietnam War. For him, gone were the goodness, innocence, romantic love and optimism that had become his and his lyricists' stock in trade. Now, disenchantment, mockery, and minimalism had become the norm.

In 1999, Rogers and Hart were each commemorated on US postage stamps. Rodgers composed more than nine hundred songs and forty-three musical shows. He undoubtedly was one of the most significant composers of the twentieth century. His life's work made a tremendous impact on popular music. Richard Rodgers, born 28 June 1902, died 30 December 1979.

Harold Arlen

Harold Arlen was born Hyman Arluck in Buffalo, New York, on 15 February 1905 but Americanised his name to Harold Arlen in 1928.

It was by accident that Arlen was chosen to write the music for the film in 1939 named *The Wizard of Oz*. The first choice of composer was Jerome Kern, who, at that time, suffered a heart attack and a mild stroke. As a result, Arlen composed 'Somewhere Over the Rainbow', with the lyrics brilliantly written by Edward Yipsel (Yip) Harburg. The song in the film was sung by Judy Garland and, from that moment onwards, would always be associated with her. It made her a star, and yet that too was an accident, simply because the deal made by MGM with Twentieth Century Fox was to borrow Shirley Temple for the part. That deal however, fell through. The song, as we all know now, won the Academy Award.

As a young boy, Arlen sang in the choir of the synagogue with his father, who was the cantor. It was his mother, however, who encouraged him to play the piano, and he soon learned to improvise as a pianist. He soon revealed a fascination for popular music and also learned to arrange music and sing. Perhaps more than any white composer, Arlen had an early fascination with jazz, which was clearly reflected in his music. He went further than his friend George Gershwin in using black African influences combined with white styles, with a touch of Semitism.

Arlen dropped out of school at fifteen and played the piano in Buffalo cafés with his own trio known as The Snappy Trio, growing into a quintet The Southbound Shufflers. Later, he became a singer, pianist, and arranger in an eleven-man ensemble called the Buffalodians. His first songs were 'My Gal, My Pal' and 'I Never Knew What Love Could Do!' Neither of these songs was published.

When Harry Warren heard Arlen playing, he introduced him to a young lyricist, Ted Koehler, and Warren asked him to write lyrics for an Arlen song he had heard. The song was 'Get Happy'. When George Gershwin heard it, he went backstage to congratulate Arlen on having written an outstanding piece.

Arlen soon found employment, this time with Remicks Publishing House in Tin Pan Alley. But in 1930, he was hired to write songs for the Cotton Club in New York's Harlem. It was here he established his reputation as a fine composer, with Ted Koehler providing the lyrics. Some of these songs were 'I've Got the World on a String'; 'As long as I Live'; and, the most important, 'Stormy Weather' in 1933.

Following the Wall Street Crash in 1929, many composers moved across the country to Hollywood. It was here that Arlen wrote probably his most memorable piece 'Blues in the Night', partnered with Johnny Mercer, who wrote the lyrics for Warner Brothers. They even named the film after the song, which was nominated for the Academy Award, losing out to Kern's 'The Last Time I Saw Paris' from the film *Lady Be Good*.

His other good songs in that period were 'Let's Fall in Love', with lyrics by Koehler; 'Ac-cent-Tchu-Ate the Positive', with lyrics by Mercer; and 'This Time the Dreams on Me', also with Mercer. In 1947, the song 'Hooray for Love' became popular after it featured in the film *Casbah*. Of those songs, the two that stood out for me were 'Let's Fall in Love' and 'Ac-cent-Tchu-Ate the Positive'. The latter song became very popular in this country during the war, and I can still remember most of the lyrics today.

In 1946, Arlen wrote the music for the film *St. Louis Woman*, and the outstanding song was 'Come Rain or Come Shine.' Arlen wrote scores for other pictures, notably *A Star is Born*, with a song 'The Man that Got Away'. The film starred Judy Garland, and the lyrics this time were written by Ira Gershwin in 1955. The song was nominated for an Academy Award that year.

Like Harry Warren, Harold Arlen was completely unknown to me as a young man; hence, so was most of his music. The films he scored were for the most part never identified with Arlen, and it was this lack of publicity that promoted my ignorance of him. Nevertheless, I can appreciate his wonderful talents, and I really enjoy playing and, at the same time, trying to sing the lyrics.

Harold Arlen, without doubt, had an astonishing melodic gift, coupled with a harmonic accompaniment that was unusually sophisticated. It appeared that his musical inspiration derived from his melody line and his superb ability as an improviser. It is for these incredible gifts that Arlen figures in any context as an American great.

Following the early death of his wife, Arlen remained largely inactive for the last two decades of his life and died at home in New York City on 23 April 1986 at the age of eighty-one.

CHAPTER 12
Lyricists of the Glory Years

When I was a young boy in Junior School, I was considered reasonably bright by my teachers, but rather wild. It was, therefore, somewhat surprising that I developed a keen liking for poetry, even to the point of writing it. My first real attempt was about the Charge of the Light Brigade during the Battle of Balaclava on 25 October 1854, during the Crimean War with the Russians.

Maybe I had already read the poem 'The Charge of the Light Brigade' by Alfred Lord Tennyson, but I had no recollection of so doing. I duly presented my poem rather proudly to my class and teacher, Miss Pomroy, only to have my ears boxed for cheating (which I hadn't).

My next poetic effort was about my dog Mac, a mongrel my father had brought home as a stray. For the next twelve years or so, Mac and I developed a wonderful relationship, perhaps only possible between a young boy and his dog. The poem called 'Mac' extolled his many virtues and our mutual love and affection. We would walk the mountain together every evening after school, and when we rested, Mac would place his paws across my chest, and I would read him the poem. He loved it, and his tail would wag furiously.

My third attempt occurred when my younger sister, Gillian, asked me to write a short complimentary poem in her large diary. She was so unimpressed by my effort she stopped talking to me for a week.

When I went to the grammar school, my English teacher was a Miss Caldicott. She was a gem. She encouraged me to read books and write poetry. She introduced me to the poem 'The Highwayman' by Alfred Noyes, and I well remember the line 'over the cobbles he clattered and clashed in the dark inn yard', and so I learned the meaning of the word 'alliteration'.

Rodgers and Hart

The first piece of sheet music where the lyrics both astonished and delighted me was in the song 'There's a Small Hotel'. I was a mere thirteen years of age when I first played that song, and the words so excited me that I was drawn to the names at the top of the first page. Lorenz Hart had written the words, and the music had been composed by Richard Rodgers. It was the neatness of Hart's words and how he repeated them that attracted my attention:

> There's a small hotel
> With a wishing well
> I wish that we were there together
> And through the window
> You can see a distant steeple
> Not a sign of people
> Who wants people?

The song was used in the 1936 musical show *On Your Toes* and also in the film version of the Broadway Musical *Pal Joey* in 1957, with its fine Frank Sinatra-Nelson Riddle collaboration.

Lorenz Hart was one of the most famous lyricists of the golden age of the American Song Book through the 1920s and the 1930s. Hart has often chaffed at the banality of Tin Pan Alley song lyrics, but his own lyrics were acclaimed as the cleverest and helped transform the musical comedy from a 'revue' to a more dramatic form of musical. It was Hart's lyrics, both intricate and sophisticated, exemplified in 'Manhattan' in 1925, that began a new era in popular song. Perhaps it was then for the first time that people began listening to the lyrics of the song.

Hart undoubtedly had a remarkable talent for polysyllabic and triple rhymes. He also had a remarkable ability to find rhymes in the most unlikely places and, more often than not, blended the rhythms into natural speech—quite remarkable really! He used Rodgers musical pauses and repetitions to form what I considered a very witty lyric, for example:

> We'll bathe at Brighton
> The fish you'll frighten
> When you're in
> And then
> Your bathing suit so thin
> Then
> Will make the shellfish grin
> Fin to fin

And another example:

> The city's clamour can never spoil
> The dreams of a boy and goil.

Without doubt, Hart had a technical sophistication that few, if any, other lyricists could match.

Many of Hart's lyrics, like the verses of 'Manhattan', were both playful and funny. Yet his lyrics suggested a vulnerability beneath the surface that led to a wonderful poignancy.

Lorenz Hart was born in Harlem, New York, the elder of two sons, to Jewish immigrant parents. Through his mother, he was a great grandnephew of the German poet Heinrich Heine. He attended Columbia University and, in 1919, through a friend, met Richard Rodgers. The two joined forces to write songs for amateur and student productions. However, in professional terms, they were largely unsuccessful. But just at the point of quitting the musical business, they came up with 'Manhattan', which proved an immense hit across the globe. Their future was thus ensured.

When the pair was in a Paris taxi in the company of two ladies, they just missed a collision with a truck that suddenly emerged from a side road. It was a near-run thing, and one of the ladies exclaimed, 'My heart stood still!' Rodgers wrote the words on a piece of paper and later composed a piece of music that Hart completed with the most sublime lyrics. The verse of the song, or release as some people call it, read as follows:

> Though not a single word was spoken
> I could tell you know
> That unfelt clash of hands
> Told me so well, you knew

'My Heart Stood Still' was written in 1927. Two years later, the duo wrote 'With a Song in My Heart', with more astonishing and beautiful lyrics:

> Just a song at the start
> But it soon is a hymn to your grace
> When the music swells, I'm touching your hand
> It tells me that you're standing near

Such lyrics were undoubtedly the outpourings of a hopeless romantic. Hart stood just under five feet tall and really saw himself as an undesirable freak. He was also a closet homosexual who had to pursue a secretive and tormented lifestyle, often reflected in his lyrics. He stood as a lonely figure, and many of his lyrics conveyed a heart-stopping sadness that reflected his conviction that he was too physically unattractive to be loveable. Yet he made an immeasurable contribution to the American popular song that will stay with us for many years to come.

My favourite songs of Rodgers and Hart are 'Blue Moon', 'I Didn't Know What Time It Was', 'Isn't It Romantic?' 'It's Easy to Remember', 'Manhattan', 'My Heart Stood Still', 'The Lady is a Tramp', 'There's a Small Hotel', 'This Can't be Love', 'Thou Swell', 'Where or When', and 'With a Song in my Heart'.

Altogether, the pair wrote more than five hundred songs and twenty-eight stage musicals. In 1940, MGM made a film of Hart's life called *Words and Music*. Mickey Rooney played the part of Lorenz Hart, but the details of his life's work were heavily edited and romanticised. Lorenz Hart died in New York City of pneumonia from exposure on 22 November 1943 after drinking heavily. He is buried in Mount Zion Cemetery, Queens County, New York.

Rodgers and Hammerstein

When Oscar Hammerstein was turned down by Jerome Kern to make his musical *Oklahoma*, he turned to Rodgers and Hart. While Rodgers could visualise the possibilities of the show, Hart regarded it much as Kern had, a cowboy musical in the middle of a world war. Additionally, Hart was physically unwell and had neither the strength nor the appetite for the project. As a result, Rodgers took Oscar Hammerstein as his new lyricists, which gave rise to the birth of a new age in musical theatre. Hammerstein and Rodgers appeared to be perfectly suited in a way that Rodgers and Hart had never been.

However, I'm not alone in recognising the special quality that Hart brought to his songs like, 'My Heart Stood Still', 'With a Song in my Heart', and 'Thou Swell'. They have a freshness and inventiveness that appears absent from Hammerstein's lyrics, which tended only to speak of uncomplicated optimism for the future. Certainly, I enjoy playing Hart's music far more than Hammerstein's, although the latter is pleasing on the ear and, in the light of history, more popular.

Certainly, as a young boy the music from *Oklahoma* would always remain in my heart as familiar and universally loved. Its melodies almost became meshed into our collective memories, and just about everybody I knew seemed to know some of the songs. Hammerstein on one occasion said, 'Do you realise how difficult it was for me to follow behind Larry Hart! I was such a great admirer of Larry's that I never thought I could do it.' Well he did do it and did it well, bringing a great deal of happiness and hope to a war-torn world.

Hammerstein was undoubtedly a great lyricist, but his greatest contribution was as a librettist, probably the best that Broadway has ever known. In terms of lyrics and unlike Hart, it could take Hammerstein a week to write a single lyric—a couple hundred words at most. When he wrote 'Oh What a Beautiful Morning', the original line was, 'The corn is as high as a cow pony's eye.' Hammerstein, not satisfied, walked over to a neighbour's cornfield and saw that the corn was much higher than he had thought. Hence the lyric became 'as high as an elephant's eye'.

Rodgers and Hammerstein revived the tradition of the libretto and the lyrics coming first, as had been the practice of Gilbert and

Sullivan, European operetta, and opera. In America however, the process had been reversed, as with Rodgers and Hart and many others who wrote their songs to satisfy the 'dance craze' of the early twentieth century. It seemed simpler to let the composer go first.

With Rodgers and Hammerstein, the words did not *always* come first. In fact, in some of their songs—like 'People will Say We're in Love', 'If I Loved You', and 'Getting to Know You'—Rodgers's music came first. However, when the lyric was completed first, Hammerstein would send it by messenger to Rodgers (no email then), who would set the lyrics to music, usually in a matter of minutes, much to Hammerstein's feigned annoyance. Without doubt, Rodgers had the precise mind of a musical genius, while his partner's habits were completely methodical.

Hammerstein often wrote about sudden love as he himself had experienced it. Clearly his most famous song on the subject was 'One Enchanted Evening'. In early 1927, he crossed the Atlantic in the liner *Berengaria*. During the captain's cocktail party on the first night at sea, he spotted his wife to be, Dorothy, across a crowded room. Such things, it appears, do indeed happen!

Back in the sixties, I took a job teaching educationally subnormal children (1960s terminology). The inadequacies of such children have been well documented, but nevertheless, they still retained the ability to surprise. I was simply amazed at their knowledge of the countryside. They taught me the names of trees, birds, and insects. They could identify various speckled and coloured eggs, and they also had an easy knowledge of flowers and their Latin names, which left me floundering and humble. This leads me to one of Hammerstein's quotes, 'If you became a teacher, by your pupils you'll be taught.' I was never able to meet with the man, but what he said enthralled and enamoured me to his beliefs.

In the musical *South Pacific*, the love stories were shaped by questions of race. Yet all the initial prejudices between the various characters faded in the face of something that's really important in life. That thing is love. The *King and I* is about cultural differences. The Welsh governess and the Siamese children know nothing of each other at the beginning. Yet again, all race and colour faded in their getting to know and love each other.

Hammerstein didn't appear to belong to any church, but he had a strong faith in humankind and in the belief that, in the long run, good would always triumph over evil. In politics he said that, at times, he tried to vote Republican but always wound up voting Democrat.

Broadway in the forties and fifties loomed far larger in the American cultural landscape than it does today. Television was in its infancy, and the musical was still a major source of popular music. As a colossus in the musical business, Hammerstein wore his authority lightly. He and Rodgers were household names across the world, though. When their musical *Cinderella* for television was broadcast on 31 March 1957, 107 million tuned in, almost two-thirds of the entire US population.

Many people forget that it was in the musical *Show Boat* where Hammerstein made his name, and it was that show that was the precursor to *Oklahoma* sixteen years later. *Show Boat* is the oldest Broadway musical that can still hold its own today, with its extraordinary score by Jerome Kern (his greatest) illuminating an America of the past, while it was *Oklahoma* that represented the present. Today *Oklahoma* remains as enduring as ever, with more than a thousand productions per year worldwide.

Rodgers and Hammerstein produced *The Sound of Music*, which, for more than a decade, held the box office record for a movie musical, even surpassing that of *Gone with the Wind*. Hammerstein wrote his last lyrics, 'Edelweiss', for *The Sound of Music*. In the film, it was sung by Captain von Trapp as a small form of defiance in the face of the German invasion of his country, Austria.

It was appropriate that this was the captain's goodbye to his fellow countrymen before fleeing to Switzerland. It would also be the last goodbye for Oscar Hammerstein, who would pass away some nine months after the making of *The Sound of Music*. By the time of his death, the American musical had become one of the major art forms.

Oscar Hammerstein was born 12 July 1895 in New York City and died 23 August 1960. He was sixty-five years old.

Ira Gershwin

Ira Gershwin was born Israel Gershowitz on 6 December 1896. He was the elder of the two brothers who were as totally unlike each other as any two brothers could be, but they formed a wonderful complementary team that brought pleasure to millions. Together, George and Ira created one of the most prolific songwriting partnerships in American popular song history.

It was in my early teenage years when I first purchased the sheet music for a Gershwin song. There on the top of the lead page were the famous names George and Ira Gershwin. I presumed then that Ira was the name of his sister, as I knew two local girls called Eirwen, not too dissimilar to Ira. I was not the only one, it appears, to hold this misconception. When the Gershwin brothers arrived in California for the first time, George Gershwin was acclaimed as the greatest American composer of all time. He had bridged the huge chasm between popular music and classical music with this *Rhapsody in Blue* in 1927 and *'American in Paris'* in 1928. A young female journalist in a local Californian newspaper had been denied a ticket to the Gershwin reception. She wrote a piece about it anyway, extolling the great George Gershwin and his beautiful wife, Ira. It was surely good for a laugh, although I doubt whether her editor saw it that way.

Ira was extremely proud of his brother George and had no desire to ride on his famous 'coattails'. So early in his career as a lyricist, he adopted the pseudonym of Arthur Francis, a combination of the first names of his younger brother and his sister Frances. Sometime later when George was asked, 'Who's this Arthur Francis?' he answered, 'Oh, he's a clever college kid with lots of talent.' However, Ira dropped that name in 1924 because, by this time, everybody knew him as a Gershwin.

When a piano was hoisted up into the Gershwin apartment, primarily for Ira to learn and play, it was George who joyfully took up the keyboard duties. It was Ira who was the studious one, with a great love of books. He was fortunate, in that he attended a school where he would study the classical poets. It was there that he befriended a classmate E.Y. (Yip) Harburg, who was also to become a famous lyricist. Harburg would, in fact, write the lyrics for the number one hit song of the twentieth century, 'Over the Rainbow'.

Playful rhyming verse became an essential part of Ira's lyrics, which were soon seen to match the high energy of his brother's music, who played with great skill and a pure enjoyment. Ira, being a New Yorker, soon learned to combine the colloquial everyday talk with his acquired literary light verse and wit. In this, he was eventually to match the other two golden pair of lyricists, Lorenz Hart and Johnny Mercer. Harburg and Ira were not alone in their admiration for society verse. Dorothy Field (the only standout woman in the field of music at that time) and Howard Dietz were among others who followed this trend.

Ira was very well pleased when some of his poetic lyrics were selected in the *Oxford Anthology of Light Verse*. Colloquial idioms could be lifted into the most romantic lyric and were dubbed by H. L. Mencken as a new American language. Lyricists like Ira took the new American vernacular, incorporated it into the new songs, and made the phrases sing.

Tin Pan Alley had established a rigid formula for popular songs. Indeed, most of the songs of the golden age are built on a thirty-two-bar line structured into four eight-bar units—in other words in an AABA format. In words, this sequence required between fifty and seventy-five words. It was on such parameters that love, in love, out of love, unrequited love, lost love, and so on were set.

In a P.S. to the forward of his book *Lyrics on Several Occasions*, Ira wrote, 'Since most of the lyrics in this lodgement were arrived at by fitting words musically to music already composed, any resemblance to actual poetry, living or dead, is highly improbable.' Ira always insisted that the music pre-recorded the lyrics. He also said that it took many years of experience to know that a note could take, or not take, a certain syllable. He also held that many a poetic line could be unsingable—in other words, some lines looked good when written but were awkward when sung. A song is the joint art of words and music, two arts under emotional pressure coalescing into a third. The relation and balance of the two arts is a problem that has to be resolved anew in every song that is composed.

Ira had heard a comedian in *Lady Be Good* clipping his syllables from certain song words. Consequently, he decided to use this device in the song "Swonderful'. Ira's most ambitious work was to write the lyrics to *Porgy and Bess*, an American folk opera, as George had described it. In this, he was assisted by the author of the novel *Porgy*, Dubose Heyward and Dubose's wife, Dorothy Heyward. The team spent most of 1934 and 1935 working on *Porgy and Bess*, with Ira acting as editor of the libretto and also writing some of the lyrics. *Porgy and Bess* was produced on Broadway in October 1935 but did not win the immediate enthusiastic or critical acclaim that was hoped for. Later, of course, it became a great commercial success.

Porgy and Bess was a collaborative effort by everybody. George felt that there was a spot where the music could have been lighter. Accordingly, George went to the piano and began to improvise. After a short interval a more cheerful melody emerged. At that moment, Ira said, a title popped into his mind, and 'I Got Plenty O'Nuthin' emerged. Ira said that he shook his head in wonder at the reservoir of musical inventiveness, resourcefulness, and craftsmanship that George could resort to; and regardless of what procedure was used, the reluctant music sang so naturally that no listener could tell which had come first, the words or the music. After George's death, which affected Ira very badly, he eventually worked as a lyricist with Jerome Kern, Harry Warren, and Harold Arlen. His lyric writing remained undiminished in in quality as expressed in songs like 'Long Ago and Far Away' and 'The Man that Got Away'.

Ira Gershwin was born in New York City on 6 December 1896 and died on 17 August 1983 in Beverley Hills, California, USA, at age eight-six. Some of my favourite Gershwin songs are 'Love Walked In', 'Love is Here to Stay', 'They Can't Take That Away From Me', 'Embraceable You', 'But Not for Me', 'Oh, Lady be Good!' 'Someone to Watch Over Me', 'For You, For Me, For Evermore', and 'Embraceable You'.

Johnny Mercer

Johnny Mercer was born in Savannah, Georgia, on 18 November 1909, and he became a leading American lyricist and songwriter. He became a co-founder of Capital Records and wrote lyrics for over 1,500 songs. As a young boy, he had an early exposure to African

American playmates and servants, and it was this exposure that was unique among the white lyricists of his generation. Music fascinated him as a child, but he had no formal musical training other than to sing in the choir as a six-year-old. His talent was in creating the words and singing but not in playing music. He was a great lover of jazz and blues and, at the age of nineteen in 1928, moved to New York, when a chance meeting with Hoagy Carmichael resulted in his first big cheque for the song 'Lazy Bones'. His future as a lyricist and songwriter became assured when he moved to Hollywood in 1935. His first big song that became a hit was 'I'm An Old Cowhand' from the Rio Grande. For this song, he wrote both the music and the lyrics, and it was sung by Bing Crosby in the film *Rhythm on the Range* in 1936. A year later he wrote 'Goody Goody', and later he produced a standard with 'Too Marvellous for Words', this time for Warner Brothers and followed up with 'Hooray for Hollywood'.

By 1938, he had revived his singing career when he sang a duet with Bing Crosby titled 'Mr Crosby and Mr Mercer', which became a hit in 1938. In that year, he also partnered Harry Warren and wrote the lyrics for 'Jeepers Creepers' recorded by Louis Armstrong, followed by 'You Must Have Been a Beautiful Baby'. In 1939, a fateful year, he wrote 'Day In, Day Out' and, one of my favourites, 'Fools Rush In'.

Like Irving Berlin, Mercer was a close follower of the changing language and cultural fashion. And by 1941, he began to display a sophisticated wit and the Southern vernacular that characterised his best songs. This was all too evident in 'Blues in the Night', where he wrote the lyrics to Harold Arlen's music. This piece was a jazz and blues influenced composition, which allowed Mercer to use his sophisticated idiomatic lyrics to the best effect. Who else could have written the line 'My mama done tol' me'? In 1942, he wrote 'That Old Black Magic', which became a best-selling single when Sinatra sang it, backed by the Axel Stordahl orchestra. In 1944, he wrote the song 'Dream', in which he inserted the line about smoke rings rising in the air, as a perfect song to close out the Chesterfield Tobacco programme. When the Pied Pipers recorded it, everybody seemed to want to record it, and it sold over a million copies of sheet music. In 1946, he wrote the lyrics for the song 'On the Atchison Topeka and the Santa Fe', a composition by Harry Warren. It proved a big hit for Judy Garland in the 'Harvey Girls', winning Mercer the first of his four Academy Awards for the best song. He then wrote the lyrics for 'Laura', 'Satin Doll', and 'Midnight Sun', after they had all become hits.

In 1961, Mercer wrote the lyrics for the song 'Moon River' for Audrey Hepburn to sing in the film *Breakfast at Tiffany's* and the 'Days of Wine and Roses'. Both pieces were composed by Henry Mancini. Both pieces earned Mercer his third and fourth Oscars for best song.

Johnny Mercer was honoured in 1980 with his portrait on a stamp issued by the United States Postal Service, and in 2009, Clint Eastwood produced a documentary film on Mercer's life called 'The Dream's on Me. 'In that year a Bronze Statue of Mercer was unveiled in Ellis Square, Savannah, Georgia, his home town and birthplace. Philip Furia wrote a biography of Johnny Mercer in 2004 named *Skylark*. In the course of his career, Mercer wrote more than a thousand songs. Of these, eighteen would be nominated for the Academy Award for Best Song, and four would win the Oscar. Johnny Mercer was born 18 November 1909 and died 25 June 1976, at sixty-six years old.

Johnny Burke

My first encounter with Johnny Burke's lyrics occurred when I was a young boy and I heard the song 'My Very Good Friend the Milkman'. It was a novelty song that stretched back to the 1920s, and it was sung by Fats Waller. It was one of a number of songs by Harold Spina with Burke as the lyricist. He then went on to write the lyrics for 'Pennies from Heaven' and 'One Two, Button your Shoe' with Arthur Johnston. In 1935, he joined up in Paramount Pictures with James V Monaco, and the pair was assigned to write songs for Bing Crosby films. They wrote the music for the first road picture—'Road to Singapore' in 1942 and scored a hit with 'Too Romantic'.

When Monaco left Paramount, Burke teamed up with James Van Heusen, and their climb to the top began. Together they scored the songs for twenty Bing Crosby films including, *Road to Morocco* (1942), *Road to Utopia* (1945), *Road to Rio* (1947), and *Road to Bali* (1952). In fact, the two partners spent almost their entire time at Paramount writing for Bing Crosby. In fact, Crosby claimed he owed much of his success to a lyricist he dubbed 'the Poet'. Crosby said, 'One of the best things that ever happened to me was a 145-pound leprechaun named Johnny Burke.' Burke wrote the lyrics for 'Penny from Heaven', setting the standard for a string of hits. Burke said he learned to write lyrics for Bing Crosby by paying attention to his conversational style and taking phrases directly from his speech patterns.

Burke wrote or collaborated on more than four hundred songs and had the distinction of being the only lyricist to have had five out of the top ten songs on 'Your Hit Parade' at the same time. His songs included the music in forty-two films and also the scores four for Broadway musicals. For the Crosby film, *Going My Way*, Burke and Heusen wrote 'Swinging on a Star', which won the Oscar for the best film of 1944. The story behind the song is interesting. Jimmy Van Heusen was at the Crosby's home one evening when one of Crosby's children confessed that he didn't want to go to school the next day. Crosby rebuked the child and said, 'If you don't want to go to school, you might grow up to be a mule.' Heusen took the idea to his partner, and Burke turned out the suitable lyric that won the Oscar. In 2002, the song was placed in the Grammy Hall of Fame.

In 1995, Johnny Burke's life was depicted in a Broadway Musical Revue, *Swinging on a Star*, showcasing the works of the prolific Hollywood lyricist. The material in the show highlighted Burke's craftsmanship as a witty wordsmith and a consummate romanticist. Burke, like Harry Warren, was not a household name, as they both concentrated their musical efforts on Hollywood films and not Broadway.

Johnny Burke was born in Antioch, California, on 3 October 1908 and died in New York City on 25 February 1964 at fifty-five years old.

Some of Johnny Burke's songs include (with Harry Spina) 'My Very Good Friend the Milkman', (with Arthur Johnston) 'Pennies from Heaven' and 'One, Two, Button Your Shoe', and (with James Monaco 'Only Forever', 'An Apple for the Teacher' and 'Scatterbrain'. With Jimmy Van Heusen, he wrote 'Polka Dots and Moonbeams', 'Imagination', 'Moonlight Becomes You', 'Going My Way', 'Sunday, Monday or Always', 'Swinging on a Star', 'It Could Happen to You', 'Suddenly It's Spring', 'But Beautiful', 'We're Off on the Road to Morocco', and 'It's Always You'.

P. G. Wodehouse

I was surprised, indeed amazed, to find some years ago that P. G. Wodehouse had been a librettist and lyricist between 1905 and 1935 for musical shows on both sides of the Atlantic. Today, of course, he is largely remembered as the champion of chinless wonders and powerful bossy grande dames. His theatre life as a librettist and lyricist spanned three decades, and in early 1906, Seymour Hicks (actor-manager) invited him to become the resident lyricist at the Aldwych Theatre in London. Hicks had already recruited the young Jerome Kern to write the music. And the song Wodehouse and Kern wrote, 'Mr Joseph Chamberlain', for a time became the most popular song in London.

A milestone in Wodehouse's life occurred when Kern introduced him to Guy Bolton, who became his closest friend and collaborator. Wodehouse preferred the music to be written first, fitting the words to the melodies. Their shows made them enormous fortunes and played an important part in the development of the American musical. Richard Rodgers, the composer, wrote 'Before Lorenz Hart, only PG Wodehouse had made any real assault on the intelligence of the song listening public.' Certainly, Lorenz Hart thought very highly of P. G. Wodehouse as a writer.

It was Bolton, Wodehouse, and Kern who moved American musicals away from the traditional European operettas to more intimate productions, using witty integrated books and lyrics. The following was written about the trio:

> This is the Trio of Musical Fame
> Bolton and Wodehouse and Kern
> Better than Anyone Else You Can Name
> Bolton and Wodehouse and Kern.

In the 1920s, Wodehouse collaborated on nine musical comedy productions on Broadway and in the West End of London. In 1927, Wodehouse provided the lyrics to the song 'Bill', which appeared in the 1927 musical classic *Showboat*, composed by Jerome Kern. The song was only once heard in the show, but it became one of the musical's most famous. The show was made into a film in 1936. The film, not in Technicolor, was remade in 1951, with Ava Gardner playing a lead role. For the singing, however, her voice was dubbed by Annette Warren. Shirley Bassey also recorded the song in 1959.

In 1934, Wodehouse worked with Bolton on the book for Cole Porter's 'Anything Goes' but not on the lyrics (Porter always wrote his own lyrics).

Wodehouse started writing his books in 1908. At a young age, he had consoled himself by reading books, which delivered him into an imaginary world of his own. His word play was a key element in Wodehouse's writing, using puns, metaphors, and mixed metaphors. He saw life as a comic vision, and he became a humourist of the first order, using a kind of comic poetry.

I first read a Wodehouse novel while in my early teens. The book, entitled *Mike* enthralled me, as the story revolved around the sport of cricket in an English public school setting. At that time in my life, cricket was an all-consuming passion of mine, and that one story led me to read almost the complete works of P. G. Wodehouse. When the character Mike was sent by his father to another school, owing to his lack of academic progress, the reader is introduced to another huge character in the form of Psmith. The *P* in Psmith is silent, as in psychic (or, as one of my more lyrical friends remarked, as silent as the *P* in bath). Psmith it appears had been 'sent down' (fired) from Eton. He was an immaculately dressed tall figure who wore a monocle. He had an elaborate manner of speech and was characterised by his navigation through wild adventures whilst always appearing completely unruffled. Psmith is featured in four P. G. Wodehouse novels. *Mike* was published in 1909, and the three other Psmith novels were *Psmith in the City* (1910); *Psmith Journalist* (1915), set in New York; and, finally, *Leave it to Psmith* (1923), set in Blandings Castle.

To avoid double taxation in America and Britain, Wodehouse went to live in France with his wife. He turned down the offer of an aircraft seat to fly out when the Germans invaded, as it meant leaving his wife behind. He was subsequently imprisoned and was freed when Paris was liberated in 1945. Wodehouse loved America and went to live there in 1947 and never left. His British knighthood had been denied him by the British establishment for some years. The reason, it appears, is that it gave currency to the Bertie Wooster image of the upper-class English character. However, in 1974, Harold Wilson, the British prime minster, secured a knighthood for Wodehouse, and it was announced in 1975 at the same time as Charlie Chaplin received his.

His novels have been described by some to be as living in a fairyland.

Wodehouse clearly understood human nature very well, and he had the ability to create humorous situations that stood firm against the forces that control our lives.

P. G. Wodehouse, born 15 October 1881, in the United Kingdom, died 14 February 1975 in Southampton, New York, at ninety-four years old.

Alexander Dubin

Alexander Dubin, commonly known as Al Dubin, came from a Russian Jewish family who emigrated to the United States when he was in his early years and he grew up in Philadelphia. Dubin sent his first set of lyrics to M. Witmark & Sons, a leading music publishing company at the time. In 1909 he began working for them on a full-time basis as a lyricist. When the film-maker Warner Bros. purchased the song-publishing companies Witmark, Remick, and Harms, they inherited Dubin's services.

In 1929, Dubin wrote the lyrics for 'Tiptoe Through the Tulips', a piece as singable today as it ever was. The music was composed by Joe Burke.

In 1932, Dubin teamed up with Harry Warren on the film musical *42ⁿᵈ Street* and provided four songs for the film, including 'You're Getting to be a Habit with Me', 'Young and Healthy', and 'Shuffle off to Buffalo'. Between 1932 and 1939, they wrote sixty songs for Warner Bros. musicals, including *Gold Diggers of 1933*; *Footlight Parade*, starring James Cagney; *Roman Scandals*, starring Eddie Cantor, and *42ⁿᵈ Street*, set in New York during the Depression. The song 'Lullaby of Brooklyn' was written for *Gold Diggers of 1933* and won the Academy Award for Best Original Song of 1936. 'I Only Have Eyes for You' was another hit by the duo. In 1935, the pair wrote twenty-seven songs for eight films, and in 1936, they wrote a further fifteen songs for six more films.

The Warner Bros. work ethic was now taking its toll on Dubin and Warren. As a result Harry Warren begged the company to hire Richard Whiting and Johnny Mercer to take the pressure off Dubin and himself. In their typical penny-pinching manner, the company only hired Johnny Mercer and, consequently, an uneasy three-way partnership persisted for two more films in 1938.

Dubin began to have treatment for his eating, drinking, and drug use, which, combined with his marital problems, caused him to miss time at work. When he returned, he wrote three more musicals with Warren, and one of their songs, 'September in the Rain', became a jazz standard.

Unable to cope with his reduced status at work, he asked the company to release him from his contract, which was granted. For the next few years, he worked infrequently, and his last contract was on the Broadway show *Laffing Room Only* with composer Burton Lane.

He collapsed on a New York street on 8 February 1945 and died in hospital three days later from pneumonia, coupled with drug overdose. He was fifty-three years of age.

Dorothy Fields

Dorothy Fields was the only woman songwriter who achieved equality with all the male composers and lyricists mentioned in this book. She was held in high esteem by her colleagues as a superb librettist and lyricist, who wrote 400 songs for Broadway and Hollywood during her fifty-year span in the music business. She was born in Allenhurst, New Jersey, on 15 July 1905 and grew up in New York City. Her father, Lew Fields, was a Jewish immigrant from Poland who became one of the most influential theatre producers in history. Between 1904 and 1911, he produced forty Broadway shows.

Dorothy Fields, without doubt, was the only woman major league song writer of the golden age of American popular song and stood virtually alone among men for fifty years or so. Her career really began when she teamed up with Jimmy McHugh. The pair produced hits that are still ingrained in Western culture today, among them 'On the Sunny Side of the Street', 'I Can't Give You Anything but Love', and 'Exactly Like You'.

In the 1930s, Fields began working with Jerome Kern after RKO Pictures assigned her to write the lyrics for the film version of *Roberta*. Kern's sixteen-bar melody became 'Lovely to Look At'. Field's lyric is restrained and contemplative with a matter-of-fact wisdom that looks with hope into the future as expressed in the final chorus:

> Lovely, never, never, change
> Keep that breathless charm
> Wont you please arrange it?
> 'Cause I love you
> Just the way you look tonight

However, I have always considered the song's introduction or the release as the most beautiful part of the song:

> Someday, when I'm awfully low
> When the world is cold
> I will feel a glow just thinking of you
> And the way you look tonight

Clearly, the Kern-Fields song has a real depth to it, and Fields said, 'When Kern played that melody to me, I had to leave the room because I started to cry.' In my humble opinion, such lyrics could only have been written by a woman. There is a certain magic to them, a certain nostalgia that I cannot recall in any other song. It was no surprise therefore that the Motion Picture Academy presented Kern and Dorothy Fields with the Oscar for the best song of 1936. It was the first time in history that the Academy had honoured a female songwriter. She was a mere thirty-year-old woman at that time—a quite remarkable feat!

The film, *Swing Time* would be the pinnacle of Field's work and would mark the pinnacle of her Hollywood experience. The film featured Fred Astaire and Ginger Rogers. It used to be said that he gave her class, and she gave the partnership the sex. Perhaps the same could be said for the partnership of Kern and Fields. In 1938, Irene Dunne the actor introduced the Kern-Field's standard 'You Couldn't Be Cuter' in the film *The Joy of Living*. However, that song somehow seems to have passed me by.

In 1938, Fields returned to New York to work as a librettist with her old friend Arthur Schwartz on a Broadway show *Stars in My Eyes*.

She also got married for the second time and produced two children, a boy, David, born in 1940 and a girl, Eliza, born in 1944.

In 1946, Fields approached Oscar Hammerstein with her idea for a new musical based on the life of the famous 'sharpshooter', Annie Oakley. Hammerstein and his partner, the composer Rogers, agreed to produce the show, and Kern and Fields were signed to write the songs. Sadly, Kern died before he could begin work on the project, and Irving Berlin was hired, albeit reluctantly, to replace him. It must have been disappointing, doubly so for Fields, as she greatly admired Kern; now, she would also be deprived of the opportunity to write the lyrics for the show. However, Fields and her brother wrote the book *Annie Get Your Gun*', and Berlin, as he always did, wrote the lyrics and the music for the new musical. The show was a huge success and ran for 147 performances.

When Fields returned to New York from Hollywood, she concentrated on writing the librettos for a number of musicals together with her brother, Herb Fields. They wrote three shows for Cole Porter, who had little interest in the books for the shows and generally just handed over a batch of songs and said, 'Here, fit them in!' Like Irving Berlin, he too always wrote his own lyrics. The shows were *Let's Face It* (1941), *Something for the Boys* (1943), and *Mexican Hayride* in 1944.

Unlike George and Ira Gershwin or Rodgers and Hart/Hammerstein, Fields collaborated with a number of companies but never received a permanent identification as one half of a specific team, which has no doubt resulted in her name not being well known today. The same applied to the composer Arthur Schwartz, who worked with a number of collaborators. In 1951, Fields and Schwartz worked together on *A Tree Grows in Brooklyn*. What she and Schwartz wrote was her best musical score to date.

In the 1960s, the fallout years began. Fields's friend Arthur Schwartz was now living in London, and Broadway was now largely in the hands of a new generation. Also, 1960 brought the death of her old friend and the emotional links to Jerome Kern, when Oscar Hammerstein succumbed to cancer just a few months after the opening of *The Sound of Music*, marking the termination of the Rodgers and Hammerstein era.

After all this professional inactivity, Fields met Cy Coleman at a party, and he asked her if she'd ever consider writing some songs with him. He was surprised that here was this legendary figure waiting about to be asked. As a result, she wrote the songs 'Big Spender' and 'If My Friend Could See Me Now'. Both the songs are vintage slangy, street-smart 1920s Dorothy Fields, with the maturity and expertise that only a Broadway veteran could write. In Coleman, Fields had found a perfect collaborator. His energy and her experience lent their work a mastery and polish. The continuing success of *Sweet Charity*, with its musical hit songs, 'Big Spender' and 'If My Friends Could See Me Now', were promptly recorded by Barbara Streisand and consequently entered the national consciousness through radio and television. For Fields, it meant her rejuvenation and personal and financial success at the age of sixty.

Dorothy Fields wrote more than four hundred songs and worked on fifteen stage musicals and twenty-five films. She was a fine pianist and a lifelong lover of classical music. She died of a heart attack on 28 March 1974 after a career that spanned nearly fifty years.

Thirty-five years after her death, Barak Obama, in his inauguration speech as the United States forty-fourth president on 20 January 2009, gave a nod to the lyrics of Dorothy Fields. 'Starting today we must pick ourselves up, dust ourselves off, and begin the work of remaking America,' he said. This alluded to Fields's lyrics in the song 'Pick Yourself Up' from the 1936 film *Swing Time*, 'Pick yourself up, dust yourself off, and start all over again.'

Mack Gordon

Mack Gordon was born in Warsaw on the 21 June 1904. His birth name was Morris Gittler, and he was born to a Jewish family who went to the United States when Gordon was a young boy. He was a singer, a comedian, and a skilled writer. He teamed up with Harry Revel for much of the 1930s. He wrote 'Time on My Hands' for Vincent Youmans, which was used in the Marilyn Miller biopic *Look for the Silver Lining* in 1949, when it was sung by Gordon MacRae and June

Haver. It was also used in the 1953 film *So This is Love* and sung by Kathryn Grayson.

Some of Gordon's top songs include 'Did You Ever See a Dream Walking?' 'Goodnight My Love', 'I Had the Craziest Dream', 'Mam'selle', '(I've Got a Girl in) Kalamazoo', 'It Happened in Sun Valley', 'Serenade in Blue', 'May I', and 'At Last'.

In addition, the following songs were all nominees for Academy Awards: 'Down Argentina Way' in 1940, 'Chattanooga Choo Choo' in 1941, '(I've Got a Girl in) Kalamazoo' in 1942, 'I'm Making Believe' in 1944, 'I Can't Begin to Tell You' in 1946, 'You Do' in 1947, and 'Wilhelmina' in 1950.

Mack Gordon wrote the lyrics for 'You Never Know', with composer Harry Warren, which won the Academy Award for Best Original Song in 1943. It was used in the film *Hello Frisco, Hello*.

Gordon also wrote the lyrics for 'The More I See You' and 'There Will Never Be Another You'—two favourites of mine and both written by Harry Warren. Both songs are outstanding, and I can never fathom why they weren't at least nominated for Oscars.

Mack Gordon was a Jewish American lyricist who wrote music for Broadway but mostly for Hollywood films. He was nominated for the Best Original Song Oscar nine times in eleven years, some of which are listed above. He was listed by many to be the top Hollywood lyricist in the 1930s and 1940s. His contribution amounted to 120, which appeared in fifty films.

Mack Gordon was born in Warsaw on the 21 June 1904 and died in New York City on 1 March 1959, at fifty-four years old.

CHAPTER 13
Light Music Marvels

I grew up with an understanding that there were three classifications of music—classical, light music, and popular music. In this section of my narrative, I have tried to remain faithful to these divisions. However, it is a difficult task, as some classical music, for example, Rachmaninoff, could be described as popular; some popular music could be described as classical, take Gershwin; and some light music can be called either.

My subject here is light music and is perhaps so called because it appeals to a wide audience, is easy to listen to, and is of a shorter duration (thirty minutes or so) than operatic or symphonic type music.

It was Jacques Offenbach, a German Jew living in Paris, who began a one-act comic musical format, which he called operettas. Soon he further developed this concept as a full- length musical. Viennese audiences loved the works of Offenbach, and soon the native composers followed this style. Perhaps the most memorable of these was Johann Strauss (the composer of 'The Blue Danube'), who soon became known as 'the Waltz King'. He wrote 'Die Fledermaus' ('The Bat') in 1874, which became his most frequently performed work. In 1905, Vienna gave the world another huge hit with 'Die Lustige Witwe' ('The Merry Widow') by Franz Lehar, but more of that later.

In the United States, the Boston Pops Orchestra emerged in the nineteenth century, founded in 1885. This orchestra played lighter and shorter pieces by Leroy Anderson, Ferde Grofé, and George Gershwin.

Today, light music is now understood to be somewhere between the two other genres, although it is generally understood that the boundaries are often blurred. British light music can be said to have started in the bandstands of our seaside resorts. It was also played in the best hotels, and its golden age stretched roughly between the years 1925 and 1955. Much of this type of music often appeared as theme music on the BBC—for example, Arthur Wood's 'Barwick Green', the theme music for the radio programme *The Archers* seems to have been on our radios forever.

Indeed, light music found a ready outlet on the BBC. When the light programme was formed at the end of World War II, light music took off, particularly through programmes like *Music While You Work* and *Friday Night is Music Night*. The latter programme still adorns the airways and can be found today on Radio 4. Today Sidney Torch is accepted as the creator of *Friday Night is Music Night*, which began its long journey on the radio in 1953. Torch was famed as an orchestral conductor, and it was he who conducted the BBC concert orchestra for almost all the Friday night shows until he retired in 1972. Vilém Tauský was another conductor closely associated with the programme. He arrived in Britain in 1939, and he deplored the British snobbishness in categorising music and musicians. In his home country, now known as the Czech Republic, people considered music to be just that— music! His book, *Vilém Tauský Tells His Story* was published in 1979 and is well worth a read.

Robert Farnon was yet another name closely associated with *Friday Night is Music Night*. Farnon was a Canadian-born composer, arranger, and conductor. As a child, he learned both the piano and the violin and later learned to play the cornet and drums. He joined the Percy Faith orchestra and played the first trumpet. He came to Britain during the war as the conductor of the Allied Expeditionary Forces Canadian Band. Among the songs he wrote was 'Jumping Bean', which became the most used signature tune ever, as well as 'Peanut Polka' and the 'Westminster Waltz'. He also wrote fire scores for films, including *Spring in Park Lane* and *King's Rhapsody*. He won the Ivor

Novello awards for the 'Westminster Waltz' in 1956, 'On the Seashore' in 1960, and 'Colditz March' in 1973. *Friday Night is Music Night* in 1987 was entirely devoted to his music and was retitled as *Friday Night is Farnon Night*.

In all, Farnon wrote music for more than forty films, including *Captain Horatio Hornblower* in 1951, *Road to Hong Kong* in 1962, and *Bear Island* in 1979. He also wrote the theme music for television series such as *Colditz* (1972–1974), *Secret Army* (1977–1979), and *A Man Called Intrepid* (1979).

Robert Farnon was born in July 1917 and died in April 2005 at eighty-seven years of age.

Edward White was a composer of a number of novelty tunes, the most famous being 'The Runaway Rocking Horse' (1946) and 'Puffin Billy' (1952). He also wrote 'Paris Interlude' in 1952. 'The Runaway Rocking Horse became the signature tune for *Children's Favourites*, a programme that ran from 1952 to 1966. It was also the theme music for the programme *Captain Kangaroo*, which appeared on the CBS television network. Finally, it was the theme tune for the American TV series *Life with Buster Keaton*.

Edward White was born in 1910 and died in 1994, at eighty-three years old.

Finally, a frequently heard name on BBC radio in those long-ago-but-not-forgotten days was Haydn Wood, who was a prolific composer of light orchestral pieces. However, he was best known for a piece he had dedicated to his wife, which became famous and known as 'Roses of Picardy'.

Haydn Wood was born in March 1882 and died in March 1959.

As a young boy, I used to listen to and be enthralled by *Dick Barton – Special Agent*, which could be heard nightly during the week between 6.45 to 7 p.m. on BBC Radio. The theme music, which started and ended the programme, was Charles Williams's 'Devils Galop' (spelt correctly, as it derives from a lively country dance introduced in 1820 to Parisian Society that found great popularity in Vienna, Berlin, and London). Then there was the 'Coronation Scot' musical piece, which preceded the BBC's radio programme *Paul Temple*, a series of detective stories that occupied the airways from 1938 to 1968. This piece of music was composed by Vivien Ellis, from an idea he took from his often-taken train journey between his hometown of Taunton in Somerset and Paddington station in London. In fact, the train, the 'Coronation Scot', ran from London Euston station to Glasgow Central in Scotland. Vivien Ellis, in the period 1925 to 1958, provided the music for a number of successful West End shows in London. He wrote some superb pieces of music, including 'Spread a Little Happiness', 'This is my Lovely Day', 'Ma Belle Marguerite', and 'Over My Shoulder', which proved a huge success.

Vivien Ellis was born in October 1903 and died in June 1996, at ninety-five years old.

Nothing pleased me more than an orchestra playing beautiful melodic light music. Some years ago, I attended a concert at Millfield School in Somerset to listen to the Central Band of the Royal Air Force. As an encore, the band played two pieces by Jerome Kern, which sent my senses reeling. When I arrived back home, I went straight to the piano and played Kern's music. It was a most wonderful evening of superb music played by a brilliant band, enhanced by the presence of Johnny Johnson, the last British survivor of the Dambusters and the attack on the German dams in 1943. He was the celebrated guest, and in his honour, the band played the 'Dambusters March' by Eric Coates. Coates was a leading composer in Britain from the 1930s to the 1950s. He had trained at the Royal Academy of Music in London and, from 1910, played the viola in the Queen's Hall Orchestra under the baton of Sir Henry Wood. However, after leaving this post, he devoted all his time to writing music, for which we all should be grateful.

It was customary when I was young that, on Saturdays when we had returned from seeing my grandparents in Maerdy, my father would light the lounge fire. This was my father's job, and I would sit near the fireplace to watch the comedy show that was about to begin. The paper would catch fire, as would some of the sticks; then after a short time, the fire would show signs of faltering. It was now the fun began. My father would then hold a double side of newspaper across the fireplace to draw up the flames. A few minutes later, the fire would begin to roar and then the newspaper my father was holding would burst into flames. My mother would scream, and my father would curse and then beat out the flames, until a certain normality to the proceedings returned. After one such effort and sometimes two at him trying to set himself alight, we would all take our seats at the table, and tea would be served. We would then make ourselves comfortable and tune the radio to listen to *In Town Tonight*. The programme would be introduced by 'Knightsbridge March', written by Eric Coates.

Some years later when I was at my boarding school, the delightful matron would allow me to use her radio. It was then that I became familiar with the theme music for the programme *Desert Island Discs* and its introductory music called 'By the Sleepy Lagoon', also composed by Eric Coates.

My musical memories of the late 1930s and war years seemed dominated by the organ recitals on the radio. Before the onset of war, the name I remembered as the sublime organist was Reginald Foort, who played the original BBC theatre organ. His reign began in May 1923, with a long series of cinema organ recitals, which continued until July 1939 when he had completed his 1,000[th] performance.

In 1938, Sandy MacPherson became the staff organist of the BBC when he succeeded Foort. Sandy played throughout the war years and was very popular with the public. He maintained his position until July 1952. Sandy MacPherson was a soft-spoken Canadian, and he completed over 6,000 organ recitals for the BBC before his retirement. His organ-playing series included programmes like *Sandy's Half Hour* and *At Your Request*.

The third organist I remember was Reginald Dixon, who was the resident organist at the Tower Ballroom Blackpool. For almost fifty years, his signature tune was 'I Do Like to Be Beside the Seaside'. My school days began at nine o'clock each weekday morning, so I missed the following programme, which was *Housewives' Choice*. Reginald Dixon, apart from his Blackpool duties, also presented this programme on a number of occasions.

I was about thirteen years old when Mr James, my piano teacher, made the suggestion that I should learn to play the pipe organ in the local chapel where he was an esteemed deacon. I found myself sitting in front of this monster with its numerous keyboards, knobs, and levers. Looking back over the years, I see now that the organ controls were not dissimilar to an aircraft cockpit. Furthermore, instead of a pair of rudder bars of an aircraft, the organ had beneath your feet another wooden keyboard, which, of course, you learned to play with your feet. Moving your feet across the keyboard was much like copying the style of Fred Astaire in his dance routines. Sitting there as a young boy, I felt like I was facing and controlling a large beast. In some ways, playing this large organ was not dissimilar to flying an aircraft. Indeed, the coordination of hands, eyes, and feet is necessary in both, and the two require and similar skills (organists, please note!). I have no recollection of how many lessons I had on the organ. But I did succeed in mastering it in some small way and certainly enjoyed the experience, and it was fun!

The Scottish Variety Orchestra had been established by the BBC in 1940 and was based at the BBC studios in Glasgow. On one particular evening, I heard the orchestra playing a piece called 'Serenata' that stunned my senses. From that moment in time, it has remained one of my favourite pieces of music. I later learned that it had been composed by an American, Leroy Anderson.

It was about ten years later that I heard another startling piece of his. It was in 1952, and I was in the Royal air force hospital of Little Rissington in the Cotswolds, Gloucestershire, home of the Central Flying School of the RAF. I was suffering from a grumbling appendix when I heard for the first time 'Blue Tango'. Anderson had written the music in 1951 and recorded it the same year. It was an extremely popular piece of music and sold over a million records worldwide. It became the first instrumental music to reach number one in the hit parade. He also wrote 'Belle of the Ball' and 'Plink Plonk Plunk', among others during the year.

Anderson never wrote popular music. Nor did he set out to do so. Yet his compositions achieved huge popularity. He himself described his music as 'concert music with a popular quality.' Perhaps that is as close as anyone can get to defining it. Although I have included his music in the light category, it nevertheless almost defies classification. It inhabits the 'no man's land' between all three genres. It certainly reflects Anderson's sense of humour and sensibilities that appear way ahead of their time, ignoring the normal standard pattern and constructs. Anderson's music is wonderfully tuneful, melodic, and extremely enjoyable. As an example of his craft, he wrote 'Jazz

Pizzicato' in 1939, when nobody had ever written a pizzicato for jazz before. Teachers can teach techniques, but it is left to the pupil to develop his or her own style. Anderson certainly developed his own unique style of composition.

Anderson's music was first recognised when 'Jazz Pizzicato' was played by the Boston Pops Orchestra, conducted by Arthur Fiedler. At the end of World War II, Anderson became the Pops' full-time arranger when he was still a captain in the United States Army Intelligence Service. At that time, all musical compositions stayed under three minutes duration, the then recording limit.

Fiedler now began expanding the programme for the Pops. Before Fiedler's arrival on the scene little twentieth century music had been played. Rossini overtures were quite common, but Fiedler now expanded the repertoire by playing music by, for example, Gershwin, mostly his popular tunes, show tunes first heard in Broadway musical shows. Whatever the critics thought of Fiedler's music, the orchestra was stretched as never before with a far greater variety than hitherto. Anderson's music certainly played an essential part in this developing process. As a result, everybody now found something to enjoy. Anderson had never been interested in writing popular songs or classical music. Rather, he had drifted into his own brand of light composition. People say that only good music survives the test of time. And for me, I am quite sure that Anderson's music clearly satisfies that criteria.

Anderson was born in Massachusetts in June 1908. His parents were both Swedish by birth and it was his mother who introduced him to the piano. Following grammar school, he studied music at Harvard University, and he became director and arranger of the university band between 1931 and 1935. He learned to play the double bass, the tuba, and the accordion, as well as the piano. He spoke five languages and, during the Second World War, became a translator and interpreter. He had been assigned to military intelligence as an officer in Washington DC. There, he was chief of the Scandinavian desk. He chose a musical career after the war, rather than a future in the US Army—a decision that many of us worldwide who enjoy his music are very grateful for. His many other musical pieces include 'Fiddle-Faddle', 'Forgotten

Dreams', 'Jazz Legato', 'Sandpaper Ballet', 'Serenata', 'Sleigh Ride', 'The Waltzing Cat', 'Summer Skies' and 'The Syncopated Clock'.

Just a mile or so from the city centre of Cardiff, the capital of Wales, traffic lights indicate the crossing of two major roads. A few yards from the lights on Cowbridge Road East, there stands a house with a single blue plaque attached. It reads as follows: 'Ivor Novello was born here 15th January 1893. He was a composer, dramatist, actor, and man of the theatre.' Apart from his writing and acting skills, Novella was the most successful composer of British musicals in the twentieth century. He was born David Ivor Davies, and he adopted his mother's maiden name Novello as his professional surname. Although he trained on the piano and organ, his successes were as a songwriter. At the beginning of the First World War in 1914, he wrote the musical piece 'Keep the Home Fire Burning', which proved to be an immense hit that brought him fame and fortune.

In 1916, he joined the Royal Naval Air Service as a trainee pilot but clearly lacked the aptitude and, consequently, spent the rest of the war in a desk job at the Air Ministry.

With his classic good looks, Novello became a film idol and played the romantic lead in *The Call of the Blood* in 1920. In 1923, he went to America and made his first American film for D. W. Griffiths (a fellow Welshman) in *The White Rose*.

By 1935, he turned once more to music and wrote 'Glamorous Nights', the first of a series of popular musicals with Christopher Hassell writing the lyrics. This show became his greatest triumph, and the music was superb. Novello was a sentimentalist but had a natural Welsh wit. He was anything but highbrow, although some of his songs, like 'Shine Through my Dreams' and 'Fold Your Wings', bordered on operatic music. However, he loved the operetta style of the melodies of Franz Lehar.

His show, *Crest of the Wave*, opened in September 1937 with its most popular piece, 'Rose of England', a rather pompous and wildly patriotic piece of music. His next musical was called *The Dancing Years*, which ran throughout the war from 1939 to 1945. This was followed by *Perchance to Dream*, with its leading number 'We'll Gather Lilacs', which became a great hit. I have always regarded the piece as one of the most beautiful romantic tunes ever written by anyone. It remains as fresh today as it did when it was first sung in the West End all those years ago. Novello wrote both the musicals and the words for the piece.

Despite its undoubted success, it was the musical *Oklahoma* by Rodgers and Hammerstein that now represented the future of musical theatre. Undoubtedly, however, Novello continued much in the same vein. And his next musical, *King's Rhapsody*, written in 1955 was, perhaps, his finest work of art, with the musical score of 'Some Day My Heart Will Awake'. The British public loved it, and it proved a certain antidote to the six years of war.

Novello's musicals were *Glamorous Nights* (2 May 1935), also made into a film in 1937; *Careless Rapture* (11 September 1936); *Crest of the Wave* (1 September 1937); *Dancing Years* (23 March 1939), made into a film in 1950; *Arc de Triomphe* (9 November 1943); *Perchance to Dream* (21 April 1945); *King's Rhapsody* (15 September 1949), made into a film in 1955; and *Gay's the Word* (16 February 1951).

Ivor Novello died on 6 March 1951, at just fifty-eight years old. In terms of musicals, he ranks as good as any and better than most.

In 1955, in Novello's memory, the International Songwriting Awards was established. They are presented each year by the British Academy of Songwriters, Composers, and Authors. In 1952, a bronze bust of Novello was unveiled in Drury Lane. And in 1972, to mark the anniversary of his death, a memorial stone was unveiled in St Paul's Cathedral, London. In 2005, the Strand Theatre, also in London was renamed the Novello Theatre, with a plaque set in his honour at the theatre entrance. Finally, on 27 June 2009, a statue of Novello was unveiled outside the Wales Millennium Centre in Cardiff Bay, a mere mile or so from his birthplace.

In 2001, Novello was portrayed in the film *Gosforth Park* by the actor Jeremy Northam.

In 1956, I had taken a teaching post at Seaford, a small coastal town between Eastbourne and Brighton on the south coast of the country. Soon after my arrival there, I was asked to play football for Eastbourne Town, who played at the Saffrons. After home games, I would join some of my friends at the Sussex Hotel in the town, but my musical interest attracted me to visit the Grand Hotel, which stood on the seafront.

When I'd lived at home with my parents during the war years, more often than not, we would sit on a Sunday evening to listen to the light music being played from the Palm Court of the Grand Hotel, Eastbourne. This programme had started on the BBC as early as 1925 and ran on Sundays continually from 1943 to 1973. The orchestra played its Sunday concerts from the lounge hall of the Grand Hotel, and I was disappointed to discover that the hotel never did have a Palm Court.

Later, the orchestra played its Sunday concerts from the concert hall at Broadcasting House, London, where it was usually hosted by violinist Albert Sandler, until 1948 when he was replaced by Tom Jenkins. Max Jaffa took over the orchestra later. And finally Reginald Leopold directed the orchestra until the programme ceased in 1973. The programme was reviewed in the 1980s under Max Jaffa and again in 1995 for a one-off celebration.

I remember a visit with my family to Florida's Disney World and a ride that took in a visit to the haunted ballroom, where an orchestra of skeletons could be seen playing their musical instruments. I have no recollection of the music they were playing, which is unusual, as I tend to put music and places together in my memory. However, the music they should have been playing was the aptly named *The Haunted Ballroom* by Edward Geoffrey Toye. He had composed the music for the Sadler's Wells Ballet Company in 1934, which featured Alicia Markova, Robert Helpmann, and Margot Fonteyne.

Toye had studied at the Royal College of Music, and, although a brilliant pianist, he became famous in music circles as a conductor. He became a governor of the Old Vic Theatre and also at Sadler's Wells Theatre in 1931. He composed *The Haunted Ballroom'* in 1934, and it became his best-known piece of music. It is a lovely and serene piece of British light music, even though it was composed for the ballet. It is a sublime piece of romantic music and so unworldly that it is a most perfect piece of music for Disney World's Haunted Ballroom.

When my parents were in their courting stage, they visited the theatre, probably in London, to see *The Merry Widow*, a most wonderful operetta by Franz Lehar. Indeed, it was so popular that it conquered the English-speaking world and caused my father, at unexpected moments, to break out into song. The piece that so entranced him and many others was 'Vilja' from the show, which, in its own German language, is 'Die Lustige Witwe'. I would have enjoyed my father singing it in German, the last lines of the operetta being:

> Vilja, O Vilja, was tust du mir an?
> Bang fleht ein liebkranker mann!

Translated into English, it means:

> Vilja, O Vilja, what are you doing to me?
> Begs a lovesick man!

Sometimes a piece of music is infinitely better sung in its own language. Sadly, my father could not speak German.

When I reached my teens, I received a present from a friend in the form of a music record titled, 'Girls Were Made to Love and Kiss'. This music was also written by Lehar, and it's a piece that has remained a favourite of mine. It was from the musical show *Pagini*.

Lehar was born in Hungary in April 1870, the son of a bandmaster in the Austrian regiment of Infantry. It was his father who gave him his first lessons in music. He grew up learning to play the violin, but his ability at conducting was a self-taught skill.

In 1902, Lehar became the conductor at the historic Vienna Theatre an der Wien. He was always closely associated with a famous Austrian tenor, Richard Tauber, and composed a number of operettas with roles especially written for him. A piece that became very popular with my family was 'You Are My Heart's Delight' ('Dein ist mein ganges Herz'), and his finest waltz was 'Gold and Silver'.

During the Second World War, Lehar had an uneasy relationship with Adolf Hitler. Lehar himself was a Catholic, but his wife was Jewish. Hitler greatly admired Lehar's music, and because of their close relationship, Hitler saw to it that Lehar's wife became classed as an honorary Aryan by marriage. It was this arrangement and classification that allowed her to be saved from the extermination camps.

'You are my Heart's Delight' was from the musical *The Land of Smiles (Das land des Lacheins.* The lyrics were written by Paul Knepler and Bela Jen Bach. The English translation was written by A. P. Herbert in 1953.

Franz Lehar died in October 1948 at the age of seventy-eight. Richard Tauber, having been attacked by Nazi thugs because of his Jewish ancestry, spent the years of the Second World War in London. He was born in Linz in May 1892 and died in London in January 1948, the same year as Lehar. He was only fifty-five years old.

Robert Stolz was born in Graz, the largest city in Austria after Vienna. As a brilliant pianist, he toured Europe at the age of seven playing Mozart. He was fortunate in having wonderful musical credentials, in that his father was a musical conductor and his mother a concert pianist. In 1905, he became the musical conductor at the famous Theatre an der Wien in Vienna and soon became the leading conductor at a time of the golden age of Viennese operetta.

At the same time, he continued to write his own operettas, including a favourite of mine 'Frühling in Wien'. Another early composition was 'Adieu mein kleiner Gardeoffizier', from his operetta *Die Lustigen Weiber Von Wien*. This soon became known to wider audiences following its inclusion in the musical *White Horse Inn*.

During the Second World War, as a Jew, he was lucky to be in Paris. And when the Germans arrived, he was befriended by a young lady who purchased for him a ticket to journey to America. Whilst in the United States, he achieved fame with his Viennese concerts, such as A Night in Vienna, held at Carnegie Hall. He also received two Academy Awards nominations for the song 'Waltzing in the Clouds' and the film *Spring Parade*. Gus Kahn wrote the lyrics, and Deanna Durban sang most beautifully the best original song of 1941. Stolz also wrote the music for the film *It Happened Tomorrow*, which was nominated as the best dramatic film score of 1945. Stolz returned to Vienna after the war and remained there until his death. He had composed over forty operettas during his lifetime.

Robert Stolz, born in August 1880, died in June 1975, at ninety-four years old. He is buried next to Johannes Brahms and Johann Strauss II in Vienna's Zentral Friedhof cemetery. And a statue of him has been erected in the Weiner Stadtpark. In 1970, he was awarded the honorary medal of the city of Jerusalem and, a year later, the Jerusalem medal for his assistance to fellow Jews escaping the Nazis in World War II.

Some of his music includes 'Salome' (1920), lyrics by Arthur Rebner; 'Das ist der Frühling in Wien" (1921), lyrics by Arthur Rebner; 'Madi' (1923), lyrics by Alfred Grunwald / Robert Gilbest; 'Adieu, mein kleiner Gardeoffizier' (1930), lyrics by Walter Reich; 'Zwei Hertzen im Dreivierteltakt' (1930), lyrics by Walter Reich; 'Wenn die Kleinen bluhen' (1932), lyrics by Bruno Hardt-Warden; and 'Waltzing in the Clouds' (1940), lyrics by Gus Kahn.

Nothing takes me back to the heyday of light music more than the theme of *Music While You Work*. The music, thankfully, can be heard today on YouTube. The theme music for Dr Finlay's casebook of the 1960s is also a reminder of my courting days. It was composed by Trevor Duncan and was titled 'March from a Little Suite'.

Finally, even the late-night shipping forecast had its own theme music, entitled 'Sailing By' by Ronald Binge. However, I always missed it, as I would be fast asleep in bed.

CHAPTER 14
Towards the Rainbow's End

Some three years ago, in 2016, I found in one of my many books of music a piece called 'You Stepped Out of a Dream'. It was composed by Nacio Herb Brown, a name totally unfamiliar to me, while the lyrics had been written by Gus Kahn. There was no book available on Nacio Herb Brown, like, for example, on Irving Berlin, Jerome Kern, or George Gershwin. Consequently, I had no knowledge of the scope of his music. Brown had begun writing songs as a hobby, and soon his reputation grew after he wrote 'Doll Dance' (the song can be heard on YouTube), which became a hit. This led to an invitation by Irving Thalberg, then the chief producer at Metro Goldwyn Mayor film studio, for him to write songs for them. However, at that time, Brown was working in real estate, at a time when California house building was booming. Consequently, he rejected the offer. But following the Wall Street Crash of 1929, he saw Thalberg again and joined MGM, in what was to be a long association with that film company. It was, of course, the heyday of the lavish Hollywood musicals.

Brown met Arthur Freed in a music store, and they began working closely together. They usually agreed on a song title and then fitted the melody and the lyrics together. Freed had been born into a Jewish family in Chicago and began work as a song plugger and pianist. In that city, he met Minnie Marx, the mother of the Marx brothers. He teamed up with them and toured the Vaudeville cities as a singer and writer of musical material. In 1921, he collaborated with Brown on the song 'When Buddha Smiles'. When Freed joined MGM in 1928, he was assigned to work with Brown. For the film *Hollywood Revue of 1929* they wrote, 'Singing in the Rain'.

Some time ago, in May 2018, I awoke one morning and began singing a song called 'You Were Meant for Me (I Was Meant for You)'. I can honestly say that I had not heard that song since I was a young boy, something like seventy years before. Neither did I have the musical piece in my quite extensive library of music. I remembered the words of the first line and the last line of the song, which was, 'I'm content, the Angels must have sent you, and they meant you just for me!' Perhaps it was the repetitive sounds of *sent* and *meant* that somehow reminded me of the song. The brain is clearly an amazing piece of engineering, and mine allowed me to remember the song. The song was also written by Brown, and the lyrics were written by Arthur Freed.

The lyrics of 'You Stepped Out of a Dream' were by Gus Kahn in 1940. By that time, Arthur Freed had moved into film production. The music was written in 1940, and by that time, Arthur Freed had compiled an impressive list of standards with Brown, including 'You Were Meant for Me', 'All I Do Is Dream Of You', 'Alone', 'Good Morning', 'Paradise', 'Pagan Love Story', 'Temptation' and 'You Are My Lucky Star' etc.

Freed had worked as an assistant producer, uncredited, on the film *Wizard of Oz*. Later, his legendary 'Freed unit' produced around fifty films for MGM, including *Lady be Good* (1941), *Meet Me in St. Louis* (1944), *Easter Parade* (1948), *On the Train* (1949), *Annie Get Your Gun* (1950), *An American in Paris* and *Showboat* (1951), and *Gigi'* (1958). In that year, Gigi won the Academy Award for Best Picture. And when *Singin' in the Rain* was made and released in 1952, it was only a modest hit. Since that time, however, the film has gained legendary status and is now regarded by the critics as the best musical ever made and the best film from the Freed unit at MGM. In a list of fifty greatest films, *Singin' in the Rain* is placed twentieth, and in 1989, the United States Library of Congress selected the film for preservation in the National Film Registry. In 1967, a special Honorary Academy

Award was presented to Arthur Freed for his distinguished service to the Academy of Motion Picture Arts and Sciences, and he was inducted into the Songwriters Hall of Fame in 1972.

Earlier in this piece, I mentioned the name Gus Kahn as the lyric writer for one of my favourite piano pieces. 'You Stepped Out of a Dream'. The music appeared in the 1941 musical *Ziegfeld Girl*, sung by Tony Martin while accompanied by the iconic image of Lana Turner walking slowly down a 'grand staircase'. At the height of her popularity in Hollywood, a band would strike up this tune every time she walked into a restaurant.

As a lyricist, Gus Kahn was prolific, and during his career, largely in the film industry, he would write more than four hundred songs. He had been born in Koblenz, Germany, of a Jewish family on 6 November 1884 and arrived with his family in Chicago in 1890. His catalogue of music contained some of the greatest collection of songs in the early twentieth century.

By 1933, Kahn had become a full-time motion picture songwriter, and some of his songs are listed as 'Pretty Baby' (1915), 'Toot, Toot, Tootsie (Goodbye)' (1921), and 'Yes Sir, that's My Baby' (1925). For me, however, his greatest lyrics were written with Isham Jones for the song 'It Had to Be You', which Johnny Mercer called 'the greatest popular song ever written'. It has appeared in over forty films, including *Casablanca'* (1942), *Mr. Skeffington* (1944), and *Annie Hall* (1977). It has been recorded by countless artists, including Bing Crosby, Billie Holiday, Ray Charles, Ella Fitzgerald, Dean Martin, Frank Sinatra, and Michael Buble with Barbra Streisand.

Gus Kahn collaborated with some of the finest musicians of his day, including Vincent Youmans, George Gershwin, Jerome Kern, Sigmund Romberg, and Harry Warren. However, his primary collaborator was Walter Donaldson. Among their songs was 'Dream a Little Dream of Me', which was recorded by Frankie Laine in 1950, the Mamas and the Papas in 1968. It also appeared on the soundtrack of the film *Beautiful Thing* in 1986.

A Kahn piece, a favourite of mine, 'Waltzing in the Clouds', was composed by Robert Stolz for the 1940 film, which featured Deanna Durbin. As I have spent many hours of my life flying in clouds, perhaps it is not surprising that I rather enjoy that piece of music. And it leads me conveniently now to write about that wonderful Austrian composer Robert Stolz, who wrote 'Waltzing in the Clouds' for the film *Spring Parade*.

If I were to write a thriller, my story would tell the tale of Robert Stolz. Yet no books about his life are available throughout the UK library service. Nor is one available through Amazon books. So, in my account here, I concentrate on his fame as a musician, composer, and conductor. Stolz was born in Graz, Austria, with all the musical advantages awaiting him. His father was a musical conductor, and his mother, a concert pianist. She presumably taught the young Stolz the rudiments of piano playing, and he must have reacted well, as, by the age of seven, he was able to tour Europe playing Mozart. He studied at the Vienna Conservatory. Following his time there, he held several successive conducting posts before succeeding Arthur Bodansby at the Theatre an der Wien in 1907.

After serving in the Austrian Army in the First World War, Stolz moved to Berlin around 1930 and devoted himself to writing music for the film industry. The first of these films was *Zwei Herzen im Dreivierteltakt* (*Two Hearts in Waltz Time*), which became a popular favourite. An earlier composition 'Adieu mein kleiner Gardeoffizier' became a worldwide hit, largely through film, and it was included in the operetta *The White Horse Inn*.

With Hitler coming to power in Germany, Stolz returned to his native Vienna but remained active in Berlin. Using his car to travel between the two countries, he used the opportunity to smuggle Jews across the border hidden in the boot of his car (or as the Americans call it, the trunk of his car). He did this successfully twenty-one times without being caught. And as a result, he was honoured in 1971 with the Jerusalem Medal (for the flight assistance to Jewish citizens).

The German invasion and annexation of Austria (The Anschluss) took place in March 1938, by which time Stolz had made his way to Zurich, Switzerland. It was, without doubt, the best move he ever made. Immediately, the Nazis went about dissolving Jewish Organisations and Institutions in Austria, forcing Jews to emigrate. By the end of 1941, 130,000 Jews had left Vienna, with 30,000 of them moving to the United States. The majority who stayed behind became victims of the Holocaust. More than 65,000 Jews were deported to concentration camps, and as few as 2,000 survived to the end of the Second World War.

In the meantime, Stolz had made a further move to Paris, where, after the German invasion, he was interned as an enemy alien. Good fortune again appeared on his side when he met a young lady in a Paris café who obtained the money, which allowed Stolz to take a boat passage to New York; this stroke of fortune certainly saved his life.

I first heard his name when some of his music was played on BBC radio in *Friday Night is Music Night*. I had his name stuck firmly in my memory since that time, and I have played many of his compositions, among them 'Das Ist Der Frühling in Wein' ('Springtime in Vienna'), with lyrics by Arthur Rebner; 'Zwei Hertzen im Dreivierteltakt ('Two Hearts in 3/4 Time'), with lyrics by Walter Reisch; 'Das Lied Ist Aus' ('Don't Ask Me Why'), with lyrics again by Walter Reisch; and, finally, 'Wenn di Kleinen Veilchen bluhen' ('Wild Violets'). 'It's Foolish but It's Fun' and 'When April Sings', both sung by Deanna Durban in *Spring Parade'* (1940), with lyrics written by Gus Kahn, were also his.

Stolz achieved fame while in America and conducted a concert of Viennese music called A Night in Vienna at Carnegie Hall. As a result, he received many invitations to compose music for shows and films. In 1946, Stolz returned to his homeland, Vienna, where he remained for the rest of his life. At ninety years old, he was made honorary citizen of Vienna and was only the second musician to be so honoured after Richard Strauss. Following his death in 1975, Stolz received the honour of lying in state in the foyer of the Vienna State Opera House, and he was buried near Johannes Brahms and Johan Strauss II in Viennas Zentral fiedhoff. Further, the Austrian authorities erected a statue of him in the Weiner Stadt Park. Some of his last words were as follows: 'When my melodies have found a place in the hearts of men, then I shall know that I have fulfilled my mission and that my life has not been in vain.'

Robert Stolz was born 25 August 1880 and died 27 June 1975, at ninety-four years old. Note that the Austrian government declared that Anschluss 'null und nichtig' on 27 April 1945, and Austria once more became a separate country but divided into zones controlled by the

Allied Commission, which lasted until 1955. In that year, an Austrian State Treaty was passed, which restored sovereignty to its people.

Hoagy Carmichael was a towering figure in the popular music business in America from the early twentieth century. He was born Howard Hoagland in Bloomington, Indiana, on 22 November 1899. He was one of the two great composers from the state of Indiana, the other being Cole Porter. Yet their music and lyrics were as different as chalk and cheese. Cole Porter left Indiana and never looked back. Hoagy, on the other hand, was a home-town boy, and his songs spoke of rural Indiana with its lazy rivers, rocking chairs, and buttermilk skies. Without doubt, he was a country boy, unlike most of his contemporaries. Hoagy's melodies speak of nostalgia, of an America that had long disappeared. Cole Porter was clearly not one to gaze at the moon. Nor would he be a fancier of the local rhubarb pies. His river was the Seine, and his pie would have been made from caviar. Hoagy's America was of the past, when the country was still pastoral.

Hoagy Carmichael was taught to play the piano by his mother. Then he attended university and took a law degree, which was awarded to him in 1926. When in university, he fell in love. But when that feeling was not returned, he sat down and composed what was to become his greatest song, 'Stardust'! In 1928, when the song was played slowly, it became popular. In 1928, the publisher Irving Mills prevailed on him to provide lyrics for the music, and Mitchell Parish became that lyricist. Parish had written lyrics for almost six hundred songs, including 'Stars Fell on Alabama', 'Stairway to the Stars', and Glenn Miller's 'Moonlight Serenade'. The music of 'Stardust' had languished until the arrival of Parish's lyrics. At that stage, it took off and became the most recorded popular song in history.

In 1935, a recording of the song by Artie Shaw and his orchestra sold over two million copies, and it became a major hit. Since that time, it has been recorded more than five hundred times and the lyrics translated into forty languages. Tommy Dorsey and Benny Goodman recorded the song on either side of the same record. Perhaps, it was the only song ever recorded that way.

In 1930, Hoagy wrote 'Georgia on my Mind', which was recorded on 15 September that year in New York by Hoagy and his Orchestra with Bix Beiderbecke on muted cornet and Hoagy providing the vocals. It was a part of Beiderbecke's last recording version. The song's lyrics were written by Stuart Gorrell. In 1960, he recorded the song on *The Genius Hits the Road*. And on 7 March 1979, Charles performed the song before the Georgia General Assembly, after which it was adopted as the state song on 24 April 1979. In 1932, Hoagy wrote 'Lazy Bones', the lyrics provided by Johnny Mercer. Paul Robeson recorded it on 8 September 1933, Tex Beneke in 1950, Dick Van Dyke in 1963 and Nellie McKay in 2018, among many others.

In 1936, Hoagy began writing songs for Hollywood films. 'Small Fry' was sung by Bing Crosby. In 1938, Hoagy composed the song 'Two Sleepy People', with lyrics by Frank Loesser. In 1946, he produced 'Ole Buttermilk Sky', with lyrics by Jack Brooks, which appeared in the film *Canyon Passage* and in 1951, with Johnny Mercer once more writing the lyrics. He also wrote the lyrics for the song 'In the Cool, Cool, Cool of the Evening', which won the Academy Award for Best Original song of 1951.

Hoagy appeared in many films as a singer and pianist. He also became a successful character actor. In 1957, he wrote 'My Resistance is Low'. Hoagy had a very individual piano style and singing voice. And I well remember him singing 'The Old Music Master' in 1943 in the film *True to Life*. He appeared in a number of films, including *To Have and Have Not*, *Young Man with a Horn*, *The Best Years of our Lives*, and *The Las Vegas Story*.

Hoagy died on 27 December 1981, at eighty-two years of age.

Perhaps it is not surprising that many people of the older generation know songs like 'Home on the Range', 'Bless 'Em All', 'Tea for Two', and 'Tiptoe through the Tulips' but have little or no idea who composed them or who wrote the lyrics. 'Tea for Two', for example, was composed by Vincent Youmans. The song appeared in the show *No, No, Nanette*, which was Youman's greatest triumph. I consider that his piece 'Time on my Hands' is also a magnificent song, which is still popular to this day. Astonishingly, he used just four notes to create the melody and repeats them continually throughout the piece. Unlike Jerome Kern for example, Youmans, was an absolute miser with notes. Nevertheless, he tells his story more than adequately.

Youmans only composed about a hundred songs in his short life, but their small range of notes produced an energy typified in

'Hallelujah', a song he wrote while in the United States Navy in the First World War. It so impressed John Philip Sousa that it was used in all United States military bands, until there was hardly an American serviceman who was not familiar with the melody.

Vincent Youmans was born on 27 September 1898 in New York City, and he was only four years of age when he began learning the piano. Even at that age, he demonstrated a marked gift for music. And after World War I, he decided on a career in music. His first song on Broadway was 'Who's Who with You?' His efforts now attracted the attention of Max Dreyfus, head of Harms, a publishing company, where his services were utilised as a song plugger and staff pianist. In 1922, Youmans wrote his first complete score for a Broadway musical in collaboration with Paul Lannen, called *Two Little Girls in Blue*, with lyrics by Ira Gershwin, who was then trading under the pseudonym of Arthur Francis.

Youmans's last success on Broadway was *Hit the Deck* on 25 April 1927. In this, he rewrote 'Hallelujah' and a second hit, 'Sometimes I'm Happy'. Two great songs were written for the show *Great Day* in 1929. They were 'More Than You Know' and 'Without a Song', with lyrics by Edward Elisa and William Rose. In 1932, Youmans went to Hollywood and wrote the score for the very first film that featured Fred Astaire and Ginger Rogers, *Flying Down to Rio*. Among the songs were 'Carioca' and 'Music Maker Me', with lyrics by Gus Kahn and Edward Elisa.

In 1934, he began to suffer from tuberculosis, which eventually killed him. It is somewhat remarkable that many of his great hits were songs developed from simple themes. 'Tea for Two' was a perfect example of this.

Undoubtedly his fame would have been far greater had he a top-class lyricist as a permanent partner. George Gershwin had Ira, Rogers had Hart and later Hammerstein, and Harry Warren had Al Dubin and later Mark Gordon. Youmans never used a regular lyricist and tied himself to lyricists who were merely adequate. Indeed, the lyrics for 'Tea for Two' were not just adequate, they were positively ludicrous. Every time I play and sing that song, I stop when I come to the release and can sing it no more. How Youmans allowed that to happen baffles me completely, and in the light of history, he certainly deserved better.

Vincent Youmans died in Denver, Colorado, on 5 April 1946, aged a mere forty-seven years.

Sammy Fain was born in New York City on 17 June 1902. He came from a Jewish family, and his father was a prominent cantor. Sammy was a self-taught pianist and started to compose songs while in high school. He soon found employment as a staff pianist for the music publisher Jack Mills and published his first song 'Nobody Knows What a Red-Headed Mama Can Do', with lyrics by Al Dubin. In the 1920s and the 1930s, he contributed numerous songs that became part of the Great American Song Book. When he began working with the lyricist Irving Kahal, they wrote the song 'You Brought a New Kind of Love to Me', which proved most apt, as they continued their partnership for seventeen years before Kahal died in 1942.

In the 1930s, the partners wrote songs for many Hollywood films, the most famous being 'I'll Be Seeing You', which was published in 1938 and became a much-loved song throughout the Second World War. It had great emotional power, and I remember both my mother and my aunt crying when they heard that song a short time after their brothers departed for war. I think the last few lines are unforgettable:

> And when the night is new,
> I'll be looking at the moon—
> But I'll be seeing you.

I was only a young lad at that time, but I will never forget those times and those words. For all of us in war-torn Britain, it was Vera Lynn's recording that brought lumps to our throats and tears to our eyes. The song featured in the 1944 film of the same name, which starred Ginger Rogers and Joseph Cotton. However, it was Bing Crosby singing it that made it a hit during that time. The song has been recorded and played by many artists—too many to mention here in full. However, it was recorded again by Vera Lynn in 1962 and again in 1966 in her album *More Hits of the Blitz*. Willie Nelson also recorded it in 1994, and Cassandra Wilson in her album *Coming Forth by Day* in 2015.

Kahal quite enjoyed working in parallel with another lyricist, and two classics were written 'Let a Smile Be Your Umbrella' and 'You

Brought a New Kind of Love to Me'. Both were co-written with Pierre Morgan. Kahal also co-wrote 'That Old Feeling' with Lew Brown.

Between the 1930s and the 1950s, Sammy Fain composed music for over thirty films. His songs were nominated nine times for the Oscar, winning on two occasions. For the Best Original Song of 1954, he won the Oscar with 'Secret Love', written for the film *Calamity Jane*. In 1955, he again won the coveted title with 'Love Is a Many Splendid Thing'. Both songs had lyrics by Paul Francis Webster. In 1958, he wrote the theme music for the television series *Wagon Train* and contributed song scores for the Walt Disney animated films *Alice in Wonderland* and *Peter Pan and the Rescuers*. A year earlier, he wrote the music for the song 'April Love', again with lyrics by Paul Francis Webster. He wrote many other songs of note, among them, 'I'll Remember Tonight', 'When I Take My Sugar to Tea', 'Happy in Love', and 'Dear Hearts and Gentle People'. In 1972, Fain was inducted into the Songwriters Hall of Fame. Sammy Fain, born Samuel E Feinberg, died on 6 December 1989 at eighty-seven years old.

A song I well remember, which I first heard in the late 1950s, was 'When I Fall in Love', first recorded by Nat King Cole on 28 December 1956 and used in the film *Istanbul* in 1957. It was released in the United Kingdom in 1957 and re-released in 1987. Its popularity stems from the lyrics by Edward Heyman, who also provided the lyrics for some other old favourites, 'Body and Soul' (1930), 'I Cover the Waterfront' (1933), and 'For Sentimental Reasons' in 1936.

The composer of 'When I Fall in Love' was Victor Young, whose young life was perhaps as exciting as that of Robert Stolz. He was born in Chicago on 8 August 1900 into a very musical Jewish family. At the age of six, he learned to play the violin. At ten, he was sent to Poland to stay with his grandfather and studied at the Warsaw Imperial Conservatory, where he gained the diploma of merit. In 1915/16 he became a concert violinist with the Warsaw Philharmonic. The First World War prevented him from returning to the United States, so he remained in Poland until 1920 before returning home.

Around 1930, he turned to popular music and composed the following songs (among many others)—'My Foolish Heart', 'Stella by Starlight', 'Delilah', 'Sweet Sue', 'I Don't Stand a Ghost Chance with You', and 'Golden Earrings'. While in Los Angeles, he came into close contact with film music and, as a result, formed his own orchestra for film work and remained in the film business for the rest of his life. He became a specialist in writing film scores, which included *Fatal Lady* (1936), *Wells Fargo* (1937), *Raffles* (1940), *Arizona* (1940), *The Outlaw* (1941), *Reap the Wild Wind* (1942), *For Whom the Bells Toll* (1943), *Frenchman's Creek* (1944), *Golden Earrings* (1947), *The Quiet Man* (1952), *Shane* (1956), and many more. His last film scores *Omar Khayham*, *Run of the Arrow*, and *China Gate* were released after his death. The last-mentioned score was finished by his long-time friend Max Steiner.

Victor Young received twenty-two Academy Awards nominations for his work in films. He was twice nominated four times in a single year but never won the award during his lifetime. His only win was for the film *Around the World in Eighty Days* in 1956, which was awarded posthumously. Young, in fact, holds the record for the most Oscar nominations before winning the coveted award.

Earlier in his life, while playing the violin in concert before Tsar Nicholas, he had so impressed the head of the Russian Federation that he had been asked to play before him in a private session. It was because of this connection that he was imprisoned for a short period, narrowly escaping death at the hands of the Bolshevik regime and, in 1920, returned to his home town of Chicago. Victor Young was born in Chicago on 8 August 1900 and died in Palm Springs, California, on 10 November 1956, age fifty-six.

Julius Kerwin Stein was born in London on 31 December 1905. When he was eight years old, he left with his family for the United States and settled in Chicago. He studied piano at the Chicago College of Music and soon displayed his talent by performing with the Detroit and the Chicago Symphony Orchestras. However, by the time he was thirteen years, he gradually moved his interest to popular music. He changed his name at the suggestion of an executive of the Music Corporation of America. And from that point, he became known as Jule (pronounced /Joo-lee/) Styne. He played piano for several bands and, in 1931, created an ensemble of his own playing in various hotels and nightclubs—including, as he said, many owned by the Mob.

He soon moved to New York and became a vocal coach and conductor, which led to a job with Twentieth Century Fox in

Hollywood coaching such stars as Shirley Temple and Constance Bennett. He went on to write cowboy songs for Gene Aubrey and Roy Rogers at Republic Pictures.

In 1942, Styne met up with Sammy Cahn, a young lyricist, and the two decided to work together. Their first song proved to be a great success. It was called 'I've Heard That Song Before', and it was written in 1943 and sung by Frank Sinatra in a film called *Youth on Parade*. The following year, they produced another hit with the song 'I'll Walk Alone', which appeared in the film *Follow the Boys*. It became one of the outstanding ballads of World War II. In the next few years, the pair wrote 'Let It Snow! Let It Snow! Let It Snow!' 'The Things We did Last Summer', and 'There Goes That Song Again,' the latter appearing in the film *Carolina Bliss*. 'Five Minutes More' and, an all-time favourite of mine, 'Time After Time' were in the film *It Happened in Brooklyn*.

The pair needed a song for a scene in which Jack Carson was to take Doris day to a nightclub in Cuba. Jule was playing a tango on the piano, and when Cahn asked him what it was, he said, 'Just something I've been playing for two years.'

Cahn asked him to play it again but more slowly. 'Once more—slower.'

Jule did, and the song became known to all of us as 'It's Magic'.

In 1954, Styne and Cahn received the Academy Award for the title song from *Three Coins in the Fountain*.

For his third time on Broadway, Styne wrote the music for the show *Bells Are Ringing*, which starred Judy Holiday in her first Broadway appearance. This was in November 1956, and it featured two songs that are memorable—'The Party's Over' and 'Long Before I Knew You.' The lyrics were written by Betty Camden and Adolph Green. Arthur Freed produced the motion picture of the same name, which was highly successful and also starred Judy Holiday.

In 1959, Styne wrote the music for another smash hit on Broadway, *Gypsy*, an adaptation of Gypsy Rose Lee's autobiography, which starred Ethyl Merman. The standout songs for me from that show was 'Everything's Coming Up Roses' and 'Some People'. In 1964, Styne composed the music for *Funny Girl*, which starred Barbra Streisand and included the songs 'Don't Rain on My Parade' and

'People'. Styne also wrote scores for television and ballet and produced a revival of *Pal Joey* and *Will Success Spoil Rock Hunter?* He was also actively involved in the revival of *Gentlemen Prefer Blondes*, which opened at the Goodspeed Opera House in East Haddam, Connecticut.

It's estimated that, by 1987, he had written 2,000 songs, had published 1,500, and had managed at least two hundred hits. Clearly Jule Styne was a versatile, prolific songwriter, whose songs became known across the globe. His classic Broadway musicals included *Gypsy*, *Gentlemen Prefer Blondes*, and *Funny Girl*. As a composer, he was a flexible collaborator. At one time, he said, 'You write as well as who you write with.' And he almost always allowed the lyricist to set the tone for the musical score.

In 1990, Styne was among five artists honoured by the John F. Kennedy Center for the Performing Arts in Washington for their cultural contributions to the nation. In 1992, he received the New Dramatists Lifetime Achievement Award. Jule Styne died on 20 September 1994 in Manhattan, New York, at eighty-eight years of age.

Apart from winning the Oscar with Styne for 'Three Coins in the Fountain', Cahn had four further wins with composer Jimmy Van Heusen. They were for 'All the Way' in 1957, 'High Hopes' in 1959, and 'Call Me Irresponsible' in 1963. In the course of his career, Cahn was nominated for thirty-one Academy Awards, five Golden Globe Awards, and an Emmy Award. In 1988, the Sammy Film Music Awards was started in his honour. He won this because he had received more Academy Award nominations than any other songwriter.

Some of these nominations were, in 1942 'I've Heard That Song Before'; in 1944, 'I'll Walk Alone'; in 1948, 'It's Magic'; in 1950, 'Be My Love'; in 1952, 'Because You're Mine'; in 1960, 'The Second Time Around'; and in 1964, 'My Kind of Town'. Some of his other songs and favourites of mine include 'Come Fly With Me,' written with Jimmy Van Heusen; 'Day by Day', with Paul Weston and Axel Stordahl; 'I Should Care' with Weston and Stordahl; 'Love and Marriage' with Heusen; and, finally, 'The Things We Did Last Summer'.

Sammy Cahn was born on the lower East Side of New York City to parents who were Jewish immigrants from Galicia and then a part of the Austria-Hungary Empire. He said, 'Lyric writing has always been a thrilling adventure for me and something I've done with the kind of ease that only comes with joy!'

Sammy Cahn died at the age of seventy-nine at Cedars Sinai Medical Center in Los Angeles. He was described as one of the last American songwriters to embody the can-do spirit of Tin Pan Alley. He wrote the lyrics for 'High Hopes', which became a campaign song for John F. Kennedy in 1960.

In 1928, the Republican President Herbert J. Hoover, early in his presidency, confidently stated, 'In America today, we are in the final triumph over poverty than ever before, in the history of any land?'

Scarcely a year later, on 24 October 1929 (Black Thursday), there occurred the most devastating Wall Street stock market crash in United States history. It followed the London Stock Exchange crash of September, and it began a twelve-year (or more) depression that affected all the Western industrialised countries. The result in America was catastrophic, when 13 million people became unemployed and 20,000 companies went bankrupt, resulting in the closure of over 1,000 banks. In addition, and sadly, over 23,000 people committed suicide in one year, the highest ever recorded up to that time. The Depression that took place in the 1930s spread across the globe, helped in the rise of the Nazi Party in Germany, and helped create the Second World War.

Being born into poverty is no fun, and those who have experienced it have little difficulty recalling its bitter memories at any time in later life. Yip Harburg was one such person. Born of Russian Jewish parents in the Lower East Side of New York on 8 April 1896, Isidore Hochberg—later to be known as Edgar Yipsel 'Yip' Harburg (he was called 'Yip' from an early age)—was one of many who lost not only his company but also his job and all his money in the Depression.

However, his career took a sudden and unexpected turn when he met Ira Gershwin, when both of them attended and became friends at New York City College. Both boys were fans of the witty rhymes of Gilbert and Sullivan and collaborated in writings for the college newspaper. From that moment, they became lifelong friends. Although Yip Harburg was ruined by the stock market crash, that disaster gave him the opportunity to begin his songwriting career through the help of a financial loan from Ira.

His breakthrough began in 1932 when he and composer Jay Gourney were asked to contribute material for a new musical revue called *Americana*. The music was based on a Russian Jewish lullaby, which had been sung to Gourney by his mother when he was a young child. Yip Harburg, who had seen the financial ruin about him, penned the most poignant of lyrics—universally recognised as a masterpiece. The song, of course, was called 'Brother, Can You Spare a Dime?' The song was considered by Republicans to be anti-capitalist propaganda. Perhaps they objected to the following verse and its sentiments:

> Once I built a railroad, I made it run
> Made it race against time
> Once I built a railroad, now it's done
> Brother, can you spare a dime?

The song was almost dropped from the show, and attempts were made to ban it from the radio. But when Bing Crosby recorded it on 25 October 1932, the song went viral. It became recognised as the anthem of the Great Depression and was the bestselling record of the period.

Yip Harburg, like his father before him, was a socialist with strong beliefs, which were often personified in his actions and also his lyrics. He believed that all people should be guaranteed basic human rights, political equality, free education, and economic opportunity. He retained these qualities throughout his life and, in my humble opinion. should be praised for it. His views were a reflection in all probability of his early life in poverty. He has been called naive by some writers, but I could never subscribe to that opinion. In fact, I believe that anybody with half a brain and social conscience would behave and think the same way had he been brought up in poverty and seeing crying, starving children at close quarters. Harburg's philosophy and background are clearly revealed in the lyrics of his songs.

While in Hollywood, Harburg wrote lyrics for a number of composers, including Harold Arlen, Jerome Kern, Jule Styne, and Burton Lane. But his great success occurred when he was asked to score *The Wizard of Oz*, with the music written by Harold Arlen. Harburg's lyrics signified an escape from the Depression in the song

'Over the Rainbow'. The song was a simple continuation of Harburg's optimistic philosophy of life.

In 1973, he explained how the song was almost removed from the film. The story told how the film director, Victor Fleming, wanted the song removed from the script, as it was too long. Arlen reacted by taking the argument 'upstairs'. It was settled by the studio head, Louis B. Mayer, who decreed, 'Aw, well let the boys have the damn song. Put it back in the picture. It can't hurt.'

In 7 March 2001, the Association of America and the National Endorsement for Humanities ranked 'Over the Rainbow' as sung by Judy Garland as the number one song of the twentieth century. The American Film Institute broadcast the one hundred greatest songs also of the twentieth century, also with 'Over the Rainbow' ranked as number one. In April 2005, the United States Postal Service issued a commemorative stamp recognising Harburg's accomplishments. His stamp photograph was surrounded by a rainbow and lyric from 'Over the Rainbow'.

The partnership between Arlen and Harburg continued producing fine songs like 'It's Only a Paper Moon' and 'Last Night When We Were Young'. They then crossed America to Broadway to write the musical *Hooray for What!* This was followed by *Bloomer Girl*, the show addressing slavery, the women's reform movement, and the horrors of war. This was well before the civil rights movement and feminism. These were all were daring topics for 1944.

Harburg went on to write another masterpiece, *Finian's Rainbow*, in 1944 with composer Burton Lane. The show became one of the most enduring works of the musical theatre and has, since that time, been produced endlessly across the world. The standout songs were 'How Are Things in Glocca Morra?' 'Old Devil Moon', and 'Look to the Rainbow'. The show embodied Harburg's hopeful philosophy of life.

Harburg also wrote the lyrics with Earl Robinson to 'Free and Equal Blues'. The song scored the United States Army segregationist policies, which, during World War II, even separated white and coloured blood supplies. Harburg's lyrics quoted a doctor saying, 'A molecule is a molecule, son—and the damn thing has no race.'

In 1968, *Finian's Rainbow* was made into a film starring Fred Astaire and Petula Clark. The screenplay was written by Yip Harburg. The musical was a fantasy about racial injustice and, in the late 1940s, was way ahead of its time. It was to be Astaire's last major movie musical. Harburg's witty and elegant lyrics saw Astaire as a transplanted Irishman to the American Deep South. He was sixty-nine years of age when he took the part in *Finian's Rainbow*.

Astaire was born in Omaha, Nebraska, in 1899. And when he was auditioned by a casting director for RKO Pictures in his youth, was purported to have said, 'I can't sing, can't act, but I dance a little.' His birth name was Frederick Austerlitz, having both German Lutheran and Austrian Jewish parents. Well, Astaire, always a favourite of mine, could certainly sing, and his dancing was among the most gracious ever seen on the screen. As I said earlier, *Finian's Rainbow* was Astaire's last major movie musical, and how well he performed.

Harburg was nominated, together with Fred Saidy, for the Best Written Musical by the Writers Guild of America. *Finian's Rainbow* was based on an idea from James Stephens's *The Crock of Gold*. It became an allegory of racial oppression. In it, the boycotted politician Billboard Rawkins is turned black and has to live under state and local laws that enforce racial segregation in the United States (laws that continued to be enforced until 1965). Harburg's biographer, Harold Myerson, wrote, 'Though the spirit of the thirties hangs over *Finian*, there is no other comparable work that approaches its use and mixture of fable and fantasy, comedy and music.'

The songs from the show—'How Are Things in Glocca Morra?' 'Old Devil Moon', and 'If This Isn't Love'—quickly became standards, and the show ran for over two years. Bing Crosby recorded these songs as did Gracie Field, Barbra Streisand, Julie Andrews, and Rosemary Clooney, among many others. The show and the music were favourites of President John F. Kennedy, which shouldn't surprise anyone who knows of his Irish background.

In the early 1950s, McCarthyism swept across America, and Yip Harburg was blacklisted as a Communist, which he was not, and his passport was confiscated. For twelve long years, he was not allowed to work. In spite of the blacklist, however, Harburg continued to write poetry and musicals, including '*The Happiest Girl in the World* in 1961.

It was to be his last musical. He was seventy-two years of age. He never gave up his battle against injustice. His personality combined a sense of social outrage with his optimistic view of life, an example to many.

His lyrics are well worth remembering and some are recorded here as follows: 'The greatest romance in the life of a lyricist is when the right word meets the right note', and, 'I am one of the last of a small tribe of troubadours who still believe that life is a beautiful and exciting journey, with a purpose and grace which are well worth singing about.'

Yip Harburg was known through his professional life for the social commentary of his lyrics. He was a romantic with a cynical view of love as the following lines indicate:

> When I'm not near the girl I love
> I love the girl I'm near.

Harburg belongs to a small group of musical lyricists who wrote unforgettable words to music and, without doubt, helped to change the American theatre. Throughout his life, he was a champion of racial and gender equality and an ardent critic of religion. At one time, he was quoted as saying 'No matter how much I prove a point, I cannot quite believe in God. But I do hope to God, that he unswervingly believes in me.'

Yip Harburg was certainly a dreamer. But then the world has been built by dreamers. Orville and Wilber must have dreamed of flight long before they took to the air. There are countless other examples. Yip Harburg must have dreamed that one day we would all be able to fly over the rainbow to a land where all our troubles would melt like lemon drops. May all of us always dream of such a possibility.

Yip Harburg died on 4 March 1981, at eighty-four years of age, in a car crash in California. May his spirit live on forever.

Epilogue

When I first decided to write this book, I had every intention of including film music in its pages. I have to say, however, that this became impossible, owing to health reasons and an extended hospital stay. Films played an important part in my early life and provided me with excitement and adventures enhanced by the music, far removed from my day-to-day experiences. I saw one such film, called *Dawn Patrol*, which starred Errol Flynn, David Niven, and Basil Rathbone. I was spellbound by the flying action, which stimulated my early interest in aviation. Many years later, I met David Niven whilst flying based in the West Indies. He was there to make a coffee bean advertisement, and we met at Pearls Airport, Grenada. I told him how the film had motivated my first interest in becoming an airline pilot. He appeared pleased that the film had such a positive effect on my life. Indeed, *Dawn Patrol*, by all accounts, was the finest film made about flying during the First World War.

It appeared that I must have watched a large number of Warner Bros. films and, without fail, always remained behind to read the film credits. Who had written the music for the film was always a question on my mind? Soon, one name became familiar to me, and I felt unable to complete this book without mentioning his name. Early in my life, I regarded him as something of a musical genius. I could not have envisaged then that today I would find myself delving into the life of a man who became known as 'the father of film music'. His name, of course, was Max Steiner—or, to give his full name, Maxmilian Raoul Steiner.

Steiner was born on 10 May 1888 of Jewish heritage. His birth took place in Vienna, Austria, and he was the only child in a theatrical family. His godfather was the famous composer Richard Strauss. It's no surprise, therefore, that Steiner grew up into a musical boy wonder. When he entered the Vienna Imperial Academy of music, he completed the four-year course in one year, winning the Gold Medal of the Imperial Academy.

He began his professional life conducting operettas in a number of European countries when he was a mere fifteen years old. When he arrived in London, he conducted Lehar's *The Merry Widow*. He remained in London for a number of years, conducting music in a variety of theatres including the Adelphi.

When the Great War or World War I broke out in 1914, Steiner was interred as an enemy alien, as Austria had sided with Germany in the First World War. Fortunately for Steiner, his professionalism as a musician had created a large number of admirers, including the Duke of Westminster, who was not only very rich but also a powerful political figure. It was he who provided Steiner with the necessary help to organise passage to the United States of America. Subsequently, he arrived in New York with just thirty-two dollars in his pocket.

Soon, he was working on Broadway, composing, conducting, and arranging music for a variety of shows, and this continued for a number of years until he was approached by a director of RKO Pictures and signed a contract with that company.

In 1921, he arrived in Hollywood, California. In 1930, he orchestrated his first film, *Rio Rita*. A year later, he was made a director of RKO's new musical production department. In 1932, Steiner was asked by David Selznick, a new producer at RKO, to add music to his film *Symphony of Six Million*. It was a turning point in Steiner's career and a hugely significant one for the film industry. Until that moment, little music had been used for underscoring dialogue, as the film producers were afraid that audiences would ask, 'Where is the music coming from?' (unless, of course, there was a musical source on the screen). This may appear quite ridiculous today but not so in the thirties.

If *Rio Rita* had been a turning point for Steiner, then *King Kong* (1933) became a breakthrough. Oscar Levant, a brilliant pianist and wit, called the film a symphony accompanied by the movie. The music score fitted perfectly into the film, and Steiner's name became one of the most respected in Hollywood. By 1937, Steiner had left RKO and signed an extended contract with Warner Bros. There he would score fourteen Errol Flynn movies, the first being *The Charge of the Light Brigade* in 1936, the first of 140 films for his new company over the next thirty years. In 1938, he provided the music for *Dawn Patrol*, mentioned earlier.

In 1939, Selznick borrowed Steiner from Warner Bros. to write the music for his next film, *Gone with the Wind*. He wanted Steiner to use old classical pieces of music to save money, but Steiner was having none of it. For the three-hour film, Steiner ignored Selznick's wishes and composed an entire original score in the three weeks available to him. The score is ranked number two by the American Film Institute—the second greatest film score of all time. And 'Tara's Tune' is still one of the most recognisable pieces of music in the history of film music.

Steiner wrote the music for over twenty Western films, so it's no wonder that, as a young boy, I kept seeing his name appear on film credits. Altogether, he composed, conducted, and arranged the music for more than three hundred films, and he was still working away in his seventies. Today, one may find his life's archives at Brigham Young University in the state of Utah in the United States of America. There one may also find his unpublished autobiography *Notes to You*, written during 1961/1962 and, of course, copyrighted.

His first use of the Warner Bros. fanfare composed by Steiner himself fronted the film *Tovarich* in 1937. And it was the American Film Institute who ranked the music for *Gone with the Wind* and *King Kong* numbers two and thirteen respectively on its list of the twenty-five greatest film scores. Steiner was nominated for twenty-four Academy Awards, winning just three—*The Informer* in 1935, *Now, Voyager* in 1942, and *Since You Went Away* in 1944. In my view, he deserved far greater credit for his efforts. His awards should have included *Casablanca* in 1942, *Gone with the Wind* in 1939, and *A Summer's Place* in 1959. All this music can still be heard today on YouTube.

Some of my favourite Steiner films include *Angels with Dirty Faces*, 1938; *The Dawn Patrol*, 1938; *Charge of the Light Brigade*, 1938; *Dodge City*, 1939; *Sergeant York*, 1941; *Captains of the Clouds*, 1942; *Casablanca*, 1942; *Arsenic and Old Lace*, 1944; *Key Largo*, 1948; *Operation Pacific*, 1951; *The Caine Mutiny*, 1954; and *A Summer's Place*, 1959.

Max Steiner died on 28 December 1971 in Hollywood, California.

He will always remain one of the greats of motion picture history, and his music will continue to thrive. Undoubtedly, he was a musical genius. I find it fitting that I should end this book by describing this man and his music, a man I seem to have known all my life.

Bibliography

Albright. H (1991) Pearl Harbor: Japan's Fatal Blunder, Hippocrene Books, New York

Barnet. C (1992) Those Swinging Years: Autobiography of Charlie Barnet, Da Capo Press

Beach. E. L. (1995) Scapegoats, Airlife Publishing LTD, UK

Bergreen. L (1990) The Life of Irving Berlin, Penguin Group

Buckingham. W.E. (2004) D-Day: The First 72 Hours, Tempus Publishing

Burgess. M (1980) Gracie Fields, W.H. Allen, London

Cahn. S (1974) I Should Care, Arbor House, New York

Carell. P (1992) Stalingrad, Verlag Ullstein, Frankfurt

Childs. R.B. (2010) Cory, Cory, Hallelujah, Prima Vista Musikk Ltd

Danchev. A (2001) Alanbrooke War Diaries, Weidenfeld & Nicolson, London

Duchen. J (1996) Erich Wolfgang Korngold, Phaidon Press LTD, London

Firestone. R (1993) The Life and Times of Benny Goodman, Hodder and Stoughton, London

Forezyk. R (2010) Erich Von Manstein, Osprey Publishing, Oxford

Freedland. M (1978) Biography of Jerome Kern, Robson Books LTD, London

Furia. P (1990) Poets of Tin Pan Alley, Oxford University Press, New York

Furia. P (2003) Skylark, St Martin's Press, New York

Gannon. M (2001) Pearl Harbor Betrayed, Henry Holt and Co, New York

Gavin. J (2003) On to Berlin, Presidio Press, New York

Gershwin. I (1959) Lyrics on Several Occasions, Omnibus Press LTD, New York

Gill. B (1971) Cole, Dell Publishing, New York

Harrison. N (1960) Songwriters, McFarland and Co, Jefferson, North Carolina

Hart. L (1970) History of the Second World War, Cassell & Co LTD, London

Jablonski. E (1988) Gershwin: A Biography, Simon and Shuster, New York

Kemp. A (1982) German Commanders World War II, Osprey Publishing Co, London

Kimmel H.E (1955) Admiral Kimmel's Story, Henry Regnery Co, Chicago

King. C (2002) In the Mood, Caxton Editions, London

Layton. T.E (1985) And I was There, William Morrow & Co, New York

Lyman. D (1986) Great Jews in Music, Johnathon David, New York

Lyman. D (2009) A Fine Romance, Random House Inc, New York

Nolan. T (2010) Artie Shaw, King of the Clarinet, W.W. Norton & Co LTD, New York

Palmer. C (1990) The Composer in Hollywood, Marion Boyars, London

Peyser. J (1998) The Memory of All That: The Life of George Gershwin, Billboard Books

Pope. W.M (1951) Ivor: The Story of an Achievement, Hutchinson, London

Prange. G.W (1981) At Dawn We Slept, McGraw-Hill, New York

Prange. G.W (1981) Miracle at Midway, McGraw-Hill, New York

Sandford. H (1972) Tommy and Jimmy: The Dorsey Years, Da Capo Press, New York

Schneider. W (1999) The Gershwin Style, Oxford University Press, New York

Scott. M (2008) Rachmaninoff, Sutton

Seacrest. M (1992) Somewhere for Me: Biography of Richard Rogers, Bloomsbury Publishing, London

Sheed. W (2007) The House That George Built, Clearway Logistics Phase 1a

Sidran. B (2012) There Was a Fire: Jews, Music and the American Dream, Unlimited Media, Ltd

Simon. G (1976) Glenn Miller and His Orchestra, Da Capo Press, Boston, Massachusetts

Steely. S (2008) Pearl Harbor Countdown, Pelican Publishing, Gretna, Louisiana, United States

Suskin. S (1992) Show Tunes, 1905-1991: The Songs, Shows and Careers of Broadway's Major Composers, Limelight Editions

Sweetman. J (1982) The Dambusters Raid, Cassell

Tiomkin. D (1959) – Please Don't Hate Me, Doubleday, New York

Walker. L (1989) The Big Band Almanac, Capo Press, Boston

Way. C (1991) Glenn Miller in Britain Then and Now, Battle of Britain, Prints International LTD

Wegele. P (2014) Max Steiner, Rowman & Littlefield Publishing, Lanham, Maryland

Whiting. C (1989) The battle of Hurtgen Forest, Leo Cooper LTD, London

Wieder. J & Einsiedel. M (1962) Stalingrad: Memories and Reassessments, Arms and Armour Press, London

Wilder. A (1972) American Popular Song, Oxford University Press, New York

Wilk. M (2008) They're Playing Our Song: Conversations with America's Classic Songwriters, Easton Studio Press, New York

Zinsser. W (2001) Easy to Remember: The Great American Songwriters and Their Songs, David R Godine, Boston

About The Author

John Howard Evans was born before the onset of the Second World War in the mining community of the Rhondda Valley in Wales. He started learning to play the piano at the age of eight years and by thirteen had passed the senior examinations of the London College of Music playing classical music. Somewhere along the way he became attracted by American popular music largely the music of Gershwin, Kern and Porter.

In his early years he was classed as a 'delicate child' owing to asthma and overcame this handicap by virtue of his ability to play soccer and rugby well. The war saw him develop a keen interest in flying and he completed his two years National Service in the Royal Air Force in the early fifties.

His mother led the way in his choice of profession and he then spent three years training to be a teacher at St Pauls College, Cheltenham, Gloucester. His first teaching post was at Seaford County Secondary School in East Sussex. Here he was successful and spent approximately five years in that post, but now flying was again 'tugging at his sleeve.'

Consequently John resigned his teaching post, returned to Wales and began serious study to become an airline pilot. Later he developed a great interest in the business of aviation and in the course of the next twenty years or so saw him start four regional airlines in the UK and became Chief Executive of a Government airline in the Caribbean. He also held most of the airline senior positions including Chief Pilot, Chief Training Captain and he also became an approved UK Civil

Aviation Authority Flight Examiner. In his career he totalled in excess of 10,000 accident free flying hours.

During the writing of this book John suffered an accident which saw him having his left leg amputated and spent 16 weeks in two hospitals. He was in the midst of a house move when all this occurred and as a result all the working notes he used in researching this book were lost as was his memory. At one stage he was even unable to play the piano for a number of weeks. Showing admirable fortitude he completed the book and made every effort to cite sources hence the extended bibliography.

John has asked the publisher to remove or change any omission in this respect. Also, he states that any errors in the text are all his own and he asks for the readers forbearance.